Angus&Robertson

Twenty-seven-year-old Scotsman David Mackenzie Angus stepped ashore in Australia in 1882, hoping that the climate would improve his health. While working for a Sydney bookseller, he managed to save the grand sum of £50 – enough to open his very own second-hand bookshop. He hired fellow-Scot George Robertson and in 1886 Angus & Robertson was born.

They ventured into publishing in 1888 with a collection of poetry by H. Peden Steele, and by 1895 had a bestseller on their hands with A.B. 'Banjo' Paterson's *The Man from Snowy River and Other Verses*. A&R confirmed the existence of Australian talent – and an audience hungry for Australian content. The company went on to add some of the most famous names in Australian literature to its list, including Henry Lawson, Norman Lindsay, C.J. Dennis and May Gibbs. Throughout the twentieth century, authors such as Xavier Herbert, Ruth Park, George Johnston and Peter Goldsworthy continued this tradition.

The A&R Australian Classics series is a celebration of the many authors who have contributed to this rich catalogue of Australian literature and to the cultural identity of a nation.

These classics are our indispensable voices. At a time when our culture was still noisy with foreign chatter and clouded by foreign visions, these writers told us our own stories and allowed us to examine and evaluate both our homeplace and our place in the world. – GERALDINE BROOKS

About the Author

Ion L. Idriess was born in Sydney on 20 September 1889. His father was a mines inspector and sheriff's officer and for the first years of Idriess's life the family lived in various towns in rural New South Wales, eventually settling in Broken Hill. After his mother died of typhoid in 1905, Idriess ran away to sea as a bosun's mate, and then went bush and tried his hand at opal mining. In 1910 he began to write for the *Bulletin*'s 'Aboriginalities' page, using the pen name 'Gouger'.

During World War I Idriess served in Gallipoli, Sinai and Palestine, and it was his experiences during these campaigns which became the basis for *The Desert Column* (1932). His first book, *Madman's Island*, was published by Angus & Robertson in 1927 but his first major success was *Prospecting for Gold* (1931), which is reported to have sold 2000 copies in the first two hours of its release.

Idriess spent much of his life roving Australia, collecting material for his true-life stories: he wrote *The Cattle King* in 1936 after travelling throughout Sidney Kidman's empire and spending time with him, his family and staff.

Ion Idriess is undoubtedly one of Australia's best loved and most prolific authors—he published more than fifty books over forty years, all with Angus & Robertson, and in 1968 was awarded an OBE for his contribution to Australian literature. He died on 6 June 1979, at the age of eighty-eight.

Also by Ion L. Idriess

THE CATTLE KING

ION L. IDRIESS

AUSTRALIAN CLASSICS

A&R Classics
An imprint of HarperCollins*Publishers*

First published in 1936 by Angus & Robertson Publishers
This edition published in 2013
by HarperCollins*Publishers* Australia Pty Limited
ABN 36 009 913 517
harpercollins.com.au

HarperCollins*Publishers*
Level 13, 201 Elizabeth Street, Sydney, NSW 2000, Australia
Unit D, 63 Apollo Drive, Rosedale, Auckland 0632, New Zealand
A 53, Sector 57, Noida, UP, India
1 London Bridge Street, London SE1 9GF, United Kingdom
2 Bloor Street East, 20th floor, Toronto, Ontario M4W 1A8, Canada
195 Broadway, New York, NY 10007, USA

National Library of Australia Cataloguing-in-Publication entry:

Idriess, Ion L. (Ion Llewellyn), 1890–1979
  The cattle king / Ion L. Idriess.
  978 0 7322 9695 7 (pbk.)
  978 1 7430 9932 2 (ebook)
  Kidman, Sidney, Sir, 1857–1935. Cattle trade – Australia.
  Ranchers – Australia.
A823.2

Cover design by Darren Holt, HarperCollins Design Studio
Cover images by shutterstock.com
Typeset in 10.5/12pt Times by Kirby Jones
Printed and bound in Australia by Griffin Press
The papers used by HarperCollins in the manufacture of this book are a natural,
recyclable product made from wood grown in sustainable plantation forests. The
fibre source and manufacturing processes meet recognised international
environmental standards, and carry certification.

Publisher's Preface

Ion Idriess has been described by scholar Colin Roderick as 'an instrument through which the genius of the land speaks'. From childhood his imagination was caught by the wilderness of the Australian bush, and by the time *The Cattle King* was published in 1936 he had covered vast tracts of Australia by horse, camel and mailman's truck. He had roamed the immense deserts of the west, through the centre and the Northern Territory into the Kimberley, and traversed the northernmost fringes of the Great Barrier Reef, along the northern coast to the Timor Sea and Indian Ocean. Thus Idriess developed a natural affinity for the land, which gave his writing such strength and life.

Kidman's remarkable life greatly inspired Idriess's pioneering instincts: here was a man who had run away from home aged thirteen with a one-eyed horse and five shillings in his hand, and through sheer tenacity and enterprise had eventually created a mighty cattle empire, fighting droughts, bushfires, floods and plagues of vermin to do so. Sidney Kidman recognised the knowledge and love of the bush that Idriess would bring to his story and in 1935 invited the writer down to South Australia to spend time with him, effectively commissioning the book. The result is a fitting tribute to the spirit and courage of the Cattle King.

Idriess had not only spent time with the white men who were learning to tame the Australian bush. In 1913 he had headed north to the Cape York Peninsula and become the prospecting mate of two leaders of a tribe of Aborigines. Later, in the Torres Strait after World War I, he again came into contact with Aborigines, who taught him something of their deep spirituality and legends. These teachings were to influence Idriess's writing—he felt it vital to record the impression they had made on him and to illustrate what could be learnt from their customs and their profound knowledge of the country. In other ways, however, the treatment of Aborigines in *The Cattle King* rings a discordant note in our now more thoughtful world, and serves as an important reminder of the cruel indignities inflicted by the white pioneers who were colonising Australia.

Idriess's writing naturally reflects the spirit of the land with a simplicity of philosophy comparable to that of Henry Lawson. He has an inherent talent for bringing alive parts of the country that remain a fascinating mystery to most Australians. One London publisher described Idriess as '[a] writer [who] carries the spirit of Australia in his book. All boys and all those whose youth is still in them would be richer for reading him.' Colin Roderick, the late scholar and chronicler of Idriess's work, agreed, and perhaps the final word on Idriess should go to him: 'The closeness of his work to Australian life brought renewed vigour into Australian literature... In this he resembles Walter Scott, who first led the English man in the street to read poetry. Greater poets followed Scott and finer prose writers will no doubt succeed Ion Idriess. But none will ever be able to take from him the pioneering honour which is his by common consent.'

Sydney, 2001

3

"I'll *Never* Give In"

Upon his knees he gazed to the skies: "Please, God, direct me where the water is."

He plodded on only to stumble, but steadying himself went more resolutely forward. He tried to forget that queer buzzing in his ears. His face felt big and hot and the skin was tight. He battled on for several miles, then suddenly realized he was on bullock tracks. He followed them with a trembling hope. They led to a precipitous slope. Wonderingly he gazed up. Surely even thirsty cattle would never climb such a place; it ended high up, on a wall of rock. Doggedly, he followed on. In the sunset shadows he could hardly distinguish the tracks. Then he heard the chirping of birds like faint tinklings in the sky.

Trembling with excitement he climbed, snatching at the bushes, clawing higher among the rocks. At the foot of the cliff gleamed a pool around which hundreds of waxbills and sparrows were quarrelling and playing and bathing. He dashed in among them and fell in the pool and imagined he was drinking it dry, dry, dry. Actually he could not swallow, he just lay there until the water brought life to his lips, feeling to his throat. At last he splashed up and laughing, stumbling, falling, almost rolled down the slope to run back to Russ. The man lay still, huddled there in the dark.

"I've found water, Harry! Oh, Harry, water!"

But he had to shake Russ, to lift his head and shake him again and again. When Russ understood, he staggered and swayed there, clutching the boy. They reached the rock-pool late in the night.

Very quiet by the fire among the rocks the boy lay thinking. Water! the most precious thing on earth. It was life. Lack of it meant death to every living thing. This realization was eventually to mean fortune to him.

Russ had given in. If he had given in too, they would never have found water; they would be dead. He let the lesson sink in. "Never give in!" he whispered. "I will never give in."

Next day brought hunger. It was the boy who trudged back to where they had abandoned their swags, but the dingoes had torn everything to pieces, even his threadbare rug and towel. He trudged back to the rock-hole.

"Stiff luck," growled Russ, "we nearly perished of thirst, looks like we'll perish of hunger."

"No jolly fear," replied the boy. "We're not dead yet."

He collected some heavy sticks. Rues watched wonderingly. When the waxbills were thick as flies around the pool the boy let fly and disabled thirty. They roasted the birds on the coals and ate everything, legs and all, everything except the tiny burnt beaks. "Get some more, boy, when they come back at sundown," encouraged Russ. "We'll need all our strength."

Next morning Russ had regained confidence. "I remember that range in the distance." He pointed hopefully. "We should drop down into Poolamacca over that range. It is thirty miles from here. Come on."

Russ was right this time. That evening they saw the station lights blinking through the bush.

"It is a blessing to see it," sighed the boy.

"Thank God!" answered Russ, "every bone in my body is one big ache, I can barely put one foot before the other. You are a wonder, boy. How do you do it?"

"Oh, I just keep on going."

"Luckily for me," admitted Russ. "Listen! the dogs are barking. We'll soon be there."

By the slush lamp in the station kitchen they ate a ravenous meal, after which Greasy Jack, the cook, congratulated the boy on his "breaking in" to the bush. "Your brother'll be along in the mornin' young un," he added, "and if he don't kill you for running away from home I'll get you a job offsidin' for me. What! You're asleep. The poor kid does look done in."

The "young un" was to learn a lot about station cooks, but Greasy Jack's damper was the best he ever ate.

German Charlie rode across next morning from his shanty away down by the creek. A little blue-eyed German; a likeable rogue. As he listened to the story they heard the light footfall of George Kidman. A black-bearded man, his face wrathful, strode into the kitchen and glared down to the boy's smiling "Hullo! George."

"You young ass! Why did you run away from home?"

"Because I wanted to."

"Oh, did you. Well, you'll go straight back."

"I'm not going back."

"Oh, you're not?"

"No, I like it too much."

"Oh, you do, do you? Well, this is a man's country, not a boy's."

"I can do a man's work."

"What!"

"Ho ho," broke in German Charlie. "The young un has got, what youse call it? Grits! He might handy be about the blace."

"Handy my eye," growled George. "What would *he* be handy at?"

"Shooting the bushrangers in the hills," laughed old Charlie, "or hunting wild blackmans. Leave the boy mit me."

"Yours isn't the responsibility," answered George sourly. "I've got enough on my hands without being burdened by a schoolboy." He frowned at the kitchen floor.

15

"Well, I don't see how you can get him back to Adelaide under six months," sniffed Greasy Jack, "and by that time he'll be a man."

He would have been sent straight back home could the elder brother have done so. But there were no trains out there in those days, and neither ration wagon nor traveller might be leaving for the south-west for six months to come. George Kidman was a stern man, a droving contractor working on the fringes of settlement. He glared at the boy, puzzled what to do with him. Then abruptly left the kitchen.

"Youse win your battle," smiled German Charlie. "George he know not what he do. Py George he good brother mit you; he make you work like a horse."

"Until he does," growled Greasy Jack, "you skip out to the woodheap and get busy with the axe."

The boy obeyed with a light-hearted whistle.

At evening in the men's hut all hands yarned for a while, sprawled on the rough bunks or sitting smoking over the long plank table. From the narrow escape of Russ and the young un, the talk drifted to grim incidents showing how every year the bush claims its tally. Then to yarns flavoured by strong personal romance was a natural diversion where every camp had its "character".

"The nearest I come to perishin'," said Greasy Jack thoughtfully, "I come near to starvin' too. It was away out on the Barcoo an' I was makin' for Teatree, 200 mile away. No stations in between and only three waterholes, the last one so full of dead bullocks that the water was crawlin'. I slings me swag away an' goes straight over them sand-hills, knowin' me chance of ever reachin' Teatree was dead as doornails. On the third day I was crawlin' an' prayin', when there comes flyin' over the sky a mob of pelicans; a proper mob they was too. They passed me flyin' so low one after the other that I counted three thousand seven hundred an' eighty-seven of 'em! I was perishin' an' dazed an' let 'em go at that. They was heavy loaded, flyin' tired an' low, their pouches hangin' like a 'roo carryin' a joey. As they passed me the leader lets out a despairin' squawk an' out drops a fish from 'is

16

beak. Every one of th' line squawked an' dropped a fish until they was like silver raindrops fallin' away over the horizon. You can bet I scrambled for a fish like a drownin' man snatchin' a straw. That fish was kickin' when he was slidin' down me neck. Well, I knows them pelicans must be makin' for water an' I tracks 'em by the fish they dropped right to Bancannia Lake, twenty-five mile away."

They smoked a while, musing. Then a tall, lean stockman put down his pipe, stretched, yawned, and turned down his blankets. He undid his belt.

"I say, Greasy."

"Yeh!"

"I saw some of your friends the pelicans on Bancannia Lake yesterday."

"You don't say now!"

"Yes. I thought you might get us some fish for breakfast."

In the days that followed the lad worked hard for the old cook, but he felt restless; wanted to be up and doing. No wonder. All men were restless. The year marked a big forward movement in each colony. The building of railway lines, roads, bridges and telegraphs. This year, 1870, ushered in the last phase of exploration—a new move forward of occupation and development. South Australia, a colony of huge dimensions with a population of only 184,000, cheerfully commenced the construction of a telegraph line right across the continent from Port Augusta to Port Darwin, passing through that country which only John McDouall Stuart had yet traversed. In New South Wales men had already pushed west of the Darling and were creeping out into the semi-arid "corner", that north-west area bordered by the sandhills of northern South Australia and the barely-known country of extreme south-western Queensland.

Queensland, with its small population of 115,000, was just regaining confidence after the disastrous financial depression of the late sixties. Her pathfinders had spread over the rich central downs and out into the west; and were to follow the Charters Towers and Palmer rushes which later ushered in a reign of roaring prosperity. Pastoralists, recovering from the depression and cheered by a rise in wool-prices, with horse and packhorse, dray and bullock-wagon, were slowly spreading over the little-known country of the Cooper, Diamantina, and Georgina. Indeed, the ever restless leaders among these men were already gazing still farther west and north-west towards the dim haze of the Barkly Tableland. Victoria, perhaps the most blessed with a dependable rainfall and evenly productive land, was already comparatively populated by the gold-rushes of the Roaring Fifties. Among her many interests she turned attention to overlanding herds of cattle and sheep right north to the Aramac district in Queensland and then towards the lesser rainfall country of the farther west. Western Australia, with its 25,000 inhabitants busy with occupation and exploration over its vast area, little dreamt of the gold-reefs and nuggets that were to transform its fortunes.

No wonder, then, that boy Kidman sat musing on the Barrier Range, and gazing towards the north; that men on the east coast gazed towards the west; and those on the west looked inland to the east.

Prominent among the men who acted were the pastoralist-explorers, those who followed the first explorers or who found tracks of their own. Every State bred its pathfinders. Some made epic treks of 3000 miles with horses, cattle, and drays, across huge areas of unknown country, partly waterless, partly a land of almost uncrossable rivers and mountain ranges, and peopled by hostile natives. These treks are comparable to the great pastoral treks of history. To one huge tract of country already traversed by Burke and Wills ten years before, the first of the pastoralist pathfinders had already come. This was the extreme south-west of Queensland, including parts of the Northern Territory and South Australia.

This long-isolated area has provided a rich, though grim, chapter in our bush history. Its story is not written yet, although it may influence our destiny. The south-western portion of this area includes the "desolation" that took the hearts out of some of our toughest explorers. It turned them back again and again; it claimed the lives of several as it has taken the lives of numerous men since. Yet, under certain conditions most of it can bloom like the rose. Its habitable area has fattened millions of cattle and sheep—but only under certain and rigid conditions.

This area begins, approximately at Lake Torrens in South Australia and extends north, verging slightly west, 500 miles; then east 250 miles to just across the Queensland-Northern Territory border; then back south nearly parallel with the border but spreading slightly east as it covers the Queensland-South Australian "corner"; then down the border of those States to the South Australian-New South Wales border; thence it turns south-west by Lake Frome across to Lake Torrens.

Full of potentialities for good or ill, this area leans slightly away from the centre of the continent. Which is why, perhaps, an old explorer called that part of it including Lake Eyre the "dead heart". Excepting the lake, only in drought does it deserve the name. Its southern portion embraces the great salt-lakes system. These chains of lakes, mostly gigantic claypans, stretch right down through South Australia. Their shallow expanses only fill when, at long intervals, the yellow floods come creeping down from the Three Rivers. The intense radiation and evaporation which then follow probably have a beneficial effect on rainfall in this portion of inland Australia. A harsh land indeed. And men who battle for a living there must constantly use their wits against the grimmest phases of nature.

The northern boundary of this area embraces the Simpson Desert. This really is desert; a small area of waterless, red sand-ridges which to this day man has failed to penetrate, and over which only the planes of the Defence Authorities, and of a geologist, have flown.

But down along the "corner", where the three States mentioned meet, this area is a garden after rains or floods, with a herbage surprisingly rich in strengthening and fattening properties. Being, however, in the low rainfall belt, its floods generally do not come from the heavens directly above. These come down three great courses (the Georgina, Diamantina, and Cooper), whose watersheds are hundreds of miles to the north and north-east. Boy Kidman was to learn more of them when he met the observant stockman, Mudmaps, and from the aborigines. These waxed fat for three or four years after a flood had filled the lakes. But they had to hunt for their lives in the dry periods. By natural means, generally the flights of birds, they knew when the yellow flood-waters were again coming creeping down hundreds of miles away. And this though the sky was brazen, and not a drop of rain had fallen for, perhaps, years.

The seasonal or near seasonal floods of these once great rivers, slowly coursing down through the continent to spill into the chain of salt lakes, are what has kept this area of country "alive". Coming in from the west across Central Australia are also the Finke and Macumba. Mighty rivers in ages past, now their dry, long-choked courses rarely carry even seasonal waters to the lakes. Once, when the chain of lakes was an inland sea, and long-extinct monsters roamed the land, they shed their waters into it.

From the South Australian side, the gamest of land-seekers had pushed into portion of this country some years before boy Kidman first saw it. Now others were coming from the east, crossing the areas already taken up, and pressing farther out into the dry belt.

That intriguing, contradictory area of country was to have a mighty influence on the fortunes of boy Kidman. It was barely known then; Australians as a whole know very little of it to-day. Its geographical position, peculiarly isolating it from any State while running along the extreme boundary of three, has kept it almost to this day outside the interest of all but a few pastoralists. Yet this very geographical position was strategic, awaiting a man with keen foresight and almost phenomenal knowledge of local, "inside", and coastal conditions, to take advantage of it.

That had already happened, and in a surprising, though unfortunately illegal way. A very large mob of cattle from a pioneer station in Queensland's far north, simply vanished as if the earth had swallowed men and beasts. It was one of the biggest cattle-stealing episodes in the world's history; and the leader of the gang responsible was one of the greatest bushmen Australia has ever known. He travelled straight for the southern coast, nearly 2000 miles away; followed down the Queensland-Territory border and vanished into the sand-hills. Arid, totally unknown country, except that rumour said much was desert or near desert, with water-holes unknown and blacks bad. Yet they got those cattle right to Adelaide and sold them in the saleyards there. A marvellous trip.

That track, from then on, was to be known to the bushmen of that country as the "Birdsville track". It lay 450 miles west of north from where the boy was chopping wood for his tucker on the Barrier station. Of evenings he listened eagerly to the stockmen discussing the new track and the country there.

4

In the Wake of the Pioneers

One morning George rode up to the kitchen leading a spare riding-horse. Throwing down a small yellow blanket, a quart-pot, knife and fork, and two green-hide straps, he called:

"Here's your swag. Roll it."

The boy rolled the swag, strapped it to the saddle and mounted. He smiled "So long" to Greasy Jack and passing the shanty, waved farewell to the bellowing laugh of old German Charlie.

They rode for thirty miles among the low, mulga-covered ridges that are the foot-hills of the Barrier Range. The sun shone from a glorious sky, the bluebush a sombre carpet splotched by scarlet patches of Sturt's desert pea.

"I'm going away droving," George explained at last. "I've got you a job at eight shillings a week shepherding stock for Harry Raines. You'll find it a rough job."

"Harry Raines *is* rough," replied the boy.

"What do you know about him?"

"He is as rough as the hills. Owns thirty horses, 320 old sheep that he bought from Corona Downs at a shilling a head, and fifty goats. He overlanded with his wife in an old shandrydan that was almost rattling to pieces. They came across from Swan Hill on the New South Wales-Victorian border; took a year on the trip. He is a free lance; squats down wherever the feed is good, owns no country. A smart hand with stock, and a bushman. His wife is as good a battler as he is."

"How on earth do you know all that?"

"I listened to the men talking at German Charlie's."

"H'm. You'll soon know the run of the country."

"I am going to know all Australia some day."

George stared at the serious-eyed boy riding beside him.

"H'm," he muttered. "See you don't know too much. The bush has a way with people who cannot mind their own business and a way with the know-alls too."

"All the bush is my business. I love it. And as for the know-alls — well, I can learn all, and keep it in my head."

George was going to say something, but changed his mind.

"You'll soon fall out of love with the bush when you've been with Raines awhile. You'll live like a dingo, and work like a horse."

He did. His camp was a dugout in the bank of a creek, with blackfellow Billy for company. In the cold of winter nights all he had to cover him was that little yellow rug. He and the blackfellow and the blackfellow's dog shared it, side by side for warmth. Their ration was: eight pounds of flour per week, two pounds of black sugar, one quarter of a pound of adulterated tea. That flour had been six months coming by wagon. When they sieved the weevils and hairy grubs out of it they tried to bake it, but it would never bake hard. When the grubs were red ones the flour used to bake a rusty pink.

"All a same dead bullock," chuckled Billy. "Bullock smell more better."

Occasionally the boy and Billy enjoyed a share in a goat, a feast indeed. They eked out their meat-supply by the boy minding the sheep while Billy hunted the creeks for possums. At daylight they would drive the sheep and goats away to pasturage among the hills, returning at sundown to shepherd them into a rough brush yard as protection from the dingoes.

One night a flood came down the creek. Billy leapt up with a yell and vanished. The boy struck out and grasped a half-drowned snake. He was out of that dugout with a yell that echoed Billy's. They slept on the creek-bank afterwards, the dugout being occupied by centipedes and other crawly things.

But the boy gloried in the life. Despite the rough food he began to grow, to find a laugh for each little discomfort. He developed a habit of falling asleep whenever he wished, a habit he cultivated to great advantage in after life. Soon he knew each sheep and goat as an animal with individual characteristics. He studied them, noting how like they were to a mob of men. There were the bosses among them and the would-be bosses; the fighters and the peaceful ones; the old rogues who cunningly watched for a chance to stray; those who assiduously sought their own succulent feed, and those who butted in to dispossess others of it. There were the timid ones and the venturesome ones, the sleepy ones and the wide-awake ones, and the leaders that were first out of the yard every morning, right down to the broken-horned old goat who was always the last in.

He learnt too those grasses the animals loved, the saltbush, the cottonbush, the herbage; and the grasses they would only eat when dry times came. He learnt that stock will thrive on various species of bushes and even trees. Saw that they will eat the windblown leaves of certain trees, will forage among rocks and fallen timber for seeds and nuts and pods, and certain roots. He learned probabilities and signs by means of which waterholes may be located in apparently dry creeks, and in rock-holes in valley or gorge; and that often you can dig in a dry creek-bed and obtain soakage water if you dig in the right place. He saw that the blacks, the wallabies, the wild dogs, even the horses do this. His eyes and his senses began instinctively searching the country for water and the possible location of water.

Becoming the best of friends with Billy, he studied his blackfellow mate. He never laughed at Billy except when Billy was frolicking for him to laugh. Often on the dark nights, when the wind-wafted howl of a dingo floated dismally by, Billy would shiver and whisper of devils and spirits and beings that walked by night. The boy would nod solemnly, never making the white man's mistake of laughing at aboriginal beliefs. For this sympathetic tolerance he was well repaid. With pride Billy passed the long lonely days in teaching this white lad, who was so understanding and was such a glutton to learn the only things that interested Billy.

So began that education in bushcraft which was to save his life, to make him a noted bushman, and to guide him to fortune in the years to come. Among other things he learnt to pick out landmarks; to stand upon hill or plain and, across hazy distance, note a landmark capable of identification for all time. When as far as thirty miles away from that landmark he learnt to turn around and point directly back towards it, and to their camp in the dugout by the creek; and away towards Poolamacca and German Charlie's, and right away towards Corona and Mount Gipps, and far away Menindee on the Darling. Earnestly he studied these lessons, determined never to get lost in the bush and perish as Russ had so nearly done. Billy was a hard taskmaster, a scornful teacher, but delighted and loud in praise for a job well learnt.

This boy's phenomenal memory never failed. Later he was to return time and again to a waterhole, a pad, a flat, a hill that he had seen only once twenty years before and he remembered instantly.

His duties were diversified. Sometimes Billy would shepherd the sheep while for weeks the boy scoured the country with Raines, the shrewd "squatter" seeking grazing-grounds other than his own against the vagaries of the bush and fellow men. In that way Raines found the rugged valley of Mootiwingee and sent the boy crawling down into an ice-cold cave among the bats, seeking water. Sometimes the boy rode 100 miles away alone, for there was no mail service there then. Information had to be sought and messages delivered by man and horse, or by aboriginal runner.

Billy boasted of the valour and strength of his tribe. Boasted of the "bad men", warning the boy in particular of Cheeky Jacky, the king. "By cri, he killem white man quick!" declared

Billy. This Jacky heaped scorn upon any of his tribe so spineless as to work for the whites. It was Cheeky Jacky's boast that he would marshal his warriors and drive the whites from the land. He threatened this with clashing of shield and spear at the corroboree fires at night. But so far his threats had been merely noise. His henchmen gained tucker by working for the whites; when others came King Cheeky Jacky would be no longer obliged to roam the bush hunting for himself. Still, apparently, his threats were bloodcurdling when, full-bellied, he harangued the camp at night.

The previous year floods had ravaged the Darling in north-western New South Wales. Now a bigger one came, spreading over the flat country twenty miles on either side of the river. Struggling settlers were flooded out, and some with their herds sought the higher lands farther out towards the Barrier, eighty miles west.

Then, away down in South Australia, a drought broke. Enabled to travel by the resultant grass, South Australian cattle came pouring in over the border from the Flinders Range and spread out in mobs lowing their way across the Barrier country. When the vanguard of these new land-seekers appeared, the boy saw another phase of pioneer life; the big herds, hungry and thirsty; the bullock-drays; the brown-faced horsemen seeking new land. He watched eagerly, feeling the struggle of man and bush, longing to join in before the last of the new lands was all taken up. From up on the hills he spied out over the country, and sometimes his shout before Billy's heralded the approach of yet another settler coming with his cattle, still like ants so far away.

And water! The boy had many weeks of riding with these overlanders, proudly piloting them to waterholes. Raines loaned the young un as a "kid who knows his way about". From the newcomers the boy learnt of thousands of cattle and sheep away southwest that had perished from thirst. Water! Without it the mightiest herd will perish in a few days.

After the settling of the herds, he returned to Raines and the welcome of the pioneer's wife. Whether under sunbonnet or old cabbage-tree hat that woman could smile though their only luxury was quandong—wild peach jam. Mrs Raines used to cut the fruit in halves, thread it on a string, and boil as required for jam. The quandong season was holiday time. Then the boy and Billy would harness up the horses in the old shandrydan and drive through bush the joyous twenty-five miles to the Langawirra hills. As scarlet as the desert pea was the scarlet of the quandong. Against the grey hillside, that splash of green picked out in scarlet dots was the signal for a whoop of joy. Only the hungry can understand the taste of the wild peach after months of weevily flour.

Mrs Raines had heart to sing, even though her roof was bark and leaves; and a smile for the boy as she patched his one pair of pants with bag. Bag was valuable, every stitch of cotton a treasure. She showed him how to grease his boots so that they would last much longer, and how to repair them with bullock-hide when the soles wore out. From grass she wove him a cabbage-tree hat of which he was quaintly proud. More than this. When the ration wagon went to Adelaide she ordered for him a pair of spurs. Raines was of the hard type that has pioneered Australia; his wife was one of those who mothered the sons of the coming nation. They lived hard too. "Government House" was a bough shed, and under this the woman toiled and cooked, when she had anything to cook. She was always toiling; whether through the long months, the years of overlanding, or under the bough sheds which meant home for a time. Their land was where the man found good grass and water for the time being; on it he camped his tiny flock, as Abraham pitched his tent. His wife fought the loneliness when he was absent, and faced strange blacks with no sign of the fear in her heart.

Raines paid no rent; owned no land. So he and others have spider-webbed from around the Australian coasts far into the inland. With this difference: Raines had not yet attained the real squatter stage. He was a nomad, a "claypan squatter". It required a shock to make him a genuine squatter. He received the shock.

27

Over the hills one day there appeared an aboriginal horseman, followed by a mob of cattle with a white man riding behind, his dog close by. Farther back, came lumbering a wagon. And driving the wagon a woman. The man's name was Abraham Wallace.

Wallace selected the very country on which Raines had temporarily squatted. He was unaware of Raines's presence until one day he rode upon the bough shed by the creek. There was a furious row.

But Wallace had Right with him, and the Australian is deeply law abiding. Wallace was a legitimate squatter prepared to select country by the laws of the land and make a permanent home upon his choice. Raines packed up the old shandrydan, mustered his considerably increased flock and away he rode.

Wallace formed Sturt's Meadow station, called after the great explorer who had passed that way. Raines trekked across country to what the blacks called Mootiwingee; selected country there; established a real station, and prospered.

But in this clash of the pioneers young Sid Kidman lost his job.

"I'm sorry, lad," growled Raines. "You've been worth a couple of men to me. But I've got to go out and battle again and you'll have to do the same. It's the luck of the bush."

"There's plenty of room in the jolly old bush for you and me," laughed the lad. "We'll both own stations yet."

"That's the spirit," laughed Raines. "Stick to it Sid and you'll be a squatter."

The boy rolled up his little yellow rug and started across bush towards Mount Gipps station. He whistled as he walked, while his eyes took in the pictures the bush was showing; the saltbush on the plains, the mulga and mallee on the hills; the long, steady flight of cockatoos, high up, that told they were travelling to some distant waterhole. He would watch such a flight until the birds vanished like butterflies flitting over the horizon. He might want water out there some day.

As the miles went by he trudged steadily towards the "broken hill", a black crest rising rugged and barren, a landmark for shepherd, stockman, and wanderer. He had climbed that broken hill with Billy the black boy and from its crest gazed north as Sturt had years before. The great explorer had stared north seeking the inland sea of his dreams; the lad stared into the haze dreaming of lands "far out". But neither explorer nor wandering boy dreamt that the rocky bastion upon which they stood was to prove a hill of destiny to Australia.

Mount Gipps, of 1400 square miles, established about four years before in the heart of the Barrier Range, was now the big station of the district. West of where the boy stood, until well into South Australia, was No Man's Country, while north was only now being dotted by the farther out pioneers. As the lad walked on into the heart of the ranges he felt as happy and free as the wallabies that played among the rocks. He used, in after years, to think wonderingly of that walk, for those wallabies were playing upon silver. They were sleeping, living, and eating upon a silver plate as large as a range of hills. And he walked over it; walked whistling with his few precious pounds rolled tightly in his pocket; walked serenely along beside a mountain of silver.

He secured a job at Mount Gipps at ten shillings per week as a rouseabout. This was luxury compared to the job with Harry Raines and that hole in the creek-bank. Here was a big station with the homestead, men's quarters, and outbuildings of mud and stone. Here was a real manager, and overseer, and forty station-hands. Men in leggings and spurs, riding from daylight to dark, coming home singing, and, after a wash, filing in noisily to the huge table in the big kitchen.

"What's for tea, Babbling Brook?"

"I'm not here to tell you what's for tea, I'm here to chuck it at you," growled the cook.

"And you do, too!"

"Yeh!" Rattle of plates and pannikins; a bad-tempered cook glaring over the tucker, plenty of mutton, damper, and jam, with sauce and brownie on Sundays. And all hands rolled up to the ding-dong-ding of the big bell.

The growing lad worked with a will and ate a man's meal. He took their jokes in good part and laughed as readily as he would mount an unbroken colt. In a short time "the kid" was a general favourite except perhaps with the stern overseer.

His mind developed faster than his body. In this big unfenced station he rode often for days, sometimes for weeks at a time, before returning to the homestead. And he memorized something new with every ride. Moving a mob of sheep to fresh pastures or waters, packing out the shepherd's rations, spying out the country far beyond the station borders, taking a turn with every job that forms the active life of a pioneer station. He learnt the carrying capacity of this particular area of saltbush country, the growth and endurance of stock bred in large numbers, the management of them for the cycle of the year.

And soon learnt what each employee knew of any country he had been on; learnt what the teamster knew of any route he had travelled. He grew into a good-looking boy, smart and active, blessed with a smiling willingness. He had only to ask, and information was his. He learnt to handle and ride buckjumpers in that quickest of schools, a stockyard full of unbroken, snorting horses, wild as the hills. The dust and excitement, the scurrying hoofs, the glint of a roguish eye was joy to these men. The throwing of a rope over a colt, the holding him while saddling his untamed body, the leap to the saddle, and the thrill as the animal plunged and bucked and reared! The sickening busters! But the triumph when he rode an outlaw to a standstill. They soon found that "the kid" was born to horsework and utterly fearless. They worked him then as a willing horse is worked. He laughed at it all and never refused a mount.

There came a jackeroo to the station to learn "colonial experience"; George McCulloch, a raw young Scotchman, wages one pound per week. Truth is stranger than fiction. There were two lads, each working for shillings per week, each with aims in life far apart, each on a battling frontier station, each destined to be a millionaire.

George Urquhart, the overseer, the boy stockman, Philip Charley, George Lind, the book-keeper—these also were to be pushed on the path that led not to one million, but to millions.

Cynical Fate did not let them realize the millions. She let Time shake their faith and so take back much she had given.

And another was coming who, by setting these events in motion, was to carve his name deep in the story of Australia: Charles Rasp, boundary-rider; wages one pound per week. The third near millionaire to be.

From a passing drover the boy bought a horse for thirty shillings, a poor horse apparently worn out. But it was a young horse, and the boy knew of a valley growing succulent feed. In two months that bag of bones was a fresh young horse, deep chested, fiery of eye. The boy tried unavailingly to sell him for five pounds. He swapped him eventually for two horses, dog poor. These two he fattened and sold to a tank contractor for four pounds each. The profit of six pounds ten shillings thrilled him. Thereafter, no hawk was keener for a meal than he was to make a deal. In his soft drawling voice he asked the overseer for a rise in wages. He got the sack instead.

5

The Vague North-West

Young Sid rolled his swag, received his cheque, and set off in boyish resentment over the hills again for Poolamacca. He had worked his hardest at Mount Gipps. In his pocket now was fifty-two pounds ten shillings. He longed for a good riding-horse, an animal that would give him standing among bushmen. As he walked, he fell to pondering on the stock he carried in his pocket. Four hundred old ewes at one shilling per head, nine cattle at two pounds per head, a horse at five pounds, and enough over to buy saddle and blankets. Why, men had started a station with less. A station! He gazed around at the sunlit bush. The world felt big and brave, full of unrealized possibilities. He decided to camp at the ram shepherd's shed that night in the range near the Paps. A meal and cheery yarn would be assured. The lonely old shepherd would welcome company; his dog would lie by the fire and gaze with those faithful brown eyes of his.

He did camp at the shed—alone. The shepherd had cleared out. For trees had grown faces that leered at him; their branches were arms whose weedy fingers snatched at him. He had cleared out.

There was not even a mildewed crust in the shed. He spent a hungry night, the wind moaning around this lonesome camp in the heart of the hills. A green centipede was his only company. He heard its creepy rustling on the dry bark, and when he looked closely saw the phosphorescent spots on its scales.

At sunrise he was walking again with a long, steady stride that did not ease until he saw the sun set dully red upon the roof of German Charlie's shanty down in the country below. Soon he was smiling to a boisterous welcome:

"Vot now, Sid! The young un returns. Vy vos dis?"

"Got the sack, Charlie."

"No, yes. For why?"

"Because I asked for a rise."

"Ho ho! Vot a joke! For a rise he asks und the boot they give! Vell, vell. Gom und a feed haf und talk vot vos to be done be."

Charlie gave him a job at twenty-five shillings a week to look after his cattle, a mysteriously increasing herd. This was a wonderful job, big money; Charlie owned 500 cattle and they had "the world" to run in. The bush had its own opinion about Charlie's cattle, but Charlie defended his honour. "If mens cattles they me bring," he protested, "buy them must I or you mens starve must! Mine cattles brands on all have, they vos honest be."

Nothing could have pleased the boy more than looking after Charlie's cattle. He was his own boss, on a job that he loved. All day long in the saddle, shepherding his precious 500 over unfenced country; roaming here, roaming there, twenty, fifty miles away. It did not matter. Picking out the grassy flats, locating water, watching them grow fat, learning to know each beast individually, learning the "mob temper". Often camped with only the tinkling horse-bell and his spotted dog for company, he fought the dangerous loneliness of the bush at night and eventually conquered it. But he always respected it.

As a sideline for quick fingers he plaited greenhide whips, halters, head-ropes, and fashioned greenhide hobbles. For these he found a fair sale from travelling bush-workers.

The track past Charlie's shanty was slowly developing into a rough bush road. On his visits to the shanty for rations he would sometimes find a discarded water-bag. "I'll put a patch on that jolly hole," he would murmur to the horse, "and sell the bag for sixpence." Sometimes it was an old hat he found, which when patched up proved saleable to some passing swagman.

Not much, but every sixpence counted. And two sixpences meant an old ewe.

"Are you a Scotchman, lad?" asked an idler one day at the shanty.

"No, why?"

"You're so keen on the coin."

"He's got brains, that lad," growled a lounging stockman.

"Brains! If your brains was gunpowder they wouldn't blow off your hat!"

Charlie refereed the fight.

As settlement slowly spread, the first of the tank-excavation men and well-sinkers came along with their bullock- and horse-teams and big iron scoops. A few of these contractors camped widely apart on the slowly forming stations. Charlie supplied these camps with beef. "Not his own!" so the tank-sinkers swore. But Charlie vehemently protested. "If mens rides along and sells me cattles they stolen has, how to know vos I! Them cattle buys me und to you sells und you starve not. Donner und blitzen! Mine beef cheap vos und tender."

The boy used to deliver meat to the scattered camps by packhorse, and he studied the work of the gangs. From each contractor he would ascertain the reason for his location at that particular site, whether for tank or dam, and thus learnt much of the vagaries of water that comes with the storms. He learnt of "holding" ground, of "catchments", of "silting", and other phases and problems that enter into water conservation.

More men were coming too. They were hardly in the district before they had vanished as quietly as the legendary Arab. Just an odd two and three now and again, generally from the Lachlan side 250 miles south-east where the stations were settled, a few even came from the far north down through the Queensland "corner". Great bushmen; best left alone. These were the horse- and cattle-thieves, driving their stolen animals

34

hundreds of miles to sell on the fringes of settlement. Occasionally they would make a big raid and drive the animals for hundreds of miles through bush to sell them boldly in one of the capital cities.

In the Barrier district these men rode through bush on to the Euriowie track and thence on to German Charlie's, for the bush shanty became the centre of local news, and a shrewdly unobtrusive man might frequently hear of buyers there.

Even German Charlie's shanty, crude and vicious in some respects, was destined to play its part in the opening up of the country. For travellers, such places isolated on lonely roads perhaps fulfilled a necessity of times now happily past. This particular shanty was a rude building divided into low rooms of untrimmed wood, mud, and stone. The few beds were of axe-hewn mulga; the mattresses of bullock-hide. There was a bucket of water outside if anybody wanted a wash, provided the "nigger" had remembered to fill the bucket.

The cook in days gone by had been a chef in a leading city hotel. Now, when sober, he worked miracles with his limited materials. When "on the ran-tan", which was every three months, Charlie did the cooking, or, if too busy, a black gin donned the chef's apron. He had chased her with an axe, but she took a fearful delight in her quarterly job. Facing the road was the main bar, a gloomy place with the smoke-blackened rafters low overhead. Charlie left the cobwebs up there so that he could point out the real spiders. He felt hurt when a guest shrieked at the tarantulas climbing up the wall, and he took pains, when the man grew sober, to point out to him the real spiders up on the rafters. There were no green ones amongst them, he would emphasize, and the only poisonous ones were the red-backs.

In the rough eating-house the food was plentiful and the best procurable, the tinplates and pannikins spotlessly clean. No man ever had to pay for food, not even the penniless ones. To eat cost nothing. But drink cost money.

No squatter, drover, or contractor ever liked a wayside shanty, for its doubtful pleasures periodically enticed their men away from the saltbush plains and dingo-ridden hills.

Returning with rations from the shanty to his camp boy Kidman found that dingoes had cut off twenty head of his cattle. Their tracks, already some days old, showed they had travelled helter-skelter to the north. Saddling his horse and tying food to the saddle he set off hot haste. A lonely ride of 160 miles among low hilly country scantily clothed in saltbush, past Bancannia Lake, past Cobham station right to the recently formed Mount Poole station. He hung on their tracks for five days and on the sixth caught them up feeding along the Coally Flats, a few miles from Mount Poole homestead.

Seeing that the cattle were contented on the sweetly grassed flats, he rode to Mount Poole for rations. The homestead was a picturesque place, squatting half-way up the hill by the precipitous little gorge known as Sturt's Glen. The boy rode down the creek to where several men were working under the big old beefwood-tree with the carving "J.P., 1845". With interest he laboriously read the inscription to the memory of James Poole, who died under this tree on 16 July 1845, when a terrible drought imprisoned Sturt in this very Depot Glen.

That evening at the homestead he listened for the first time in full to the story of Sturt, perhaps Australia's greatest explorer. Here, too, the boy learnt at first hand of Burke and Wills who years later had pressed on in the tracks of Sturt. Several of the stockmen present had given Burke and Wills a hand when they started off from Menindee.

"You are interested in the explorers?" asked a stockman quietly.

"I could listen all night."

"Better still, come for a ride with me in the next few days; I'm returning to Tilcha by way of Mount Sturt. You can give me a hand with some stock up there. I'll show you the country and point out places where the explorers camped."

"I'll see all the country you like to show me—the more the merrier."

Next morning he rode away with Jack McDermott. A few years previously, this quiet stockman had been employed by the Crozier brothers when they and a black boy rode farther west and formed Tilcha station on the border of New South Wales and South Australia, fifty miles south of the Queensland "corner". Tilcha was now "farthest west".

Boy and man rode along Sturt's Depot Glen, then north-west over a country of low bare hills sparsely clumped with mulga. Large flats covered with saltbush spread away to a low, dark range, in marked contrast to the white of the quartz-covered hills.

"I shouldn't be surprised if there was gold in those hills," said McDermott musingly. "No prospectors have come this way yet. For all we know there may be wealth in those barren-looking places."

There was. They had already ridden over a little of it at the Depot Glen where Sturt had camped so long. McDermott pointed out Mount Browne, not knowing he was to see the day when diggers would come swarming there. He pointed out, too, Mount Poole, and told the story of Sturt setting his men to work building a huge cairn of rocks just to keep their minds from dwelling on their fate. Following the tracks of beasts and camping when night fell, they rode to the South Australian border. There the boy saw his first real sand, leagues upon leagues of low red sand-hills, each running north and south, some among them crowned with dark, stunted pines.

"They look like some queer but pretty pictures I once saw in a book," exclaimed the boy.

"They *are* a bit unusual. Lonely, too, on a dark night under a cloudymoon with a wind whining. I've camped among them many a night, with native stockmen and dingoes for company. You may not think it, but there are mobs of birds on those sand-hills. And in a good season emus and kangaroos are fairly plentiful. The sand-hills look good now; but it's another picture when the dust-storms come. Then the limbs of the pines bend down and fairly shiver while the sun is blotted out by red dust. Sometimes on a hot day with the sun blazing through the red air it is a very inferno. When we are caught out here we have to shelter the horses between the ridges and just wait until it blows over. Luckily, we don't experience many bad storms a year."

6

German Charlie's
Race-Meeting

The boy gazed at those brick-red ridges. The mulga and other tree-growth surprised him. But he could not imagine that red sand as ever being covered with herbage, let alone flowers. And yet McDermott had assured him that, after rains, they were. Here was country new to him, country possessing a queer attraction, country about which he resolved to learn everything he could. They rode north to Fort Grey, and there McDermott showed him Sturt's tree, deeply carved. Aboriginal shepherds close by were minding the stock that McDermott was to drive to new pasturage. The boy stood staring away out over the Queensland border, his mind visioning the story as told by McDermott at the campfire of nights past. Sturt, with his horses and dray and tiny handful of men making their last attempt to find the "great inland sea". Soon after leaving here, the Stony Desert, with its brick-red stones dull and hot under a pitiless sun. The finding of Cooper's Creek, that father of all creeks, then the struggle of the long return. Then Burke and Wills, sixteen years later, pushing on from Cooper's Creek ever north until they struck the sea nearly 700 miles distant. And their return, their camels exhausted, themselves but the shadows of men, right back to Cooper's Creek and death.

Before the boy was now sand and mulga and saltbush and coarse tufted grasses, stretching dully to the horizon. He found it hard to imagine desert. Later he was to see Sturt's Stony Desert under saltbush; still later with not a tree, not a blade of grass; a thing upon which not even a crow could live. But the time was to come when he would follow the very tracks of Sturt, and of Burke and Wills right to the sea. And down that track along which both those parties had suffered untold privation he was to bring his cattle in their tens of thousands and marvel at what the seasons had done to the explorers; and what man could do against the seasons—if he only knew.

Some weeks later the boy received news and orders from German Charlie.

"Sid, mine poy, you vill to-morrow go mit der horseback und you vos tell every one dat Sherman Sharlie vos make der race-meeting ven der Mount Gipps shearing vos finish. You vos der shearers tell, der dank-sinkers and der stockmen, und everybody on der stations to gome. Dank-sinkers und rouseabouts und station-hands und deamsters. Und you vos tell them to make der news go round. Everybody's to gome I vant, Sharlie's race-meetings. There vos travellers plenty goming und men from der Lachlan mit horses. You vill ride then der horse on to Gorona und vos go all round de country von hundred miles away und more. You vill take von horse pack und tucker und their friends tell make one big meeting. Tell everybody else. Und tell them, boys are goming up mit de teams, rum, viskey, vine, everyting! Goot grog that vill drive away de dingbats und goot gompanions dat vill help 'em drink it. But mine poy," and his eyes twinkled, "don't let der squatters or der dank gontractors hear you or shoot you quick they vill."

That was a long-meandering ride to "spread der news". But to the boy it sowed the ambition to acquire one of the finest stations in the "corner". Twenty miles north was Corona, a huge station recently formed, its boundaries stretching right to the South Australian border. The overseer was W. H. Tietkins, explorer, and the manager, E. B. L. Dickens, a son of the famous novelist. They had only two small flocks of sheep and the beginnings of a herd of cattle. They lived in a little stone hut on the Corona flat.

The boy reined in his horse on a hill overlooking the hut and gazed over great stretches of hill and plain, with mulga and mallee, herbage and saltbush, cottonbush and bluebush. Behind him was the sombre grey of the Barrier Range interspersed with hills of limestone. As he looked on the low rolling hills, grass covered as far as the eye could reach, and with the green threads of gum-tree creeks winding among them, the face of this boy of sixteen, with less than £100 to his name, slowly flushed. He desired to own Corona.

The boy had the vision of a dreamer; but in him, too, was developing a far-seeing mind spurred to action by a determined will. "I'll live and grow," he murmured, "like a gum on a creek. And if ever I'm brought low I'll spring up again, like the saltbush on the plains."

On his long encircling ride he came on another and similar scene—the first rude homestead of Abraham Wallace. He heard the screeching of cockatoos, then saw them circling like white butterflies over the gums of a nearby creek. Heard the hoarse yelling of blackfellows, the furious barking of dogs. A gunshot echoed among the hills as he galloped down to the homestead. As he reined up he caught sight of a shepherd running down from a hill, a gun in his hand. The station dogs snarled towards him. Mrs Wallace called out from behind a barricaded door.

Cheeky Jacky, the big fat king, had attacked the station with spear and firestick. But the attack had fizzled out; the woman with a gun and savage dogs had stood up for the homestead too determinedly. A few spears were thrown, there had been a lot of yelling with boomerangs whizzing and clattering against the homestead, but that was all. They had broken into the storeroom, however, and stolen most of the food-supply.

"We'll be in a bit of a fix," said Mrs Wallace. "Those stores were six months on the road and only arrived a month ago."

"Shall I stay until things quieten down? Or I'll ride across to Corona and come back with some men."

"No, Sid, it's all right now," smiled the woman. "They did not succeed first time, and they will not try again. Come in and have a cup of tea. I know you like brownie."

The boy rode on his way, wondering what Abe Wallace would do. Abe was of the breed that invariably goes bull-headed into action. At present he would be in the bush somewhere, probably returning from Adelaide. He had ridden away months ago with 1500 fat sheep, determined to try his luck with the distant city market.

Abe returned just before the race-meeting, bubbling over with pleasure and hope. He had realized a capital price for his sheep and looked towards the future with optimism. But when he learnt that he had nearly returned to a burned homestead and dead wife his face changed. Hanging on the wall was an old bayonet, relic of some bygone campaign. He seized this and, mounting, galloped along to the blacks' camp down the creek. A hundred warriors were lazing about their wurlies, sleeping the midday peace away. Wallace leapt off his horse and made for the king. Now Cheeky Jacky was a large, powerful man, just spreading into fatness. In ash-daubed nakedness he lay sprawled on his chest, peacefully snoring to the hum of the flies. Wallace drove his bayonet at the unmissable target and the king leapt with a shriek that lifted the cockatoos off the trees. He ran in bouncing hops like a frenzied kangaroo, ran as he had never run before. In that astounded hush Wallace jabbed right and left at leaping targets that disappeared with anguished yells. In another moment the skyline was dotted with men, women, children, and dogs, leaving Wallace to glare alone.

They never tackled the Wallace homestead again. They understood guns, but this jabbing spike was a terror that must be felt to be believed.

German Charlie's race-meeting was craftily timed. Numerous teams were converging on the district. Those teamsters not within easy reach of the meeting camped their cumbersome

41

wagons and rode across country to the rendezvous. Shearers, station-hands, bush-workers, came riding from a radius of 200 miles. Some camped quietly down the creek, most camped around and in the shanty. A sun-tanned crowd, all in their Sunday best; tight-fitting white moleskins, leggings, elastic-side boots, belt, and spurs. Soft shirt open at the neck, sleeves rolled neatly, a spotted or black handkerchief loosely knotted around the neck. Broadbrimmed, cabbage-tree hats. Most answered to nicknames, and all who could grew a moustache and beard, carefully trimmed to the owner's fancy. The Spanish Don, a tall, handsome man with flashing black eyes and jet black hair, had his moustache and beard pruned to the last hair. To see him sitting his coal-black horse was a picture.

It was when the shepherds came down from the hills though that the wild men arrived. Each had been living in great loneliness, his sole companions the little mob of sheep he minded, his dog, and the wallabies, birds, and snakes. Among the older of these were wild-eyed men who had not had a haircut or their beards trimmed for years. They would stare for hours at the fire, or up at the stars; would converse more agreeably with their dogs than with a human being; and enjoyed having fierce arguments with particular rocks or stumps in lonely gullies. The more isolated among them only saw their fellow men at shearing-time or at German Charlie's race-meetings, for they would even avoid their lonely huts when, at long intervals, dray or packhorse came with rations.

The majority had not yet grown as "shy" as this; but time and the loneliness of their shepherd life would mould every one of them. When these men congregated together at such a place as German Charlie's the result of the sudden inflaming of the mind with rum was sometimes weird and unbelievable.

The shearers and rouseabouts were there, freshly "cut out" from Mount Gipps and Corona. A boisterous, lively crowd these men. Bush-workers from far and wide came. Many had a favourite horse to race, while each was ready to back his fancy. And all were eager for fun.

Soon, the shanty bar was overcrowded; every room was crowded. Men were lying about the veranda, around by the kitchen, down the creek, and along the dusty road. The first night had not well started before the Wild Irish Lad and Kelly the Rake were rolling over and over, each trying to gouge the other's eyes out. Kelly the Rake was the favourite in the betting until the Wild Irish Lad got Kelly's thumb between his teeth when the fight was over with a yell. Before the night was out the Broken Duke had put the Untamed Colt to sleep. And two shepherds were fighting down in the creek, snarling over one another—exactly as their dogs were biting and writhing and snarling beside them. From the dimly lit shanty, above a hum of voices came the mournful cadences of the Wild Colonial Boy singing—

Wrap me in my stockwhip and blanket,
And bury me down below
Where the dingoes and crows won't molest me,

etc., chorused now and then by rollicking laughter, following a crash as some clumsy one fell over cases, or someone equally clumsy. From the sound of things, it was going to be a great race-meeting.

7

The "Woolly Cat"

There was much saddling up on the first race-day, and preliminary riding with clatter of hoofs in dust as whooping horsemen came galloping to scatter the crowd before the shanty. Laughter and excitement that spread to the horses tied around the shanty and to the rails of the yard behind. The dogs responded in recurring fights as canine met canine. The men wary of their heels, each dog fanatically faithful to its master, who was as fanatic in its defence should a bitten man kick it in the ribs. More than one dog caused more than one fight that day, while, in prick-eared alertness, the horses stood with heels ready to lash at the dogs.

Young Kidman was busy that week of calms and turmoils; shepherding and watering the horses of the visitors, killing for the table, carting water for the cook, among a score of other duties. Meanwhile doing a brisk business selling hobbles, halters, and greenhide pack-bags. Busy, too, learning; his ears, his questions, and his memory more eager than his fingers and body. This was a unique opportunity; by far the largest gathering of men since he had left Adelaide.

There were men who had travelled on the Queensland side, in South Australia, in Victoria, in Western Australia. And their tales of country, of horse and cattle and sheep, of men and dogs, of timber, of rivers and range and plain, of town and mining-camp, of stock-routes and river "dreadnoughts" enlarged the boy's mental horizon by tens of thousands of square miles.

Almost immediately "young Sid" picked out two little groups who, while smoking and quietly seeing all that was doing, yarned together, obviously intending to drink but little. As opportunity occurred he paid special attention to the conversation of these men, and was repaid.

"Things might move in this country," he heard one man remark thoughtfully. "The country is good, despite a low rainfall. There will be failures among the stations, then successes as they learn to know the country."

"I've an idea things will move before that," said an exceptionally tall man who was as brown as a berry.

"Why?"

"Minerals."

"Gold?"

"No. They had too much of that in the White Quartz rush eight years ago. Some among that crowd tried to push in from the South Australian side and perished of thirst. Others died of fever when they got here—dry times and the waterholes full of typhoid! No, I think it will be silver this time. Pat Green brought in some likely looking stone to Menindee a week ago. He is poking about in the hills at some place the niggers call Thackaringa. There's a sour-faced chap there they call Eureka Bill, he brought in several slugs of pure horn silver. But they can't track him; he is a nasty customer, too."

"It would take time to develop even a rich show in this outlandish spot."

"Perhaps. But let them only find one and prove it. The transformation would follow nearly as quickly as a dust-storm."

They smoked in silence awhile.

"Looks as if minerals might cause a move in the Cobar district," said a wiry little bushman who was sitting on his heels. "I came across from there with a mob of sheep for Netley station on the Darling. Cobar is rough country, poorly watered

45

too. Two chaps, Hartman and Campbell, found it by accident about three and a half years ago near the end of sixty-nine they tell me. They camped one evening at a native well and were scared of the water; it was clear but greeny with a bright red rust at the bottom. Greeny-blue stains like paint down the side of the hole first attracted their attention; they thought they'd be poisoned if they drank the water. Next morning they saw 'gold' in the ashes of the fire. They raked it out and found it was beads of melted copper. The well was where the aborigines had been gouging out the ochres for war-paint. A chap called Barton came along next year and put money into it to test the place. If it proves rich enough, he'll get teams to cart machinery there."

"Things might move there then."

"Yes. Horses and cattle and sheep will be wanted, there'll be plenty of work. Teamsters have more loading than they can carry even now and the place isn't opened up yet."

"How's things in Queensland?" asked a bow-legged man who had "stockman" written all over him.

"Moving," answered a man with crow's-feet around his eyes. "The country is moving and changing. I think the shepherding days will presently be over. Wherever you go you hear talk of fences; squatters are discussing gauges of wire like they used to discuss good shepherds. Teams are carting wire all over the place. Any sort of fencer can get a job anywhere. When those fences are put up, the shepherd's job is done. Fences will bring in the boundary-rider."

"Must be good country there."

"Wonderful, in the centre and towards the west. Great rolling plains. They have just formed Aramac; it will soon be a prosperous town. The country is moving, out from the Centre towards the far south-west, the Barcoo and Diamantina. Pretty rough out there; water scarce; blacks bad too in places. But they're pushing out, and new stations are being formed pretty well every month. The first overlanders with cattle into the Territory have just crossed the Queensland border, making west. They'll have a rough time. The Territory is unknown country."

"Did you hear any rumour of a gold-rush in the Territory?"

"Yes; but only rumour. They dug gold from the post-holes while building the Overland Telegraph Line."

So, by listening and only talking in the right place at the right time, the boy learnt much.

The evening of the first day, while the crowd was arguing over the judge's decisions, he caught Bullocky Bill's eye. There was a crafty, speculative look about the crow's-feet around Bill's eyes. The lad walked quietly away. Soon he heard unsteady steps coming behind, felt a vice-like grip on his arm, a hoarse voice in his ear: "Boy, can you ride a racehorse?"

The lad faced around. The bullocky's big red beard was threateningly close to his face.

"Yes."

"Listen. I've watched you. You seem pretty slick on a horse. Will you ride Yellow Boy in the Squatter's Plate?"

"What is it worth?"

"A tenner if you win, and I'll break your neck if you lose."

"I might lose," smiled the boy. "I won't ride him unless he's got speed. I'll try him out to-morrow before any one is awake."

"Right, put it there!" They shook hands, and the boy winced to the grip.

"And I'll give you something else besides!" whispered Bullocky.

"What?"

"The pick of my bitch's pups!" He allowed this information to sink in. "The best cattle-bitch on the Darling!" he added hoarsely.

"I'll have a look at them," nodded the boy as he walked away to his tiny room. Ten pounds! If he could only win! That would mean ten pounds for his riding-horse.

If he had only known it, the gift of the tiny puppy was to prove worth far more than any ten pounds, that puppy was to prove worth its weight in gold. But then that ten pounds was going to mean a wonderful horse, two among the best friends of his life.

Bullocky Bill really thought Yellow Boy was a Melbourne Cup winner; he was prepared to fight or bet on it. Yellow Boy was a large-boned, leggy horse with a wicked eye; many a dry track had made him as hardy as a wallaby. He was a rogue and knew his way about the bush. However, he had a turn of speed, as the delighted boy proved next morning.

He won the Squatter's Plate, won it by a whisker from Lady Mag. With his face cut by flying gravel he galloped from the dust full pelt around the hill towards the gate with the ring of hoofs, the shouts of riders, the lash of whips ringing in his ears. And he beat the flying mare right on the post (the gate-post), to the roar of Bullocky Bill.

The boy took his pick of the cattle-bitch's pups, patting her head to the beseeching sorrow in her eyes. He was delighted with the squirming little thing in his hands. He had chosen it after the greatest care. The mother was famous amongst the teamsters on the Darling; this pup surely would live true to breed. There and then he christened it Nelson. And its education started almost straight away.

With his ten pounds riding-fee he bought a few days later a fine roan colt; he had admired it out on Abraham Wallace's run. He had been friends with the baby colt from the first day he saw it; the colt had come gamely up to him, gazing from big, wondering eyes. The boy's hand caressing the soft muzzle, the drawl in his voice, the smile in his eyes, brought the colt nuzzling his chest and shoulder. He loved the colt. Many years later he was to cry beside it when it died of extreme old age.

With the race-meeting over, the sober ones and those moderately so got "the kid" to run in their horses while they packed their swags. Then they rode away. For not all these men drank. Some came for the company alone, others because it was a change, others for a bit of fun and no more. The roysterers were still cutting out the remnants of their cheques. Teamsters, their heads as big as their wagons, were slowly pulling out of camp; shearers were running in their horses; station-hands were saddling up; shepherds were already drifting back to the hills. The boy rode away to his beloved cattle; they had had a whole week of roaming to themselves. The pikers among them would surely have a spread on by now.

An aboriginal found the "Woolly Cat" down the creek under the washed-out roots of a tree, coiled up in a grotesque attitude suggestive of a hairy spider gripped in a fantastic web. He was a skinny little chap who had not known a barber for years. He had died in the horrors. But he had quite a lot of money on him. They carried him back to the shanty and those not already gone gratefully postponed their departure for another day. They would give the Woolly Cat a wake. They drank his health with the last of his money and the last of Charlie's rum. That night they sat him up on the post of honour at the end of the bar, a rum-keg propped against his chest. His woolly head lolled forward on the cask, his short legs embraced it. In the hurricane lamplight, only his sharp brown nose was visible from the tangled hair. Before him on the bar were the last five of his sovereigns, gleaming dull yellow. One by one, each time *he* shouted, a sovereign tinkled into Charlie's till.

"I've heard it rattle like that before!" exclaimed the Groper hoarsely. He was staring up at the roof.

"Heard *what* rattling?"

"The gravel when it falls on the box!"

"Chuck it!" one said threateningly. "Anyway, the Cat ain't goin' to have no box, we'll wrap him up in his blankit."

"An' bury me deep down below," wailed the Singing Bird.

"A grand way to die," boomed Saltbush Bill. "Shouting firewater for his mates."

"I'd vos *nod* Virevater!" snapped Charlie, "I'd vos rum in Bundeberg make!"

"Firewater I say," roared Saltbush. "If your head was in my belly you'd be steamed curry!"

But Charlie laughed with the rest, his was the cunning that knew when to laugh. They were all thinking at once—all except the Cat.

"Spiders!" shrieked the Groper. "Spiders! Look! Crawling down his whiskers!" He crouched against the wall, his eyes starting from his head, his fingers pointing shakily. "Spiders! Spiders!" he shrieked. They rushed him; with curses they kicked him out into the night. As he raced away they breathed heavily, listening to that diminishing wail, "Spiders! Spiders!"

They turned to the bar again, peering uneasily around. Charlie was bustling, wiping a sodden counter. "Dere vos von more sovereign left," he said, "und dere vos von more drink of rum." He swept the coin into the till, "Now, what vos your drink?"

"He wasn't a bad poor blighter," said the Rose of Shannon mournfully. He stared at the Woolly Cat. "He lived in a hole in Fowler's Gap, and used to thieve my sheep—the blighter!" They drank his health and sang to him and gave him kinder names than ever they had given him through life. In the morning they planted him under a coolabah-tree and a rough board told in charcoal: HERE LIES THE WOOLLY CAT.

Then they rode away.

Out in the mulga with his cattle, the boy was whimsically thinking. He was sitting his young roan, Prince, with his right leg across the knee-pads, the horse feeding around the browsing cattle, and Nelson, the cattle-pup, toddling at his heels. He was wondering about the efficiency of swearing. Did it really help a man to do a better job? When a man swore he generally lost his temper and the more he swore the more he fuddled the job.

He had seen men fly into a fury; then all their thoughts were whirled up in a frenzy of swearing. They seemed tired after it. And thoughts meant everything. The boy had decided that if he was to make a fortune it must be with his thoughts, impossible with his hands. Why, then, abuse his thoughts? Why not hold them in leash, train them to work for him? While he could work them so they must slave for him. He wondered if a man could go through life without swearing. He smiled. It would be a job, but he would tackle it; the mental check constantly applied would keep his mind smart and wary. He would learn to drive his mind as he rode a horse, with a loose rein when all was going well, firm when difficulties loomed ahead.

He swung his leg back over the saddle and rode off around the herd. He had made up his mind never to swear.

The boy bought a teamster's cast-off bullock for two pounds. It was an old piker, worked to the very bone. He put it on succulent feed in a gully fed by a reedy waterhole, and tended it as if it were a prize beast; and the beast responded by growing big and fat and lazy. It would stand watching with mild surprise in approving eyes its young benefactor come riding up to look him over day by day. The boy sold the bullock to a tank contractor, but the money after delivery was not forthcoming. One evening the boy learnt the contractor had shifted camp to forty miles away. He saddled up and rode straight through bush all night, and at dawn located his bullock among the contractor's horses. He drove that bullock away and back to German Charlie's.

Young Kidman resolved that any deal he made would be square, and he would expect a square deal in exchange. He would fight for it if he did not get it. A week later he sold that bullock for six pounds. He was to buy cattle in tens of thousands, but the successful buying and selling of his first beast was a long remembered thrill.

Then came a job that thrilled him with delight; he was sought as a "pilot". It was indeed an honour in those days of the frontiers. A squatter was overlanding with a big mob of stock, his wagons loaded with a year's supplies. He had taken up country on the "blind", without seeing. And now he was coming—was already in the dry belt nearing his "farther out". He needed a pilot to show him the waterholes on his own country. Otherwise, stock might well perish before he located water.

Young Kidman, with black boy Billy, had gone wandering with their little herd over that very country. Not another white soul knew it. So the boy got the job—two pounds per week! A princely wage. But the honour of it; pilot to the overlanders!

Proudly he rode towards the setting sun with bearded men beside him and, following them, the lowing herd, the creaking old wagon driven by the wife of the pioneer. He did the job in a couple of months.

He was again to be sought for in these the proudest jobs of his life. He rode back bush, nearing Wilcannia. One afternoon as he hobbled out Prince and the packhorse at sundown, a swagman passed by.

8

His First Bullock-Team

"Come along and have a feed," called the boy cheerily. "You're a nice sort of fellow passing a man's camp like that."

The swagman slouched up, unslung his swag, and made his excuses. The boy bade him welcome, and in a few moments they were yarning while the billy boiled.

"They're two decent sorts of nags you've got hobbled out there," said the stranger, "especially that roan."

"Yes, not bad. Have you noticed any likely sorts in your travels?"

"Only at Momba. I passed through the run three months ago when coming across between the Paroo and the Warrego. There were a lot of horses there with some good-looking clumpers amongst them."

"How's the feed?"

"Pretty dry, but they might have had rain since I left."

Now the youth knew from the overlanders (he made it a point of knowing these things far and wide) that there had been no rain on Momba station these last two months. So that dry feed would now be three months drier. The station was heavily stocked with sheep that wanted the feed; and there being no sign of rain, the owner probably would be anxious. Those horses might be had cheapily. The owner would have the sheep on his mind. The station being rather isolated, he would not give a thought to the time and trouble necessary to drove those horses away seeking a market.

The lad had already learnt to think of things like this, and then to estimate the owner's position and the position of a probable buyer. Now, old German Charlie was always keen on a deal. There might be something in this for him too. Next morning he saddled up and rode straight bush on the 200-mile trip. He had never been to Momba before, but he knew the direction and was now a good enough bushman to find it.

When he had travelled 100 miles he rode into a dry belt, grass scarce and withered, the bushes brown. Fifty miles farther on there was spread before him a lesson which his mind had been made receptive enough to absorb, and of which he had the will to grasp the significance.

He reined up on a low ridge and stared away out over a flat bright green under herbage and grasses, stock thick upon it, all rolling fat. Cranes and ibises he could see in the distance.

Why this green grass where all else was withered? No rain had fallen for a considerable time in this area, and yet here was a luxuriant flat. Now what natural cause was responsible?

The flat was hedged in by ironstone ridges. He judged it to be ten miles across while it spread away apparently another ten miles to the south, and as far as he could see to the north. Every yard of flat country between those ridges was luxuriantly green. He turned, and rode up it to the north. At ten miles he saw the big gums of a creek and knew he had guessed correctly. Floodwaters! And yet not from local rain. He rode to the creek. It was dry, had been for a considerable time. Where the creek cut through the flat the bank was very shallow. A flood had come down suddenly and, the bank not being deep enough to confine the water, it had spilled out over the flat and had travelled twenty miles until its source was exhausted. Hence, grass over all that flat country, and not a blade elsewhere.

It was sundown. The youth unsaddled, hobbled his two horses, boiled the quart-pot, and by the cheery fire, ate his frugal meal.

Flood-waters. Flood-country. Not necessarily flood-water from a creek. He had heard of no creek "running" for a long time past. This flood-water might have come from country hundreds of miles away! Hence, if a man owned a station with flood-country upon it, he would have two strings to his bow! Local rain when it came, flood-water probably otherwise, so long as rain fell anywhere at all along the entire upper course of his big creek. The man who owned a station with a lot of low-lying, flood-country upon it might well have green feed even though his neighbours were suffering a drought.

Next evening he camped at a boundary-rider's hut. He patted the man's dog as he accepted a seat by the fire. He was fast growing into a judge of men. Many a man could not stand a stranger patting his dog, or taking notice of it in any way; other men did not mind; others again, were pleased. But the boy always found it hard to resist a yarn, a smile, or a pat to a dog. Dogs seemed to understand him, as he them.

"Country's pretty bad," he drawled.

"Yes. We want rain badly."

"I passed over a good strip of country on the adjoining run."

"Yes, flood-country. The creek came down two months ago, luckily for them. That grass is going to save the sheep."

"I didn't hear of any rain."

"There hasn't been any. That water came from Queensland, down a flood-channel of the Paroo. The rain fell more than 200 miles north of here. Big storms up there somewhere and down came a rush of water. Nothing to do any good to us though."

"But plenty of good to any man lucky enough to own a strip of flood-country."

"Yes, they are the lucky ones. Fills their waterholes too."

The youth changed the subject to horses. But he was wondering why he had never heard flood-water country being discussed before; wondering whether there were large areas of it; and if so whether men had ever definitely sought to take advantage of such; wondering why the fact and possibilities had never occurred to him before.

He saw that mob of clumpers; had a yarn with the owner and mentioned German Charlie as a prospective buyer. A cheap price was given him. Eventually Charlie bought and sold at a big profit with a handsome commission to the boy. By being companionable to that swagman he had made a nice commission; and by observation and thought he had sown the seeds of fortune. Flood-country in future years was to help him fight drought time and time again.

Dry times came, long-continued months of scorching suns and unusually fierce dust-storms. The tender grasses died first, the herbage withered, then the bushes turned brown and yellow. The waterhole began to dry up; the boy saw Charlie's cattle falling away week by week. He longed for rain while drinking in this lesson of the withering of the grass and the drying up waterholes. At last German Charlie had to send his cattle away to the Boolka Lakes to save them.

Then young Kidman, full of confidence and with £200 in his pocket, decided to battle his way alone through the world, independent of any man. He rode across to Mount Gipps and bought a small team of bullocks from Jim Bald; part in cash, the balance in payments as he received loadings. He was going in for transport. In this country, and particularly in the more settled area down east, there would be transport opportunities for many years. His first contract was to bring food-supplies from Menindee eighty miles away for German Charlie—at two pounds per ton.

He had carefully listened while Bald introduced the team. "These are the leaders, Baldy the near-side, Roany the offsider. A tractable leader he is, understands every word you say. Then comes Clancy and Peter, Jack and Todd, Mick and Reuben, Peter and Prince, then the two polers, Piker and Sauerkraut. These are both steady old coves, a bit thick in the uptake if they think you're a new chum. They'll 'put it over' you if they can. They call the two polers the pin bullocks, because they swing the turntable of the wagon! Baldy and Roany, the leaders, will follow the road well, they're tractable, they'll keep the chain tight; the rest are good pullers and know their job; the polers are quiet as lambs, and what they don't know about the pole isn't worth knowing."

Bald gave him several lessons which he learnt carefully. He had watched many a team being yoked and worked and was to find that his gift of observation and uncanny memorizing of detail was now to stand him in good stead. Still, he was to find that bullock "punching" and bullock management is an art.

So one morning, with Prince and Nelson, he rounded up his team. They strolled along, eyeing him now and again, understanding perfectly that here was a new-chum master. No one would have thought that they were measuring up the dog as well. They halted too far away from the line of yokes and chains stretched out on the ground just before the wagon. He hitched Prince to the back of the wagon, then picked up the big heavy whip, speculation in his eye as he set about yoking up his first bullock-team. These were not merely animals, they were trained animals knowing a surprising amount about humans; they were workers each to his special job. They would try the new boss out. Each would do what was wanted of him only if it were asked for in the right way at the right time in the right place. Each would exhibit an immediate bovine stubbornness if required to do anything but his own particular job. Like a lean statue of spotted blue the dog stood beside him, a gleam like coldly polished glass shining from his eyes.

Carefully, the lad held the whip in a certain way over his left shoulder, otherwise the bullocks would have taken no notice. An old crow perched up on a gum carked hoarsely down upon the team. The lad stood out in front of the wagon, the bullocks motionless, regarding him with bovine eyes. "Whee, whoa back Roany!" he called in a loud, authoritative voice. The bullocks gazed at him. He tried again, staring across at Roany's mild brown eyes. When he tried again and grasped the whip Roany walked slowly out and stood in his place on the offside lead of the yokes and chains stretched along the ground.

But Baldy turned and lumbered away, then in a moment was at the trot. In an instant Nelson flew after him, venom in his noiseless speed. In a second he had touched the heel of the flying bullock, and with the same instant had leapt back, crouching, his hair erect. But the bullock with a frantic bellow had wheeled, and shaking his bitten heel, came plunging back to his place beside Roany, pressing against him for comfort.

The bullocks had tried out the dog.

Then at the man's order each bullock strolled out from the mob and stood philosophically beside his mate. One by one he got them out in their correct places in correct pairs, each pair behind the other, the two polers in the rear. Elated by his mastery he walked up towards them, threw down the whip and picked up the leader's heavy wooden yoke. Working by memorized instruction he lifted the yoke end on to the shoulder of the near-side leader, took the bow out of the yoke, and rested the opposite yoke end on the offside leader's neck. Then brought the iron bow up underneath their necks, pushed the end through the hole in the yoke and slipped the key through the eye of the bow. Then rested the yoke on the near leader's neck, slipped the bow end up through the hole and slipped in the key. He picked up the first draw-chain, fastened it through the short ring which was in the middle of the yoke and let the chain drop over the near leader's hind quarters. He stood back and smiled, breathing heavily. He had yoked up his first two bullocks. He yoked each pair similarly, slipping the ring on the end of each draw-chain on to the hook on the yoke behind, right down to the polers. Now he had to get his team hitched to the wagon. Confidently he stood off, swung the whip slowly around his head calling "Whee, whoa back. Whey!" and the team came obediently circling towards him. He brought them right to the wagon, then turned them straight out before it until the polers were just clear of the pole then "Whey! Whoa!" and they stopped.

He walked to the polers, and with prods of the whip-handle urged them ahead of the pole. Then walked to the lead and with "Whoa, whoa back!" poked the leaders with the long handle. With a shake of their horns they stepped back close against the pair behind. Thus he stepped each pair back until he came to the polers. He instructed these to "Whey, whoa bullock! whoa back!" at the same time letting the whip-thong gently fall across their horns. The polers stepped back into place, one on each side of the pole. Feeling wonderfully pleased with himself, he unhooked the chain from the start ring of the polers, lifted the end of the pole and slipped it through the ring, hooked the chain end on to the draw underneath the pole, and fastened the pole end by the kingpin.

With a laugh he stood back; he had yoked up the team. With a last look around the camp to see he had left nothing behind he picked up the whip, swung it around at the length of the handle and brought the long thong hissing down to crack on the ground. "Gee Roany!" he called. "Gee Baldy," and the leaders bent slowly into the yoke. The chain tightened with clinkings down along the line bent to the yoke, the wagon creaked protestingly as the wheels slowly turned. She moved off. He had started his first wagon. It was an added triumph when he suddenly remembered he had not sworn once.

9

Bullock-Drays and Copper Towns

In Menindee men still spoke of Burke and Wills as if they had passed through but yesterday. From there they had started on their ill-fated expedition to the Gulf. From there, too, Howitt started out in search of them. The lettering on the gum-trees that marked the camps of the explorers and the rescue party were spread throughout the district as plainly as if marked but months ago.

The township by the river gums was a depot for station stores that came upstream in the paddle-wheel steamers, and a rendezvous for the teamsters and land seekers who were crossing the river there and pushing farther west towards the Barrier, and north towards the Queensland side.

Young Kidman, now a tall, wiry youth, completed his carrying contract for German Charlie, then returned to Menindee. His team had educated him to the fact that he had quite a lot to learn about working bullocks. He was dubious about ever becoming a "professional", even with Nelson's help. Nelson, now a full-grown dog possessed "cattle intelligence" inherited through a long line of highly-trained ancestors. His instinctive cunning in anything to do with cattle was phenomenal. Cattle-dogs were used much more in those days than now.

One day while trudging beside the creaking wagon Kidman became aware of the cracking of a whip and hoarse shouts ahead. He recognized the music, then around a bend in the road saw a team apparently hopelessly bogged. Old Bill Ross was swinging his whip in an almost crying fury. Kidman "whoa'd" his team as Bill flung down his whip and jumped on his hat, then racing to the leaders he pulled out a fiver and flourishing it before their noses threw it at their hoofs.

"There!" he yelled, "you——! I'll bet you a——fiver you can't pull the——wagon over my head."

He ran back to the wagon and lay with his head in the mud before the wheels. "Pull you——. Pull!" he howled. "Pull you——sons of——. Pull!"

There came a tightening of the chains, a creak as the bullocks bent to it, a groan from the wagon then slowly the wheels revolved. "By cripes!" yelled Bill as he jumped from the ground, "I'll lose my bet but not my——head." Then he leapt up with clenched fists howling "Oh my fiver! my lovely——fiver! They've tramped it in the mud!"

In vain, young Kidman helped him dig in the mud seeking his five-pound note. It was gone. The old bullocky's wailings were loud in the land. After two fruitless hours, the teams moved on. "If I threw up a sovereign," declared Ross, "it would come down a penny."

Next day the bullocky's dog sniffed at a muddy cake that had dropped from a leader's hoof. Then it picked up the cake and trotting up to old Bill laid it beside his feet. Bill kicked it aside, and swore at the dog. But the dog picked it up and carried it patiently along. Then old Bill broke the mud cake and there, pressed tight inside, was the fiver!

Young Kidman joined up with Harry Lord and Jimmy Lambert, who were working their teams down the Darling towards Wentworth, 200 road miles away, seeking combined loading for anywhere at all. After recent rains the flat country was a picture for thousands of square miles over plain and hill. Horses, cattle, and sheep were rolling fat, sunlit days made life a pleasure for man and beast. The creak of the wagon, the tinkle of a chain, the cheery shout, the lazy crack of the whip were music. In early morning the elusive, flute-like call of the bellbird was chorused from lagoon and waterhole by the deafening row from thousands of awakening waterfowl. The new combine obtained plentiful loading in busy Wentworth, and "Gee! Whoa'd!" their leaders back towards Menindee with supplies for George Miller, owner of Redan station.

After that contract the boy ventured alone again, carting wire for J. J. Phelpe's Albermarle station at Victoria Lake, seventy miles from Menindee.

Near Wilcannia he met John Conrick on a big bay horse, a huge man, John, with a brown beard that suited his rugged face. A man made to struggle against the primitive; a type of the fittest bound to survive. With his plant and black boys he had gone seeking new country, and had found it on the Cooper. Now he was returning into the "corner" of New South Wales to drive his breeding herd back to his new station at Nappa Merri. Of the many original pioneers in his chosen country he was one that the bush, droughts, floods, distance from markets, inaccessibility, and time did not defeat.

Young Kidman now understood how to load his wagon. It was the old time table-top type, one with comparatively small front wheels but large rear ones. The flat top of the body came well out over the wheels, unlike the box wagon with the low wheels that came into fashion later. No little ingenuity was required to manoeuvre wagon and load into position.

He had now come to a more intimate understanding with his team. But he realized that this was only while the roads were good and the feed plentiful. In dry times, or when rain came and flooded the creeks and made boggy the roads, then Roany and Baldy and company would have more to teach him.

He was not a driver like Willy Maiden, Johnny Lambert, and others who could make their teams of twenty pull from head to tail. Willy Maiden could work all day with a team, or ride all day on a horse, then dance the night through to daylight.

Young Kidman decided that bullock "punching" was not his line in life. Its method was too slow for him. He liked speed—in horses, in action, in everything. This dawdling along was like dawdling through life. Opportunity was slipping by. There was a good living in bullock-driving but he wanted much more. He felt that life was worth more than merely a living.

Life was a fight and the harder one fought the bigger the end would be. On every side he saw land under settlement and coming under settlement, the building of homesteads, the constant movement of flocks and herds travelling to stock new country still farther out. The roads were becoming alive with bullock- and horse-teams; gangs of tank excavators were scattered over the country scooping out dams for water conservation. The first settlers had settled on the river-banks—near water. Those following on their tracks were settling around the permanent waterholes of the big gum creeks farther out. Stations already settled were being developed. Already the vanguard of the fencers had arrived, and big tanks were being scooped from the earth many miles back from the river on both sides. Drovers with their plants were coming in increasing numbers to drove to distant markets the growing herds of "fats". Station-hands came singing as they rode the bush tracks sure of work.

On well-established stations squatters were building commodious homesteads, and travelling the roads in dashing four-in-hands. Big wool cheques meant big money, and it was being spent as if good times had come to stay. Banks and pastoral institutions were lending money right and left. In the established districts every township held its race-meetings, stations grouped together and held meetings on their own. Money was plentiful, comparatively easy to earn, easier to spend. But there was also a tremendous amount of development work going on throughout the country.

In all this restless movement young Kidman sensed something great, sensed a rich destiny for the country and for those few men who could seize the opportunity. Bullock-drivers were an absolute necessity, and would play a big part in this phase of development, but when it was all over the bullock-drivers would still be— bullock-drivers. He decided to sell his team and engage in some activity that would carry him along with the tide. He would stick to stockdealing, a line he believed he knew thoroughly, and by quick movements, quick deals, and quick returns, gain the capital necessary to take up country of his own.

While carting for Wynbar station on the Darling young Kidman helped them muster 2000 head of cattle. Picked cattle, picked men for mustering those cattle in the heart of the mulga scrub. They were frontiersmen all, trekking now to a frontier out in No Man's Country. The MacKinnons and Tobin had taken up country on the Georgina in Queensland. The new station was to be called Marion Downs and they were stocking it with Wynbar cattle. Kidman saw them off; saw the mob disappear in the bush heading towards the border. He saw too their rations leave in bullock teams from Wilcannia. Those rations were eighteen months on the road, for when they drew out into the sandhills there was no road. Thus has the sun shone on the wagons of the pioneers, creaking slowly along, watched over only by an eagle in the sky.

So the lad contracted for a loading to Wilcannia where bullock-teams were in demand, delivered his loading, then sold the team at a profit. "Anything doing about town?" he asked the buyer.

"Plenty. Station stores going out across the border to the Paroo on the Queensland side, loading for the new stations north and west, loading for up and down the river too. Shearing starts soon and then every team will be busy carting wool to the 'dreadnoughts'. There's plenty doing."

"Any 'outside' news?"

"Yes, I hear rumours there's gold being found away out. I don't take much notice of mulga wires but there seems to be a real rush out at some place they call Cobar, about 160 miles due east of here. It's copper there though, not gold."

The lad thought of German Charlie's race-meeting. The news he had heard then was true. If he had only acted at the time he would have been there early in the rush. But this confirmation was great. A rush of men meant business, they would have to be fed, opportunity would occur in transportation, in business. Stock would be wanted for transport, working, and food. Cheerily he filled his pack-bags with food, slung them on the old packhorse, mounted Prince and winked at Nelson. "We are bound for Cobar, Nelson, you and me and Prince and old Packy. We must ride bush to find it, so if Packy lags behind you just give him a nip on the heel. Come along." And away they started.

A week later he rode into a hut and tent town, its first street now being carved out through the trees. There was an air of activity over the low hills, where the axe was ring-ring-ringing, and wheeltracks every here and there told of roads soon to be formed, of timber to be carted to this soon to be town, of firewood to the rapidly developing mines. All men's thoughts were on copper. But the roving brown eyes of young Sid Kidman, and his shrewd questions, convinced him that there was opportunity in this place besides copper. He pitched his camp by the main "street", then next morning got busy cutting down saplings from the scrub. These he dragged to the camp and erected a bough shed. Finally he selected a chopping block from the scrub. When this was set in the middle of the shed he surveyed it with sparkling eyes, standing back and wiping the sweat from his brow. He had erected his butcher's shop in a day.

"And a jolly good shop it is too," he told Nelson. "What! You think it's not a shop until there's meat in it? Well, there jolly soon will be."

Not without an effort though. The nearest cattle station was eighty miles distant. He rode straight there. Yes, they had cattle, but how much money did he have. He showed eighty pounds. The manager let him have ten head of cows at eight pounds each. In a week he had driven them back to Cobar, killed one and had the meat hanging up on fencing-wire hooks next morning. Several early risers saw the new butcher's shop and raised a ballyhoo that went ringing out among the tents and huts. Soon the shouted "Butcher!" "Butcher!" brought men strolling down until the "shop" was crowded. It looked like a going concern.

It was, for a while. But those recurring rides of 160 miles for the meat-supply ate up a lot of time. He was not in a position to buy a mob and drove them to the township. The miners paid him by fortnightly account which was another brake on rapid expansion. So far in life, in his tiny dealings he had paid scrupulously in cash, or sharp on date. He began to realize the advantages of the system called credit.

However, the business progressed. And he learnt another phase of stock work, the actual selling of dressed beef. He had cultivated the knack of estimating the weight of a beast on the hoof, valuable knowledge to stock-dealers. Now that he was actually selling beasts by cut-up weight he learnt by comparison, so that later he could estimate to within a few pounds the saleable weight of an undressed beast. That means a great deal to the buyer and seller of stock.

Restlessly he watched for added avenues of activity. Newcomers were constantly arriving with drays and horses which some, in need of ready money, sold immediately, for the roughest of living was very dear. One hundred and thirty miles north on the Darling was Bourke, where flour at times cost £100 per ton, a small loaf one shilling. With transport cost to Cobar added, living was very dear.

As the mines developed, the companies experienced a shortage of transport to cart the smelted ore to Bourke. From teamsters anxious to try their luck in a copper venture the lad bought two teams cheaply, put a man on each, and secured a contract to cart smelted metal to Bourke. From there it would be shipped on a river steamer down the Darling to the Murray, thence meandering along the Victorian border and across South Australia to Port Adelaide.

A mining-field being an unknown phase of life to the youth, he concentrated his attention on what the men knew of "country". Some were widely travelled, and a different class of men to any he had so far worked with. They all came to the butcher's shop. As he served each new arrival he asked with a smile and in that drawling voice of his, direct but natural questions. The majority of these men were interested only in minerals and could tell him very little about stock, but each was an information bureau concerning mining-fields and towns. From them the youth learnt the populations and activities and localities of field and town; and so broadened his mind map of Australia. Mining-fields and towns, especially growing ones, need stock both for transport and beef. Here again he heard rumours, rumours that fly with surprising speed wherever mining discoveries are concerned.

The usual crowd were in his shop one morning when a man asked: "Has any one ever heard of silver away over on the Barrier Range somewhere near the South Australian border?"

"No. What's the news?"

"Don't know rightly. A bloke rode into camp last night and said there's a silver-rush out at a place called Thackaringa. Lumps of silver as big as your head they're picking up. So the mulga wires say."

Young Kidman wondered whether it would not pay him to saddle up and ride quietly away. He knew far more about the Barrier than any of these men. He realized that had he ridden for Cobar immediately he heard those bushmen talking at German Charlie's he would have "got in early" here, before the real rush started. Now, if he did not act, he might miss on this silver-rush—if there was going to be a rush.

But he did not go. Somehow he felt that his life was not to be cast for mining. Stock was his line. He loved stock, horses and cattle particularly. Doggedly he clung to the longing to be a squatter.

Kidman was now a tall, good-looking youth, with a supple body strengthened by rough bush work. Under a shock of wavy brown hair his brown eyes looked at the world eagerly and fearlessly.

Had he stayed in Cobar he should have risen to fortune with the rise of the town, for millions in copper ores were produced here. But tremendous transport problems confronted the copper companies. The field was 400 miles inland, and in the lesser rainfall belt. Not until November 1876 was the railway from Sydney to Blayney opened; even then there were 300 odd road miles between Blayney and Cobar. Under drought conditions or unusual periods of wet weather the teams could not haul at all. So a few years were to go by before the young field developed.

Among the population attracted to every mining town are a number of "fly-by-nights". Checkmating these was a constant drain on the youth's time. Before daylight he would mount his horse and ride into the bush, coming out on the one road that led to and from the town. He would strike this miles out from the town and with the dawn come riding back along it. Meeting a surprised man walking beside his dray and belongings he would pull his horse across the track and drawl from the saddle:

"Good day George, I see you're leaving."

"Well, yes."

"Well, I want my money."

And the hard stare in the brown eyes, the firm set of the jaw, would invariably bring the shamefaced reply: "Well, you can have it if you can change a cheque. I've got no change."

At which the lad on the beautiful roan which blocked the road like the most intelligent of police horses, would immediately produce a roll of notes and small change.

10

The Scotch Lassie

But opposition came in the form of Harry Gellert who had the cash necessary to buy large mobs of cattle and paddock them near the town. There would be no waste of time with him; his capital also would enable him to buy and sell more cheaply. Young Kidman immediately sold out to Gellert before that enterprising man realized his weakness.

The town was short of stores. Kidman rode swiftly to Condobolin, 140 miles south-east, bought two teams of bullocks and invested the remainder of his capital (£200) on stores. He drove the loaded teams back to Cobar, outmanoeuvring the teamsters lumbering south from Bourke. He was rushed, selling the flour at eight pounds per bag, sugar one shilling per pound, salt sixpence, small tins of jam at two and sixpence each, soap five shillings per bar. Then he sold his teams to the mines, including the teams carting smelted copper. He cleared a hundred per cent on everything.

In jubilant mood, Kidman considered his next move. He was worth nearly £1000. He felt very pleased with himself and the world. He sat on a log, Prince's bridle held loosely in his hand.

Prince who would come whinnying through the bush at his master's whistle; who would follow him up the main street of a town and play all the tricks of a circus horse.

Prince now nuzzled the tall young master who pulled his ears so affectionately. "Jolly old tinker," he smiled. "Where shall we go now. The Lachlan, the Murray, Menindee, Bourke? Well then, say Queensland and the wild and woolly Paroo? Or, how about the woollier Barcoo? No? Then how about those new silver-mines at Thackaringa? No? Well—Adelaide?" Prince prodded him on the chest and Kidman laughed. "Adelaide it is. A jolly good idea too. There's a market for horses down there." He patted the jealous Nelson, thinking as he fondled the animal.

"Nelson," he inquired, "how would you and Prince like to drove behind a mob of cattle that was our very own?" The dog answered with its eyes.

He had travelled now over much of western New South Wales, he knew the south-west Queensland border, the Victorian border country, and had travelled up through portion of South Australia. He knew of country "farther out" to be had for the selecting. But markets! that was the key to the future. Shrewdly he guessed that a man, even a poor man, who understood stock and knew just where and when to market, would be in a stronger position than the man whose time and thought were taken up in the breeding of flocks. He determined to start buying and selling while travelling to spy out future markets. So while building up his capital he would also be preparing for accumulating and selling the great mobs he dreamt of. Youthful ambition soars high. He determined to visit Adelaide and gauge the future market of this coming City of the Hills.

With Sid Kidman, to think was to act.

He rode down the Darling, with Nelson seeing that the old packhorse did not jog too far behind. In a few days he caught up with a mob of travelling cattle and recognized in the drovers his brothers, George and Sackville.

"Oh, it's you," said George.

"Yes," smiled Sid. "They're a nice mob of cattle you've got there."

"Yes," answered George complacently, "they're Sac's and mine. From Welford Downs on the Barcoo."

"You've been a long way up into Queensland then!"

"Yes. And what are you doing?"

"Looking for a job," said Sid with a smile.

"Oh, are you? That's a good looking sort of a roan you are riding."

"Not bad."

"Where did you get him?"

"From Abraham Wallace."

"Abraham Wallace!"

"Yes, before I left German Charlie's."

"How much did you give for him?"

"Ten pounds."

"Ten pounds! How did you get ten pounds when you were a kid at German Charlie's?"

"Oh, I picked it up here and there." George's eyes were fixed suspiciously on Prince's near shoulder. "Branded," smiled Sid. "And I've got the receipt in my pocket."

"H'm, I can't afford to give ten pounds for a horse. What have you been doing all this time?"

"Oh, picking up a job here and there. After you left for Queensland I got a job at Mount Gipps then at German Charlie's. I've been knocking around since."

"H'm. Well, we'll be pushing along."

"Where are you bound for?"

"Adelaide."

"What about that job?"

"What job?"

"You're short of a man."

"Well, I want a man, but I don't care about giving jobs to relatives; we are going to pick up a man farther along."

"How about giving me the job?"

"Well, you can have it at twenty-five shillings a week."

Sid smiled, he knew that for a job like this an experienced man was worth fifty shillings. And Nelson was worth a man and a boy.

71

"All right. Where do you want me to go?"

"Out on the left wing. Just poke them along, but don't go to sleep on the job."

Sid nodded, flicked his bridle-rein, delivered his packhorse to the horse-tailer, then rode out on the wing. He was going to be paid for his trip to Adelaide. But he earned every shilling.

"I'll never give a relation a job again," growled George on various occasions. "I send you on ahead to prepare camp and you haven't even got a breakwind built. And there's your saddle lying on the ground as if you were a new chum! Break a sapling, and hang your saddle on it. I wouldn't like the job of making a stockman out of you!" George was hard, but he did young Kidman good. He insisted on every strap and pannikin being kept shipshape; on cleanliness and tidiness even though they were going to camp only for a night. Every job had to be carried out with military thoroughness. Sackville was easier going; a strongly built man with good-humoured face and ways. He was a deliberate thinker, and was to prove a wise curb on the youth's headlong tactics in time soon to come.

At Menindee they turned west, slowly droving out towards the Barrier. When once in the ranges, young Kidman was surprised at the mining-camps scattered amongst the hills. For the faith and work of Pat Green was at last bearing fruit. He with two brothers at Thackaringa was really digging silver slugs. Soon he was to find Eldorado in the Pioneer mine, he was to be the forerunner of the "silver kings". Others around him wild with excitement were seeking silver too. Soon, little "silver towns" were to spring up here in a day. Sackville Kidman travelled out from the mob seeking the camps of the prospectors. Shrewdly he appraised the chance of each camp ever striking anything big. For if so he could see big business here to the ready ones.

They crossed the border a little south of several striking peaks called The Pinnacles, and droving down the Wild Dog Track eventually joined the Burra road.

As they slowly travelled south, across the dry belt, and neared the coastal country, young Kidman saw that even in a few years there had been changes. Country that had been lonely bush when he rode along here on old Cyclops was now cleared, with homes of split slabs upon it; barns and fences too; while the road was much improved and carried considerably more traffic. They spelled the cattle for a week outside the Burra and here Sid was sent across to Kapunda on a business message. He would catch the cattle up before they reached Adelaide.

But at Kapunda he met a surprise that set him dreaming of other things than stock—a Scotch lassie with the Highland bloom in her cheeks and laughter in her eyes. He started love-making with his smile, his soft drawling voice, and brown eyes that could say so much. In a few days he rode on, but smilingly promised that he would return—soon.

Sid Kidman spent his few weeks in Adelaide mostly at the horse, cattle and sheep sales, and confirmed his belief that this city would grow into a market for stock on a huge scale. He rode back into the bush hoping that in time he would help supply that market. Even with this great ambition on his mind he found time to stay a week at Kapunda. When he rode away again he had developed another and equally strong ambition— he wanted the Scotch lass too. He told her that he would return some day—soon. She laughed provocatively and admitted that she might be there. But the Scotch lass was shrewd as well as charming. She saw in this good-looking, smiling young Australian the makings of a big man. Handicapped by lack of education, still he appeared quick to learn. Quietly she decided that being a school-teacher, she would be his teacher.

Indeed she had already made an attempt, and was well pleased with her pupil. She quickly found that his phenomenal memory was to make the task easy. He only needed telling once. He was desperately eager to know anything that had to do with stock. So far as she knew it, she told him the history of stock in Australia. She had a liking for history.

Kidman returned to Menindee eagerly determined to make a start. There be found that cattle in thousands were travelling down the Darling to the Murray and across into Victoria. For the droving of big mobs horses were in constant demand. He knew just where to get them. He rode across country to Burkes Cave, bought a small mob and hurried them back. Driven horses can travel twenty to thirty miles a day to the bullocks' eight to fourteen. He sold them well, then made quick trips to the Lachlan; into the Cobar district; across towards Wilcannia, and over much of the country he had seen stocked with horses. His observation and memory were now beginning to stand him in good stead. He returned to the upper Darling with mob after mob, each mob larger than the one before. And all sold readily.

But Kidman nearly failed with one mob. He had bought a fine mob of utilities, in great condition, from two selectors on the Lachlan. He set out immediately for Thackaringa, for "mulga wires" were insistent about a rush of men to a big silver find.

Two days later he stared hard at a chestnut. He caught the horse, spat on his hand and rubbed its nose vigorously. The stain came off on his hand. The white blaze down the chestnut's nose was the only weak spot in an otherwise perfect job. He caught horse after horse and examined the brands. But only on one could he detect signs of faking. He was to learn more of this dark art in the future. He drove the horses straight back to those bogus selectors. To his relief they were still there, standing smoking by the hut door.

"Good day."

"Good day."

"These horses you sold me are all duffed. I want my money back."

"We sold you no horses."

"Why talk about it. You have a snug plant here; it is worth more to you than the money I paid you for the horses." He gazed fearlessly at the sudden threat in the taller man's eyes. "I am not afraid of you shooting me. Give me my money back and that will be all about it."

"Suppose you go and brag about how you got your money back," drawled the taller man.

"I'm not a fool. I am making my living in this district horse- and cattle-dealing. Other people's business has got nothing to do with me!"

"Why don't you go ahead and sell the horses then? There is quick money in them."

"My business is different to yours. I can't disappear in a night. If I sell one horse with a stained nose or a faked brand then my business is settled for good and all."

"Better come in and have a cup of tea," they invited.

He did so, and eventually got his money back. He rode away without once glancing behind but with a firm resolve to examine closely every horse and every brand on every horse that he bought in the future.

II

"Mudmaps"

Now, Kidman had not seen the Scotch lassie for quite a long time. He did not want to return unless he was on a job. So he loaded up the old packhorse, saddled Prince, and with a whistle to Nelson rode away north-east. Kapunda lay 350 miles south-west. On the second day out he met a mob of sheep, not a soul with them. Yes! a very faithful soul, Thackaringa Billy's wonderful dog. The sheep, all wethers, were nicely spread out and feeding contentedly along with the dog behind them—as perfect in its care, its watchfulness, its mastery of the situation as a good man. Kidman sat his horse and admired the dog's work, a dog that was to become known throughout the entire west of New South Wales. Kidman rode on and presently met a following mob of ewes and lambs, with Thackaringa Billy coming behind driving a cart loaded with baby lambs. The horse pulled up without Thackaringa's "Whoa". He was a tall, lean drover with the bushman's drawl. With a steady glance he regarded Kidman.

"Good day, Sid."

"Good day, Thack. That's a nice mob you've got."

"Not bad."

"Where are you bound for?"

"Beechworth—on the Victorian side."

"Anything doing down there?"

"English capital is pouring in."

"I see your dog ahead with the wethers."

"Yes."

"How will she know when to camp?"

"She will hold her mob and wait for me an hour before sundown."

"Water?"

"She will hold her mob at the Lily Lagoon until I come up and water them."

"Must be worth a couple of men to you."

"More."

"Which way have you come?"

"The Paroo, Queensland side."

"Any grass?"

"Plenty."

"See any horses?"

"Yes. Buying any?"

"Yes."

"Well, you ought to pick up a few good sorts cheap this side of the border."

"Thanks. How's the water?"

"Good."

"Any movement across on the Queensland side?"

"Plenty. The country is moving. Victorian capital is going into Queensland, while the Queenslanders themselves are developing their west."

"Know anything about the farthest west—Cooper, Diamantina and Georgina?"

"Only hearsay. Stations are established out there now, but the blacks are bad, water scarce, and the teams are often twelve months on the road. The country isn't the best and is isolated from markets."

"I suppose a man would need money to take up country there."

"He would. It is a big man's country. Big capital, big distances, big herds, and a heart as big as an elephant."

"What sort of country is it nearer in?"

"I've only seen the fringe. Nothing like the central country. It's good, but you want miles of it instead of acres. A horse-paddock out there is about the size of Ireland."

"I'd like to own 100,000 acres of this country."

"So would I. But they'll eat it out in time."

"How?"

"Overstocking."

"I can't see that."

"You will—in thirty years or so. This saltbush country will hardly carry a sheep to ten acres all the year round. Yet they're rushing stock on to it as if it was the one-sheep-one-acre country of the coast. Well, I must be moving. I see the dog looking back from that ridge ahead. So long."

"So long."

Kidman rode on, musing. "One sheep to the acre, ten sheep to the acre!" Land did vary. After all, it was simple to realize that 10,000 acres of any given country could only feed a certain number of stock the year round, strictly regulated by its carrying capacity and by contingencies arising from varying seasons. To overstock that country would mean to eat it out. But it did seem inconceivable that this sea of saltbush and herbage, this cottonbush, bluebush, these grasses, this acacia and mulga and gidgee could ever be eaten out. He began to visualize the continent as one gigantic paddock. A paddock not 100 years old as far as stock was concerned, a paddock of practically 3,000,000 square miles, so the Scotch lass had told him. The first stock came in the lumbersome old First Fleet, waddling across the seas like middle-aged ducks. That was in 1788. They landed one stallion, three mares, one colt and two fillies. One bull, four cows, one bull calf, for the "Public stock". But the officers of the ships also landed an odd cow or two and a sheep or two as a private investment. That was ninety-one years ago. And now those cattle and horses and sheep, with a few others introduced by other ships, had multiplied into over 6,000,000 cattle, 53,000,000 sheep, 800,000 horses. Those were the last census figures. Hardly credible it seemed.

"What did the Scotch lassie say the area of our New South Wales paddock was, Prince? Ah—310,000 square miles. And in the last census it ran over 3,000,000 cattle, 25,000,000 sheep, 300,000 horses. That is 28,300,000 head of stock in our paddock of 310,000 square miles, Prince. Sounds like a fairly well stocked paddock already but there is room for as many more. Now, Prince, we have 310,000 square miles carrying 28,300,000 head of stock. How many head of stock is that to the square mile?

"Ah, you can't say. Neither can I. Well, tell me how many stock that is to the acre? You cannot! Prince, we will have to ride back to the Scotch lass for another lesson."

He rode along, very interested in his thoughts. His "Victorian paddock" was only of 87,000 square miles yet it carried more than 1,000,000 cattle, 11,000,000 sheep, 190,000 horses. Queensland was of 670,500 square miles, feeding more than 1,800,000 cattle, 7,000,000 sheep, 120,000 horses. South Australia, excluding its Northern Territory was of 380,000 square miles with 200,000 cattle, 6,000,000 sheep, 100,000 horses. Western Australia was huge with its 976,000 square miles, yet it only carried 50,000 cattle, 800,000 sheep, 29,000 horses. And little Tasmania, he mused, an island paddock of 26,000 square miles carried over 100,000 head of cattle, 1,700,000 sheep, 23,000 horses.

Not including pigs, goats, donkeys, camels, this 3,000,000 square miles probably carried 60,000,000 of stock after ninety-one years.

Even so, this vast paddock was still very far from being stocked, let alone overstocked; millions of acres of it did not carry a single hoof. Certain other areas might be dangerously near the line.

He began to think about rabbits. What had the Scotch lassie read out to him? "A census of live stock taken at Port Jackson on 1 May 1788 included five rabbits, three of which belonged to the governor, and two to officers of the detachment."

Rabbits, breeding at a great rate. No wethers, or geldings amongst them, each pair breeding a litter every three months. He wondered what would be their total figure could it be estimated. It did not seem possible that rabbits could overrun, let alone do any damage to, the vast spaces he knew of. Still, there were persistent rumours of "rabbit plagues" down south, a few voices were loud in prophesying what a dire menace rabbits might become.

Rabbits ate grass—millions of stock, billions of animals of all kinds eating grass from the one great "paddock" every minute of the day and night. Billions of jaws working, countless billions of teeth chewing—biting, grinding, digging. He rode on, thinking.

This lesser rainfall country was a hard country, a cruel country, demanding that the survivors of the fittest must use their mentality to survive. Well, he would work physically hard but would beat the country by using his head. And would put these thoughts into action.

That sundown he rode up to a homestead and unsaddled at the men's quarters. On this station they dined at "Government House" in evening-clothes. The travelling drover was made welcome at the men's kitchen. "Grab yer tools," growled the cook, "and sit in with the boys."

"Thanks," replied Kidman, "I'm jolly hungry."

He reached for a tin plate, knife, fork, spoon, and pannikin and sat in at the long table with the crowd.

Next morning, as the youth was saddling up, a buggy and four came dashing up to the homestead. It was a neighbouring squatter travelling from town. The overseer came almost running from the manager's quarters.

"The Kelly Gang are out!" he called.

"What?"

"The Kelly Gang! They've shot a policeman and taken to the hills!"

That was how "the Bush" heard the first news of the notorious gang which for two years kept New South Wales and Victoria in continual excitement.

Just below Wilcannia young Kidman struck the junction of the Paroo, and turning north followed the trickling river, lined with its red gums and its yapunyah-trees whose blossoms gently swayed from the attentions of honey-eating birds. Two hundred odd miles farther north and he rode among turpentine-trees before entering the tiny border township of Hungerford. There he heard of horses on a station near Eulo, 100 miles farther east of north. He travelled on smartly, being more anxious to ride back to Kapunda the farther he rode from it. Invariably a late riser, he awoke now to the sweetly liquid notes of the butcher-bird and harmonious thrush. His yawn and lazily out-flung arms would cause a scamper among the ground birds or early goannas negotiating his burnt out fire. "You wretched eye pickers!" he would growl at the crows high in the tree-tops. "You get no scraps from my camp."

He gloried in the look of this country; in the different earth, different grass and shrubs, different, larger, much more plentiful timber of greater variety than in the Barrier country. So different again to the sparse timbers of northern South Australia, the beautiful timber giants of Victoria and eastern Queensland, and of coastal New South Wales. All changes in country were lessons to him, carefully memorized against the time when their carrying productivity and geographical position might be availed of.

He secured his horses, a good purchase, seventy head of fine upstanding sorts at eight pounds per head. He estimated their value to the farmers at the Burra 700 miles south in South Australia, at sixteen pounds per head when he got them there. Yes, a good purchase.

That night, as usual when camping on a station, he strolled across to the men's quarters, and squatting on his heels in the kitchen hut, joined in the general conversation. He steered it around to floods of which there were varied reminiscences.

"The Cooper is the place," drawled a stockman. "Spreads out there twenty miles wide and more."

"Does it now! That's a sight I'd like to see. Must be plenty of flooded country thereabouts."

"There is, in places. I was working at Durham Downs when the Cooper came down and overflowed the channels and swamped the country into a lake."

"Must have been some feed there afterwards."

"'There was. Clover a foot high, like lucerne fields far as a man could see."

"That's the right sort of flood."

"It is. Not the sort that 'Mudmaps' was talking about last night."

"Who was he?"

"A travelling talking-machine, knocks about this district. Everything he says he's got to say it with a mud map."

"I didn't pass him on the way up."

"No, he's cut across to Bulloo Downs."

"Walking?"

"No, he's got a couple of good sorts of mares and a good-looking baldy chestnut."

"What did he know about flooded country?"

"Everything—according to him."

"Did he come from the Cooper?"

"I dunno. His beat is around the Diamantina and Georgina farther out west."

"Is there flooded country across there too?"

"Oceans of it, according to him."

"Perhaps the jolly old tinker has never been there. What is west of the Diamantina and Georgina?"

"Desert and niggers."

"What do the niggers live on?"

"Don't know, never been there. But men who have, say it's desert and niggers."

"How's the feed between here and Charleville?"

Thus he changed the subject, for his every innocent question contained a hidden reason. He never wasted a question once he found the man addressed was not in a position to answer. He would change the subject inquiring of something which the man could answer and the answer of which he wanted to know.

But as he was talking, he was thinking.

The Cooper—flood-waters—flood-country. Durham Downs —a flood-country station on a huge scale apparently. The Diamantina and Georgina, far western rivers that these men knew nothing of. But these rivers according to Mudmaps carried a greater extent of flood-country than he dreamt of.

With word to the station manager that he would return later to pick up the horses, he set off after Mudmaps, 100 miles straight through bush country he had never been in before, country in which the blacks were not always trustworthy. But his "direction sense" was strongly developed and he could always "ride straight", he was not scared of the blacks, he sympathized with and felt that he nearly understood them. Here was an additional ride of 200 miles just for a "yarn". But the information acquired was eventually to mean the ownership of a strategic string of stations.

He saw Mudmaps's fire one evening, twinkling around a gidgee log. He rode up.

"Good night."

"Good night."

"Mind me unpacking here? I'd like to camp in company."

"Same here. Hobble your horses with mine over there; they are sociable too. I'll put the billy on."

They yarned till the early hours of the morning. Mudmaps had a sympathetic and attentive listener, which was what he loved. He was a stockman blessed with a keen sense of observation but not the gift of using what he saw. He would always be a good stockman; nothing more. His very gift would bring him trouble sometimes, for his tongue must rattle on about those things he had seen here, there, and everywhere. And a too sustained loquacity in stock or station camp is apt to jar.

Kidman, with a question now and then, an appreciative raising of the eyebrows, let him get well going. Then:

"Ever been out on the Diamantina and Georgina?"

The Three Rivers

"Yes, an' the Cooper too. I know the Three Rivers like a miser knows his gold. Better. There'd be no south-western Queensand if it wasn't for the Three Rivers."

"Why?"

"Because they bring the waters down from away up north. They flow right down nearly parallel with the border only they twist and turn like snakes. So much the better because when they overflow their flood-waters join and they turn the country into a sea in places. They run right down to the South Australian 'corner', and through it and run right on into Lake Eyre. You look at a map and you'll see how they water south-western Queensland."

"I'd like to, but I don't know much about maps."

"I'll show you. Look here!" He built up the fire, then sat back on his heels, and with a stick scraped the ground clear. "I'll make you a mud map. See, I'll draw Australia. Here is Western Australia; and this is South Australia running right up through the continent. All this top northern part of South Australia they call the Northern Territory. Now, inside the line here, running from north to south, then straight east to the coast, is Queensland, this here below is New

South Wales, and south again is Victoria. Now, got all the States?"

"Plain as daylight."

"Right. Now, this long twisty mark starting away up here towards the butt of Cape York Peninsula and running down the eastern part of Queensland about 200 miles inland from the coast, is the Great Dividing Range. Now, say that heavy rain falls anywhere north in eastern Queensland!"

"Yes."

"Well, every drop that falls across the range one pin-point towards the east must flow down the gullies and into the rivers and out to sea."

"Yes."

"Right. But every drop that falls west over that range cap must flow into the gullies and be taken by the rivers inland in whichever direction they flow!"

"Plain as a corn on a toe."

"Right. Now, see this long line I'm drawing, it starts away up here in northern Queensland, but just on the western fall of the range, and here it is running through inland Queensland for about 700 miles in a twisty south-west direction. Just 100 miles north of the New South Wales border it turns west into South Australia and runs on a twisting course 300 miles until it empties into Lake Eyre. See!"

"Yes."

"Well, that long line is the Cooper, Cooper's Creek to be particular, though it's the longest river in Queensland; it is called the Thomson River, too, but it is all the Cooper. Except for an occasional deep waterhole it is a dry watercourse, except in floods. That is why the old explorer called it a creek, I suppose. Captain Sturt found it in 1844–6; the Diamantina too. He must have been as full of grit as an antbed is full of ants. Well now, here starts another line up near where we started the Cooper, but maybe 100 miles south of it still on the west of the range. This runs roughly parallel with the Cooper and in 240 miles joins it here, see!"

"Yes."

"Well, this branch they call the Barcoo. The branch north of it to where the Barcoo joins they call the Thomson. It's really all the Cooper. See!"

"Yes."

"Right. Well, you see by all these little feeders going into the Cooper from the Dividing Range that it must drain a great part of the water-shed. And you see that it runs right through a large portion of Queensland and carries all that water away down through the driest parts."

"Yes."

"Right. Well, if you're not tired, I'll carry on and show you the Diamantina and Georgina."

"I'll listen to you all night, and all to-morrow."

"You'll do me. It's a treat to talk to a man worth while. Even that dog of yours is listening, and there's not even a mopoke croaking. Just wait till I fill my pipe and I'll get on with the lesson.

"Now, here goes for another line, not so long as the Great Dividing Range, and this line runs east and west! It is really only a tumble of low hills, no real range. This low hilly line running east and west is about 300 miles south of the Gulf of Carpentaria. Now, on the southern fall of this, nearly opposite but west of where we started the Cooper, we start the Diamantina. See, she's running now, a bit twisty here and there, west of but parallel with the Cooper. She runs south-west too, and she's running through a drier belt than the Cooper. Except for big waterholes, like the Cooper, she's mostly dry; but the old explorer must have seen her in flood, for he called her a river. Now, here she crosses the South Australian border, but farther west in the Queensland 'corner', and is running in close to the Cooper. But she doesn't join; she carries on down south into South Australia and joins Lake Eyre here, some miles north of the Cooper."

"It's plain as a pikestaff."

"No it isn't; not at all. If you were in that Diamantina, in a dozen places you wouldn't know if you were in a lignum plain. The channels break up, then join together again over miles of country. But I can't put that on a map, because they are as thick as lines on an old man's face. Now, you see over here across on the Thomson?"

"Yes."

"Well, see this line I'm starting here roughly midway between the Thomson and the Diamantina?"

"Yes."

"Well, this line is the Farrar. See, it follows down here south-west of the range and gradually draws in towards the Diamantina until it junctions with it here, just above the South Australian border."

"I see."

"Well, there you have the Diamantina. Now, we'll trace the Georgina. We've got to go north and cross the South Australian border right away up into the Northern Territory. See this dot, about 100 miles in west from the Queensland border?"

"Yes."

"Well, that is Alexandria station, one of the biggest cattle stations in the world. There's no mountain range here: this is known as the Barkly Tableland, a wonderful country of plains. Now, just about south of the station the Georgina starts as a sort of a creek and runs south here, but veering at last towards the Queensland border. See, our line crosses the border here about 200 miles down and wanders off down the far western boundary of Queensland, wriggling like a snake with a pain. Now it is gradually drawing nearer the Diamantina, pretty near a parallel course, junctioning where the Diamantina crosses the South Australian border near Birdsville."

"Yes."

"Well, away down south of where the Georgina heads, and right on the border we start another little line. It dribbles south close to the Territory border all in the sand-hill country, until here it crosses the South Australian border and seventy miles farther south junctions with the Diamantina, which is here sometimes called the Warburton."

"Yes."

"Well, this is the Mulligan. Hodgkinson found it only three years ago, when the Queensland Government sent him out to

87

look for pastoral country west of the Diamantina. I've only been on the Mulligan once, you would hardly know you were riding over a river, it is a dry river, as you understand when I tell you that just west of it is the Simpson Desert."

"Yes."

"By the way, there's a queer plant grows out there, the pituri bush. The niggers travel long distances for it. They burn its leaves, mix them with acacia ash, and make a beastly imitation of a chewing tobacco. Each tribe is jealous of its trees. There is often war over them. They're a hardy lot of bucks out there. How the blazes they live in dry times beats me. They must come in to the Three Rivers. Well, now up here north, but returning from the western fall of the low hills below Cloncurry where the Diamantina starts, the Georgina (apart from numerous creeks) has two big feeders, the Burke here, and this line running parallel to the east, the Hamilton."

"Yes."

"Right. Now there you have it, the Three Rivers, the Cooper, the Diamantina, and the Georgina. And you've got the Mulligan chucked in."

"Thanks a jolly lot. You've taught me more about far western Queensland than I would have learnt in years of wandering about."

"That so. Well, it's good to hear a man admit I can teach him something."

"You jolly well have. And there's something more you're going to teach me too."

"Just mention it."

"What area of country do these rivers flood?"

Mudmaps bent over the map. "You have it here. See, the Three Rivers run roughly parallel down through south-western Queensland, to converge gradually and cross over into the northern corner of South Australia. Eventually they flow south-west to (not always into) Lake Eyre. The rivers and their channels are anywhere from thirty to 100 miles apart; and they flow through a huge area of low-lying country. When they come right down into the south-west, in the sand-hill country, they simply flow between the sand-ridges. In a lot of places you can hardly trace a bank. The river-bed is indicated by wide flats, mostly lignum bush, by big old-man coolabahs, and big old gums in places. Now, when rain falls away up here north or away out there east the Three Rivers flood and down they come. The banks can't hold them, and out the waters spill, twenty, thirty miles to either side. When the waters of the Three Rivers meet, you can guess there are some sheets of water wherever the country is flat."

"And the flood-waters gradually sink into the ground, and drain away as the rivers recede."

"You have it."

"The sun shines out and turns what were lakes of water into lakes of grass."

"I'm proud of you."

"If rain did not fall over the western country or south-western country, but fell hundreds of miles away either north or north-east, then either one or all three rivers would come down and the flood-waters would water the south-western country."

"Exactly. There need not be a drop of rain in the south-west so far as the flood-country is concerned."

"If it rained heavily only in the east, but west of the range then the Cooper would come down?"

"Yes."

"If it rained in the north, both the Diamantina and Georgina would come down?"

"Yes."

"If it rained north and east the whole three and their tributaries would come down."

"They would. Get out your life-belts then."

"I can swim, although I don't like wet feet. What grass grows in the Three Rivers country?"

"A great deal is edible bush country. Saltbush, bluebush, cottonbush, parakeelia, cane-grass, herbage, edible vines, creepers, and plenty of grasses. All possess great strengthening, as well as drought-resisting powers. On them cattle fatten at sight."

"But in a dry season the country is very dry?"

"Worse than that. But I'll tell you something else about it. In a poor season, what dry grass or bush there is about, is sweet. It's not sour country. It has substance in it. Cattle thrive on it where they'd go dog poor on sour country, even though the grass was two feet high. But it is a dangerous country, lad. The pioneers are having a rough time out there; dead men's bones are out there already. You've got to be a bushman to make the stages."

They boiled the billy again, and talked on and on. Mudmaps, with the wrinkles in his weather-beaten face clean cut in the fire-light, talking on a subject that he loved. The young man listening, with his handsome face all attention, listening to a subject that he loved. The fire paled as dawn came cold and grey. A bird called from the coolabah-trees, its mate answered. Then little twitterings broke out close by as small birds came to investigate the camp.

"They're homely little things," said Mudmaps.

"Yes. Surprising the numbers of them."

"Yes. The birds out on the Three Rivers have a very hard time when a real dry spell sets in. They know, like the blacks, when it's coming. Lots of them fly to other country. In a real drought, it is only the tough 'local breeds' that are left. I've wished they could talk, for what they could tell us about water and the finding of water would be interesting to know."

As Mudmaps boiled the breakfast billy he said:

"Look here, you're interested in flood-country; why, is it your business? But we're on Bulloo Downs now, a lot of it is flood-country. We are a long way south-east of the Three Rivers. Still, the Bulloo is a flood-river, when it does run properly. How about riding around with me for a couple of days, and I'll show you some of the channels and point out just how these rivers flood?"

"If you're ready, we'll go right away," eagerly answered the seeker after knowledge.

And they did. Kidman saw for himself what was to develop into one of the finest stations in Queensland. In the early nineties, when Jones, Green, and Sullivan owned this station it was to carry 43,000 head of cattle. They were to send away a mob of 300 to 350 fats every fortnight, walking them to Burra 500 odd miles as the crow flies, then training them to Adelaide.

"Their cows are a yard wide on the top," said Kidman enthusiastically, "and as level as a plumber's rule."

"Yes. That comes of good grasses and good breeding. They're going to build up a herd of stud cattle at Parabeena out-station." In the early nineties the enterprising owners probably cleared £40,000 a year out of this station. Droughts were to come and probably overstocking. But far worse than these were to be the rabbits, whose teeth were to eat the very heart out of the station. But young Kidman could not see this—yet. He saw a station of his dreams, a magnificent "flood-country station". And he longed to own it.

"Is the Bulloo a long river?" he asked.

"No. It rises up near central Queensland and flows south-west about 400 miles, to overflow into the Bulloo Lakes on the New South Wales-Queensland border. It is only every few years, though, that it carries enough water to flood the lakes."

After some days of wandering among the well-grassed sand-ridges and river channels, Kidman said reluctantly:

"Look here, I've got to ride back now and get my horses and sell them. What are you going to do?"

"I'll get a job on Bulloo Downs."

"Well, stick to it."

"Why, particularly?"

"Because I might write you a letter some day, I might want to know how things are going."

"Meaning?"

"Well, you don't want to be a stockman all your life! You might be a station manager, and I might own Bulloo Downs."

"What!"

"Stick to your job, you jolly tinker. And if you stick to me I'll stick to you."

Mudmaps lifted his hat and scratched a puzzled brow. He stared around at the trees, then at the tall young fellow regarding him with such direct brown eyes. There was no reading the shadow of a smile that played at the corners of his mouth.

"Well, so help me Bob, I dunno. Who you are is your business; but if ever you buy this station, I'll ride a bull to Jerusalem. Anyway, I'll be somewhere in the country when your letter comes. I can't leave the Three Rivers, I love them." And they shook hands.

As the would-be owner of Bulloo Downs rode across country for his horses a new vista had opened out to him. The "mud map" was firmly printed in his mind. And through it there now ran, right down through south-western Queensland, that lonely Birdsville track, right through to the railway being built north from Adelaide. What a strategical and geographical position. By it, the man who could command huge herds of stock could feed a city market by a "back way". He might even grow on the Three Rivers the stock to do it.

13

Silver, Gold, and Horses

Kidman jogged his little mob along at the rate of thirty miles a day on that 800-mile ride back to Kapunda, crossing the Queensland border at Hungerford, following the Paroo down to the Darling, then from Menindee striking west towards the Barrier. He was surprised at the camps scattered amongst the hills. The silver gougers relied for their supplies on bullock-teams from Menindee. A drought was setting in which eventually prevented the teams from travelling. The diggers came near to starvation; then typhoid in the puddle-holes nearly wiped them out.

The young fellow rode on, staring up occasionally at men working on the outcrops of rocks. Would a town really develop in this isolation? But—water! Even if a miracle supplied water, how could he find water for his dream herds to travel those hundreds of miles down the south-western Queensland track to here? An impossible dream!

At that very time a tiny group, 300 miles north-east, were gazing on the miracle—water! Water from the bowels of the earth! That discovery was to prove of incalculable value to Australia, far above all the silver-mines in the continent. The Great Artesian Basin was to make scores of thousands of miles of otherwise uninhabitable country fit for the habitation of man.

Artesian water was first discovered in 1879–80 at Wee Wattah and Mullyeo, on the Killara Pastoral holding between the Paroo and Darling rivers. Pastoralists immediately realized the immense value of the discovery could it but be proved that a sub-artesian or artesian basin lay under the interior stretching west and north-west. Groups of pastoralists planned to test it out. Their efforts, later, were successful.

Young Kidman rode on day by day across the dry country, ever nearing the southern rain-belt of South Australia. When there, he feasted his eyes upon the green of the rolling hills and dales. The contrast of that lovely country to his "own country" never ceased to impress him.

He arrived at Kapunda and stayed a few days and wished he could stay more. "I am not sure whether it is the country I love to see," he drawled, "or you."

"'Tis a poor man who does not know his own mind!"

"That's why I'm here, Bell, because I'm certain!"

"The drover does not drove in vain," she said, smiling as she looked towards the horses.

"No, they are beauties. I am doing very well. Better still, I have learned of some wonderful country, and have had a wonderful geography lesson. I'll make a jolly good home for you." At the lift of her eyebrows, he laughed.

"Wouldn't you like a nice home?"

"I never mentioned it."

"Well, we are going to have it. And a lot more besides."

"If that is a promise, I shall keep you to it!"

"I'll jolly well keep it. I could keep any promise to you."

"Then make your promises big," she insisted "I love to see a man grow."

"I am going ahead despite all obstacles."

"You are planning under your bonnet."

"Yes, and talking too. I always seem to talk better when talking to you. But I have jolly big plans. Ours is a wonderful country, and I am going to grow with it."

"I know you will, laddie. But plan wisely; build surely."

"I could build a palace with you," he said softly.

He drove his horses to Adelaide where they were sold at Boase's Bazaar at an average of eighteen pounds per head. Elated at his profit of £700 he rode back to Kapunda and told the Scotch lassie all about it. With shrewd Scotch caution she advised him to go warily to his next success; then congratulated him on the beautiful hand he was writing, and for as long as he would stay in Kapunda quietly helped with his education. But a day came when he saddled up Prince, and whistling to Nelson, smiled his farewell and rode away.

Riding rapidly along the Wild Dog Track he crossed the border into New South Wales, rode south to and along the Victorian border right through the mountainous Kelly country, challenged several times by the mounted police whose swift patrols were scouting the country. The outlaws who had held up banks and towns were living by the rifle and were going to die by it. Young Kidman rode across through western New South Wales and into Queensland, buying wherever he saw a bargain, then driving the mob rapidly to a "sale". Some months later he was back on the Darling where he sold a mob to his old acquaintance, Abraham Wallace, who was starting overland to stock a new station, the Elsey, in the Northern Territory. Fred Kidman was in Wallace's camp. It was a happy meeting.

"You will be pleased to hear about Alexander Forrest, Sid," said Wallace.

"Always. What news?"

"He has discovered a big river in the Kimberley district of Western Australia, and has called it the Fitzroy. Abundance of good country. He tried to cross a great range called the King Leopolds, but was forced to travel east towards the Victoria River. He discovered another fine river, the Ord. It is only a rumour that has just come through."

"I'm jolly pleased."

"I knew you would be. Western Australia is exploring the north-western coast. In Queensland, last year Buchanan crossed the Queensland border and found Buchanan's Creek; likely to be an important watering-place. It might mean a lot to me on this trip to know it is there. Ernest Favenc has crossed the

95

Diamantina and gone right through unexplored country to Powell's Creek, on the Overland Telegraph Line. So 1877–8–9 have seen a bit more country opened up."

"It is jolly wonderful," answered young Kidman. "I would love to explore country that has not seen a white man."

"There is not a great deal left," said Wallace. "At least not in very large areas. Still, a bit more remains to be done."

Brother Fred was travelling with Wallace to stock that faraway new station. Sac Kidman was going to manage Sturt's Meadows for Wallace while he was away. Sac felt confident that something "big" would start soon in the silver camps out on the Barrier. He was going to be ready for business if it did.

When they moved off camp young Sid rode beside them. Under the rising sun, with the cattle occasionally lowing as they sought mates for the day's march, with horsemen away out around the wings and in the rear. Away behind, the cook and horse-tailer packing up the wagonette, a wisp of smoke from the still burning fire rising lazily in the morning air. A bellbird's elusive tinkle away out in the mulga, the whirring flight of top-knot pigeons. Promise of a glorious day; it was good to be alive.

When the brothers shook hands it was their last good-bye. Fred was drowned in the distant Kimberleys while crossing the flooded Fitzroy.

When Sid Kidman rode back into Wilcannia it was to find the township in the wildest excitement. "The Kelly Gang!" men were shouting across the street. "The Kelly Gang's been wiped out."

Young Kidman rode out into the bush knowing that he carried exciting news for every man he met. For all that, he received news first.

"Any news?" he drawled to the first traveller he met.

"Yes. Quite a stir. Johnny Thomson found gold in Depot Glen Creek near Mount Poole. I believe it was where Sturt the explorer camped. It seems to be only a small find. I don't think it will lead to a rush."

"That is good news. The Kelly Gang is wiped out!"

"What!"

Quite pleased, the youth gave the details.

About twelve months later, flushed with success and overconfidence, he bought a small mob of cattle and drove them towards Wilcannia. On the lower Paroo he met Bullocky Bill, with his red whiskers in need of a comb.

"Hullo, Bullocky, anything doing on the Darling?"

"My colonial! A gold-rush—two of 'em. Since Johnny Thomson found gold in Depot Glen Creek they've found the yellow stuff at Mount Browne out behind the Glen. They say there's 1000 men there already. I'm going into Wilcannia for loading for the field, it'll be a rough road, if there's any at all. Last Good Friday and Easter Monday they found gold around some granite rocks at a place they call Tibooburra, about 180 miles north of Wilcannia. Money's flowing into Wilcannia like rain off a bullick's back. Where've you been that you haven't heard the news?"

"In Queensland on the Barcoo."

"Oh! the land where the tall gins are. Well, you won't know Wilcannia when you see it."

"That is great news, Bullocky, I wish we could see the Roaring Fifties over again."

"My colonial! I'd swing into a millionaire on a bullick's tail inside of twelve months."

"And I'd get there with horses."

"I've a feeling you're going to get there whether or no, Sid. Brains were knocking about when you were foaled."

Kidman laughed. "I've still got to learn how to use them."

"You'll find that a harder job than driving bullicks!"

Positive now of a good sale young Kidman hurried his mob to Wilcannia to find the town over supplied. He sold out at a loss of £100. He determined not to waste one vain regret. He would *never* regret a loss. In future, he must take into calculation the probability that any likely market might be rushed by other men. He must think quicker and widen his mental horizon, else go down under competition.

Wilcannia was growing rapidly. Already a base of supplies for many of the western stations, a road led from it across the border into Queensland, another was starting to the gold-rush at Tibooburra, and yet another to Mount Browne. Further, there was the regular road down along the river gums to Menindee, and several others were being opened up. Stores came up-river in the "dreadnoughts" which returned downstream loaded with wool. The town, quite lively of nights with its dances to the music of piano, fiddle, and concertina, was now to leap ahead under the impetus of the two gold finds. Had Sturt only found gold at Depot Glen where he had been marooned so long, or had he only kept his sample stones from the "broken hill" instead of discarding them in the desert, how different might have been his life and Australian history.

At Wilcannia, Kidman met Bill Emmett, a famous horseman and dealer of the west. Slightly built, with a humorous twinkle in his eye, he was clean shaven—unusual in those days of beards. In addition to a great love of horses, they had much in common.

"You're a young colt," said Emmett, one day. "You need breaking in."

"You're an old horse," smiled Kidman. "I wouldn't mind taking lessons from you."

"Right!" exclaimed Emmett. "We'll go into partnership. I know a lot about horses and horse-dealing; I know the buyers; I know the country. We'll take up a selection as a base. I'll scour the country buying and selling. You look after the horses on the selection as I bring them in; and do a bit of buying and selling in the district while I'm travelling."

"That's a jolly fine idea. Just what I want too, now that I've learned I don't know as much about stock-dealing as I thought I did. When do we take up the selection?"

"Come to the Court House now."

And so began an invaluable partnership which was to teach Kidman the horse "inside out", not only singly but in mobs, to teach him judgment, at a glance, of capabilities; horse management, from that of a thoroughbred to a draught; the quick classification and valuation of a mob of horses of mixed classes and breeds. He was to learn the art of buying, selling, and trading.

The first day he and Emmett began active partnership he learned that he knew practically "nothing" about a horse. He resolved that not a solitary hint this man let fall would escape him; that he would learn for as long as this master had something to teach him. If he needed a whip, it was supplied by the memory of two bright Scotch eyes.

He learnt also, thankfulness for daily bread. Many a morning he would awake to see the shadowy form of Emmett bending over the fire in the little hut. Emmett would boil a pannikin of water, make his tea in that, then cut a slice from a gristly cheek of pig and with a hunk of damper commence a thoughtful breakfast.

"That's what I call a nice little feed," he would say in conclusion. "I'm real thankful for that."

"We can afford better, Bill," Kidman would say with a smile from his bunk.

"Perhaps so. But there's many a poor beggar this morning having no breakfast at all."

And Kidman would roll lazily from bunk to prepare his own breakfast, wondering at the deep contentment of a man thankful for wild pig's cheek and damper.

Emmett was away for weeks at a time buying and selling. If he thought there was a chance of selling horses he would ride night and day to meet the prospective buyer. At a hint from a passing stranger he would ride fifty miles to intercept some travelling drover who had mentioned he was short of horses. Soon the partners had 800 head running on their selection, which was unfenced, so the shepherding of the animals kept Kidman occupied. Left to themselves they would have joined the runaways that were to develop into the present-day brumby herds.

But the young horse-dealer had also a mind and an eye for other things. Constantly riding within 100 miles' radius of the camp, he was aware of the stream of men, horses, and carts beating through the mulga on their way to Tibooburra. He stopped a party returning one day.

"Good day."

"Good day."

"How's the gold at Tibooburra?"

"Not bad, not as scarce as tucker. The Wilcannia teams don't like going out. There's not enough diggers out there yet, and there's no back loading."

"Have they got gold to pay for stores if any teams went out?"

"Yes."

"Oh, well, I suppose the teams will go out some day. You fellows going into town for tucker?"

"Yes. How's supplies in Wilcannia?"

"Plentiful, there's a 'dreadnought' in."

"That's something to know anyway. Well, we'll be pushing on. We're anxious to get back to our claims. Good day."

"Good day. Good luck."

Kidman rode straight back to the selection forty miles away. Emmett had just returned from a long trip.

"The diggers at Tibooburra are starving for rations."

"Are they?"

"Yes."

"Well?"

"How about starting a store?"

Emmett turned from the saddlery he was putting away.

"We know nothing about storekeeping, lad."

"We'll jolly soon learn. We can't fail. The men have the gold; they want the rations."

Emmett pulled at his pipe. "There may be money in it," he said thoughtfully, "until the storekeepers come along. I know where we can pick up an old table-top wagon cheaply. You can drive a wagon?"

"Yes."

"Good. We've got the horses. We'll buy a load of rations when the next 'dreadnought' arrives. We'll build our own store and sell the rations in bulk. I know a young shaver of a lad and a reliable black boy we can put on here to mind the place while you're away, which mustn't be for long. You'll probably sell the whole load of rations as soon as you reach the field. Then you can hurry back here to the horses until the next boat arrives. I'll ride into Wilcannia to-morrow, get the wagon and make arrangements for stores, then ride straight out to Tibooburra and get a nigger to help me build the store."

So started the first ration store on the gold-diggings at Tibooburra. A quaint place Tibooburra, thirty-five miles from the Queensland border, a handful of low hills and hillocks all bare granite boulders. A sombre patch of country, somewhat of a geological curiosity, an "island" of granite apparently thrust up by some mighty hand from below. Never a rich field, it supported a few hundred men for years. To-day, it is a wee township kept alive mainly by the surrounding stations.

The ration store proving a success whetted the youth's appetite for another chance. He saw it in the much larger Mount Browne field 180 miles west of north of Wilcannia. Stores were already established on this rapidly developing field, but Kidman saw his chance in the constant stream of men walking out to it through Wilcannia. It was a long, dusty track that wound out past the low Milparinka hills away out past Poole's grave; a hot track. "Those jolly tinkers footing it along the Mount Browne track have their tongues hanging out like thirsty puppies," he remarked to Emmett one day.

"Yes, even the crows fall down on that track. I wouldn't be a gold-digger, not for all the tea in China."

"I reckon we could carry their swags out on the table-top wagon—at two pounds a head."

Emmett gazed at him.

"You've got a head, boy, and no mistake. There's more ways of making gold than swinging a pick and shovel. We'll try it. The kid and I and the black boy can manage the horses until the next boat comes up with loading for the Tibooburra store."

Kidman secured his first load immediately, a big load of swags, each a whopper, for every man had his packed with blankets, tent, pick-shovel and dish, rations, to the extreme limit. Now the crowd of men tramped lightheartedly behind the loaded wagon, talking, singing, smoking the miles away. Young

Kidman drove that team with quiet satisfaction and absolute assurance. It was only a matter of time before he would own his first station. From the horse-dealing was coming in an increasing turnover; the Tibooburra store was paying well and this present venture was like picking up money from home. Time, with opportunity, would surely bring him that station and—the lass at Kapunda.

Around a bend in the road came four spanking bays, polished harness glittering as their high-stepping action drew a classy buggy. The squatter of 1,000,000 acres dashed by with barely a glance at the dusty teamster who had bid him a smiling "good day". In a few years that teamster was to be the owner of those 1,000,000 acres.

He had grown into a fine-looking young man, well liked and admired by men for his horsemanship and bushmanship—two things which in any frontier land count for much. With his knowledge of and mastery of horses he had grown again to be a trifle conceited. But he was riding for a fall.

In Wilcannia the vegetable man, Ah Sam, had a big fat horse that pulled the vegetable cart. Young Kidman had admired that horse while in town. One day:

"How much do you want for him, Ah Sam?"

Ah Sam shook his head. "He no lookee too well."

"He'll soon look well when he's had a month on our good grass! I'll give you ten pounds for him."

But Ah Sam shook his head. "He no lookee too well!"

Kidman smiled to the wiles of the heathen Chinee, for the horse was mud fat. "Eleven pounds then," he offered.

"He no lookee too well!" persisted Ah Sam.

"I don't care a hang how he looks. I'll give you twelve pounds for him and that is my last offer."

"All li!" agreed Ah Sam resignedly.

"You've got a jolly good price, you cunning old tinker," laughed Kidman. "Well, take the cart home and unharness the horse, then bring him along and put him in with my mob. I'm driving them back to Emmett's place to-morrow."

At the selection, Emmett stared at Ah Sam's horse.

"A good sort that," nodded Kidman. "Ought to bring twenty pounds. I had a tussle with the celestial to buy him. He kept repeating 'He no lookee too well!'"

"He doesn't either," replied Emmett. "He's only got one eye."

One afternoon he was feeling lonely. Prince had come up to the hut door for a crust of damper and sugar.

"I want to sit down, Prince," he said.

Obligingly the roan went down on its knees, rolled over and made of itself a cushion for the man. Then the three communed together.

"Prince, we haven't been to Kapunda for ages. I think you remember a paddock there where the grass is green and sweet?"

Prince twitched his tail.

"Ah, you remember. And you, Nelson, don't you know a certain Scotch lassie who can always find a bone in the cupboard."

Nelson wagged his tail decidedly.

"Ah, well, I'll suggest to Bill Emmett that I drove a mob of horses to Adelaide for sale. Coming back, we'll stay a week or two at Kapunda."

When passing through the Barrier with the horses, he was thrilled. Where before he had seen tents and bough sheds, he saw a "boom". Thackaringa, a rough township rolling in money, Silverton already showing promise of a much larger town, hectic night and day under its wealth of silver. Purnamoota was booming, Johnny Stokie had found Umberumberka. The prospectors then found Apollyon Valley, and turned it into a roaring camp. Campfires twinkled far and wide, while grouped fires marked the big camps, a splash of clouded light amidst a confused hum was the township.

Charlie Nickel had gone prospecting and got lost and because the earth was all soggy and wet, had slept on a cold, hard rock. He twisted and turned on that rock throughout the bitter night; exasperated and miserable, at dawn he struck it with his pick. Then stared as a fragment rolled to his feet— silver chloride! The fabulously rich Maybell was found.

Kidman saw men swarming the sombre hills. They found the Day Dream. Hundreds of them dug up great bunches of isolated slugs. They talked and thought and lived in silver as in the fifties they had lived in gold. Slugs of pure horn silver, of native silver, rocks of chloride. Transformation in desolation where before only the howl of the dingo was heard.

Under a huge bough shed Kidman found his brother Sac starting a butchering business.

"It's a great boom," said Sac. "There are fortunes here if a man can swim with the tide. It only requires a level head and a little thought. Better settle here and try your luck."

The younger man shook his head.

"It's not in my line, Sac. I understand stock but not mining."

"Neither do many of the others who are picking up fortunes here."

"They are working on the blind. Only a few will strike it. I am working with an object in view."

"All right. Then hurry back here and slip into Queensland and see if you can pick up some cheap sheep and cattle. This crowd will be wanting them in thousands soon."

He drove his horses into South Australia, dreaming that those roaring camps he left behind were the beginning of events destined to move his unborn herds down the south-west Queensland track. He saw what those baby townships might mean to his ambitions. They might form a town right on the Barrier; out in this isolation; right on his dream stock-route. It was wonderful, a market of hungry people in the most isolated portion of that long, arid line. A man could start far up in Queensland, bring a big mob down this little-trodden track that he now knew so well; sell half them here, then drove the rest across the border and sell them in Adelaide. He would be buying his stock from an area in Queensland so far from civilization that every stockowner would welcome a buyer. He would come down the south-west Queensland track, and crossing the New South Wales border, follow the Paroo down to Wilcannia, then follow down the Darling and deviate towards Broken Hill. Or from the border he could come by way of Tibooburra, via Cobham and Bancannia Lake. At Broken Hill he could sell almost sufficient to pay for the mob. Then carry on to Adelaide—the city market that could not be supplied from the west, and but tardily from the east. His dream of supplying from the far north now looked faintly possible.

Half-smiling, his brain seething with plans and dreams, he pressed his horses rapidly on.

He sold the horses well, dawdled a while at Kapunda, then rode back towards Wilcannia.

Bill Emmett owned a string of racehorses. Naturally, for a man whose life was bound up in horses. The Quack was a noted country winner, while Slim Jim and Sunshine held winning records. Like a boy setting out on his heart's desire, he now started off to Bourke to win the big handicap with Pilot, the apple of his eye. In those days, when every town and township, mining camp, and many a big station ran race-meetings, the Bourke handicap was worth £1000. But the thrill of winning is above all money to such men as Emmett. His young partner wished him a cheery good-bye.

"If you don't win the handicap, you jolly tinker, don't ever come back."

"I'd give anything to win it, Sid," almost whispered Emmett from his horse. "If Pilot passes that winning-post first I'll be the happiest man in Australia."

Several days later, as Kidman was baking a damper, there was the sound of hoofs and rapidly approaching wheels. Presently four sweating horses drawing a Yankee thorough-brace buckboard drew up at the hut door with a grinding of brakes. The driver was Richard Wagner, of Rutherford, Hall, Whitney, Bradley, and Robertson, now principal proprietors of the famous Cobb and Co. line of coaches, originally started by Freeman Cobb in the roaring days of the Victorian gold-diggings.

"Where is the manager? Who looks after all these horses?" called Wagner.

"I am one of the managers, and I can sell you horses if you want them."

Wagner looked his surprise at this tall, handsome young fellow scarcely out of his teens.

"Oh, very well, I'm in a hurry. Run in a mob and I'll inspect."

It was a cloud of waving manes and flying tails and shining muscled bodies that Kidman ran into the stockyard, hundreds of high-spirited horses selected from a huge district. From them Wagner carefully chose thirty colts and paid fifteen pounds a head on the spot.

Kidman watched this world's expert selecting those colts. They were wild as hawks, overflowing with strength and animal spirits; fiery of eye; snorting, kicking, plunging in ceaseless attempts at a dash for freedom. These were not the type of horses generally imagined as being ready almost immediately to go into harness in a mail-coach and carry nervous passengers. But as colt after colt was drafted he noted the similarity in build, the physique that denoted endurance, the spirit necessary to stand great strain on rough roads at high speed.

When Wagner had completed his selection Kidman had learned the type of horse that would command immediate sale as a coachhorse.

That knowledge was to be worth thousands to him. Wagner's cheque for £450 was a trifle compared to the information.

When Wagner drove rapidly away Kidman stood staring after him. There was one of the men who had organized that huge carrying service which had spread out across much of known Australia. Now they were harnessing 6000 horses per day; their coaches were travelling 28,000 miles per week; their annual pay-sheet was over £100,000; they were receiving £95,000 per annum in mail subsidies. These men were accomplishing one of the big things in the world, and doing it with horses.

When Bill Emmett came riding back his face fairly shouted the news. Kidman grasped his hand then petted Pilot. For Pilot had won the big handicap.

Soon afterwards, Kidman wound up his partnership with Emmett. They parted with mutual esteem. Kidman was by far the gainer from that partnership. Emmett was a master in his line, content to make a living from it just for pure love of the business. But Kidman had the expanding mind capable of exploiting that knowledge not only in a district, but over a continent.

He had learned something else that was perhaps of even greater value. He had learned to look on life with a smile; to take the kicks with a smile, and just plod on smiling again.

14

The Rat Plague

Kidman rode away, again on his own, eager for stock-buying on a large scale. One midday when boiling the billy on the bank of the Darling he saw a swagman passing by.

"Come and have a drink of tea, you jolly tinker. It will wash the Darling dust away," called Kidman.

"Wash it down my throat more likely."

"It's all the same. Come far?"

"Up river from Wentworth, then out to the Barrier."

"Any grass down Wentworth way?"

"Not bad."

"How are things down there?"

"The squatters are building homes like as if the Bank of England was behind them."

"So it is. Behind Australia anyway. Heard any news out on the Barrier?"

"Oh, they've all gone 'balmy'. There are 'Silver Kings' to every acre of mulga, and enough mining sharks to float an ironclad."

"It's a wonder you did not stay where the work and money was."

"That kind of work is no good to me, too swift. I like an

easy, peaceful life, no excitement. The night Eureka Bill struck his silver bonanza the whole town went mad."

"What! Eureka struck it?"

"Yes. You look pleased. Know him?"

"I've only met him once."

"Once would be enough, from what I saw of him. He's a man who likes his meat raw, he chews his glass when he empties it."

"I'm sorry to hear Eureka is on the scoot."

"He's not. They don't go on the scoot out there. They drink dynamite and bust."

"What is the latest mine found?"

"Oh, there's oceans of talk about some show away out on Mount Gipps station. A broken hill it is. A boundary-rider called Charlie Rasp pegged it out."

"A broken hill!"

"Yes. Know it?"

"I've ridden around it many a time. I've climbed it, I've picked up stones and pelted wallabies there."

"H'm. It would be funny if you were throwing silver at the wallabies. You'll be sore if it turns out a big thing."

"No jolly fear, I hope it does. Mining is not in my line."

"Mine either. The water out there is nearly as dear as the champagne."

Kidman rode on, right down the Darling to Wentworth and across into Victoria, buying a few picked horses here, a few there. Then turning west, followed the Murray into South Australia. If this "broken hill" would only prove a mine that would support a town for years, then all his hopes must come true.

But he never dreamt what that broken hill was to mean to Australia.

Charlie Rasp pegged it on 6 September 1883. Rasp was a boundary-rider on Mount Gipps station, lean and sunbrowned, a thoughtful, reserved type of man. Studying a prospecting book in his spare time, again and again he was attracted by the black, sombre bulk of the broken hill. He tested its rocks by the tests explained in the little book and came to the conclusion that it was a hill of tin. In reality, it was a hill of silver. In keeping with the romantic atmosphere that hung over all the silver-fields, he pegged it out under romantic circumstances. Then breathed a sigh of relief.

"Now let those laugh who may," he said. "And let those rage who wish to."

The year 1883 also saw a great stride in railway development, the joining of the New South Wales and Victorian line at Albury on the border. It was now possible to travel right through from Sydney to Melbourne by train. It was even thought that in time it would be possible to travel from Sydney to Brisbane by train, and from Adelaide to Melbourne. Faster now, the coming nation was developing.

Sid Kidman sold his horses in Adelaide and rode north to Kapunda, pleased at the growing prosperity of the country-side.

"You will enjoy green grass now as a change from saltbush," he remarked to Prince, "and I'll have milk in my tea, and need not be afraid of wasting a drop of water."

The Scotch girl was waiting with a smile and praise for his success. He enjoyed a lazy holiday at Kapunda, in which his education was not neglected. Then one day he said:

"Bell, Prince is growing fat. Nelson yawns and sleeps all day. I am feeling so contented I could take root here."

"Why don't you?"

He pointed towards the north. "My future stations lie out there."

"Why not make a life work of stock-buying, then you could live in town at least six months of the year."

"I could never stand it, Bell. I was made for the bush. I love it."

A few days later he rode away.

With all his ambitions freshly cheered up he rode along the Wild Dog Track and north into the north-west corner. And his horses plunged on right in the teeth of an invasion—of rats. In hundreds of thousands they came, apparently from the north. Slithering across the country on some fast and furious business.

His horses shied and plunged at the bodies scurrying along the track, plunged violently in a kicking terror when rats leapt up their legs. From Mount Poole to Cobham Lakes not a wheel-track on the road could be seen; every one was wiped out under myriads of rat-tracks. On the first night he was well in among them, and dared not hobble the packhorse. Prince he never hobbled.

"I'll have to give you a chance, Packy," he said. "If I hobble you the rats will eat you alive."

He lit his fire and the rats swarmed to look at it. They began swarming around it, and he had to light a circle of fires to keep them off. Nelson, with his tail between his legs crept into the circle of fires.

"There's too many of them, Nelson," he said. "Chasing rats is great fun when there's only a score or two; but when they're in millions it's different. Hullo, here come Prince and Packy. What on earth!"

He was staring at glowing eyes upon the branches, gleam of eyes as wings swished past and a rat screeched in an owl's talons. Owls everywhere, swarms of the delicate owl following up the rats.

Prince stamped right in among the firelight, nestling his head on the man's shoulder. Then Packy came in with a plunge and lash of hoofs. He set about building fires farther out for the horses, but before complete Packy was off with a frantic plunge. Prince followed him. The man stood, listening to the clanging of the bell as the horses galloped through the bush.

"They're in for a bad night, Nelson, I'm afraid. I wonder where on earth all these rats have come from?"

They did not appear to be the ordinary cellar or wharf rat; they were slightly smaller, an unpleasant looking brown rat. A similar plague was to come in the far north many years later. Every tree branch had its owl—glaring, solemn looking things, they seemed to have no wings until they swooped upon a rat.

He rolled himself in his blanket; nothing could be done until daylight. Presently, Nelson's nose was nudging under the blanket, so the man gave him a share.

And soon they were over him, needle claws, hairy bodies pressing over the blanket, wee thuds as they hopped upon him.

His hair stood on end when he sensed them sniffing at his head. He threw out his arms again and again, but they came again and again. Wrapped snug under the blanket, Nelson never moved. Presently the man with his head muffled under the blanket became aware of a faint something, a tiny gnawing. He threw off the blanket. Heavens! Thousands of rats were gnawing his saddles! He rushed them and they scampered, he built up his fires and put the saddles in between—they had got under the flaps of the tuckerbags and the food inside was ruined. He sat up all night, keeping the fires burning, with a very scared Nelson for company.

In the morning, he left his saddles on the branch of a tree, he could do nothing else. Then, stick in hand, set out on the tracks of his horses.

That day at sundown he found them, a few miles outside the "path" of the rat invasion. When he returned to camp the ironware of the saddles was hanging up in the tree. He had to walk fifty miles into Wilcannia and buy new saddlery and rations.

The rat plague seemed to be in a well-defined swath across the country.

To spy out the farther country he rode north from Wilcannia, camping one evening among a queer maze of granite rocks. The night was made hideous by the howling of dingoes. Nelson crouched close beside him.

"They'd tear you to pieces, Nelson, old man," said the youth, "if you moved beyond the firelight. Look at their eyes—like golden coals among the rocks.

"I wonder what would happen," he mused, "if the wild dogs went down to the rat country. Would the dogs eat the rats, or the rats eat the dogs?"

He crossed the border into Queensland and rode north veering east nearly parallel with the South Australian border. Lonely country, sand-ridges and needlewood flats, claypans and clumps of mulga and acacias. A further week's travelling brought him to the great line of coolabahs that marked the Cooper. Riding beside it, but now west, he crossed the South Australian border to Coongy station.

A frontier station in a wild locality, bathed in vivid sunlight. Big distances here, big spaces, sparse waterholes. A man had to find his own tracks in this area and dry tracks they were.

The main Coongy country is on the eastern channel of Cooper's Creek. When the flood comes creeping down, it fills this channel then overflows into other channels, which slowly fill about twelve huge shallows called the Coongy Lakes. Then the water backs up, rolls slowly back into the main channel again, and rolls away south-west among the big sand-ridges and gibber plains to eventually reach Kanouna and (perhaps) Lake Eyre. When that happens all living things of the land go wild with joy: the very few white men because of the huge expanse of new grass; the black men because of plentiful game; the animals and birds and insects because easy food means fatness and love-making.

But the Coongy Lakes must be filled first. Later when their beds dry, there springs up grey and green pasturage as far as the eye can see. And young Kidman, riding day by day over the land with its flood-water country, spied out the geography of this area and was excited.

Several black hunters directed him to the rough homestead. He located it at leisure and rode up with his customary smile — to receive none too cordial a welcome. He thought this passing strange in a land where strangers were rare indeed. He camped down by the creek for a week. At this place, they were rough on any blacks who showed signs of hostility, for several stockmen in this district had "gone west" with a spear through the heart. Old Jack, the cook, was the roughest Sid Kidman had yet seen. At evenings, with all hands smoking in the big rough kitchen, Old Jack would make his johnny-cakes in the heap of coals and ashes in the open fireplace. Each man must kick his johnnies from the coals when cooked. If not, well, his johnnies burned to cinders. And if he did not like it he could cook his own. Kidman had a sweet tooth and long since had learnt to carry currants and raisins in the pack-bag. He could always get a bit of fat. So he used to make his own brownies, of which he and Nelson were very fond.

On killing day, a bullock would be shot in the bush, cut up and brought on packhorse to the homestead. It would be slung up outside on a big, old-man saltbush. Each man, as he wanted his meat, would hack off a piece to grill. The manager, however, was very particular—he would only eat corned beef grilled on the coal.

"Any one would think he was a bloomin' dook!" growled Old Jack. "He'll be polishin' his teeth next!"

"And they do that too," growled a stockman, "on the flash stations down south. What's more, they have governesses!"

"What's a governess?" asked a young fellow.

"A girl who teaches the boss's kids."

"There'll never be any governesses in this country then."

"Why?"

"Because the bosses don't have kids."

"Women will come."

"Bah! Fancy women out here in the sand and mulga."

"Fancy a woman coming into Old Jack's kitchen!"

They laughed. "What the hell's wrong with the kitchen," growled Jack as he spat on the floor.

"No woman will ever come here," sneered the head stockman. "Only black gins."

"What about when the country gets opened up?" inquired a youth.

"There's no opening up this country," growled Old Jack. "It's going to be a man's country for ever. Big places to roam in, and dust-storms, and gibber plains hot as the paving of hell."

Sid Kidman, sitting quietly, listening, knowing how fast the country was opening up far above the knowledge of these men, thought sympathetically of the first women who would come gradually into this country under present conditions. There would be broken hearts for those who could not adapt themselves.

He made friends down at the blacks' camp, which brought

him under suspicion at the homestead. Nevertheless, he always liked the aboriginal even though he was to experience several narrow escapes from his spears. Meanwhile, day by day he rode out into the station, memorizing all its advantages, its wonderful floodwater country, its great isolation. It was in a key position behind the huge Innamincka station. He rode to that great place and camped near the homestead on Cooper's Creek. There was quite a little crowd of men there, while blacks along the waterholes of the big dry river were very numerous.

Near by was where Burke and Wills had formed their depot preparatory to their dash north to the Gulf. At Mulcanbar waterhole Kidman stood under the big old coolabah where they died, while the local blacks grouped around him and told him the story. It was they who had befriended King. King who staggered after them crying for food while men, women, and piccaninnies, ran before him in superstitious fear.

The young fellow spent long hours in yarning with these particular blacks. And in later years he was able to befriend all that then remained of them.

For a month he rode over this great station; its old river-bed with little "island" supporting big white gums, their butts camouflaged by tangled masses of dark green lignum, refuge of black man and dingo, meandering far away through it.

That huge old dry bed with its many channels was a mighty river in ages past, its thick lines of greyish-green coolabahs running through tablelands weathering away in age; past weathered hillocks that once were mountains. Far away the coolabahs stretch into the haze, over the brown plains and Sturt's Stony Desert. Meandering through its leagues of white sand-hills, and further leagues of red sand-ridges. How vividly the sun shines on those reds and whites!

In the Innamincka country he found the rats again numerous but not nearly so bad; the plague had passed by, or had spent itself. He heard that at Naryilco station farther north when they first came they jumped into a tank and nearly filled it. Many thousands were still about. The local blacks were tired of eating them.

"Where this feller come from?" Kidman asked them, "this feller all the time jump up?"

They shrugged resignedly.

"That feller first time rat! Next time he jump up white man!"

Thus by reincarnation they accounted for the increasing coming of the whites.

He rode down along the Strzelecki Creek for a few days, but the country here seemed so walled in by sand-ridges, to be so inaccessible, that he doubted whether the large areas of feed country in between could withstand drought; whether, indeed, it would not in time be overwhelmed by sand. He believed it to be all camel country here, too; doubted whether wheeled transport would be practicable—certainly not in dry times. Water! How that necessity ruled the lives of men! Without water there was only one thing for every living thing in the world—Death.

The big trees of the Strzelecki stretched away south to the dry salt lakes Blanche and Callabonna. Desolate "lake", dry and grey as old age, holding deep in its parched and bitter bosom the bones of giant animals long dead.

Sid Kidman rode back thoughtfully to Coongy. He could see now that Coongy was a "strategic" station to Innamincka, yet Innamincka, in view of its size and geographical position might well dominate the Adelaide cattle-market.

The fat cattle from Innamincka would travel down the Cooper to Kopperamanna, then turn off south to Hergott Springs (Marree) then south again to Farina. Something over 300 miles probably as the crow would fly, but much farther by the track. Farina was railhead to the railway coming up north through South Australia. The three hundred and fifty more miles to Adelaide would be by rail transport. But cattle could only leave Innamincka when there were waterholes *en route*.

What an isolated position! What a desolate track along which to get cattle to market!

Those terrible tracks were to be dotted with the bones of men.

From Coongy, about 170 miles north-west lay Birdsville, farthest south-west Queensland township. A "droving" town.

The Birdsville track ran south to Farina, the Innamincka track would join it at Kopperamanna, just past the Cooper sand-hills.

At Coongy Kidman bought a few head of cattle. Later he was to meet the owner of Coongy, Norman Wilson, and form a friendship of years. Then, he was to buy £10,000 worth of cattle at a time.

But now, what a job he had droving his precious few head back to Wilcannia, then to the Barrier. Half-wild cattle ready to bolt at a shadow. And a lonely track, with only a young man, a horse, and a dog to drive them. On some nights he got no sleep at all, he dozed in the saddle by day. When he did sleep at nights, Nelson always took the watch.

Travelling towards the Barrier, with the cattle now quieter, he was intensely relieved to see that the rat plague had spent itself. The rats had vanished, the owls, too, disappeared as if the earth had swallowed them. In 1921 a plague of owls without the rats was to come swarming into western New South Wales, and vanish as they had come. Years later the same species were to return again behind another host of rats.

As Sid Kidman rode on in among the Barrier Hills he saw, but only here and there, a quite different type of rat, feverishly busy in tiny communities building nests of sticks, a pile three feet high. And underneath in tunnels were families of rats, jealously occupying separate compartments. Sitting up like wee grey rabbits with long fluffy tails before their burrows as he passed.

15

The Coming of the Silver Towns

He passed Corona homestead and then along the route through Mount Gipps, amazed at the change. A rough track formed, the frontier stations developing. Those lonely ranges over which he had roamed with Billy the black boy were now dotted with tents; a "silver town" here and there.

"Yust pure silver!" exclaimed German Charlie in hilarious welcome. "Mountains of it my poy. You vos riding over it mit old Sharlie's cattle. Blind fools vos ve. Silver all around us und ve vos sell rum to bushmens ven millionaires ve should be!"

Even old Charlie was growing with the times, building a larger shanty nearer Broken Hill. Farther along in the old Mount Gipps run the youth recognized two tank contractors at work. He rode eagerly across.

"Jimmy Poole you old tinker! Davy James! How are you?"

"Why, it's Sid! We are doing wonderful, Sid! Travelling to fortune like a racehorse to the post. By George, Sid, you've grown! Six feet if an inch and whiskers like Blackbeard!"

"Everything grows in this country," laughed Kidman. "Now tell me why you are still tank-sinkers instead of silver kings."

Their expression changed; they came closer.

"We soon will be, Sid. We'll be richer than Midas. We've got shares in Charlie Rasp's syndicate, the original Broken Hill syndicate. Do you remember Charlie—that quiet boundary-rider on Mount Gipps, who used to ride around with a prospecting book and a hammer breaking pieces off the rocks? Everybody thought he was queer because he imagined there was tin in that big old broken hill. You remember, that big ironstone outcrop we used for a landmark! Charlie was queer right enough—in the sanest way! Struck the richest silver lode in the world! Just a few of us are in it, George McCulloch, your old manager, George Urquhart the overseer, George Lind the book-keeper, Philip Charlie the young station-hand, Jim here and myself. We've put in seventy pounds each to sink Rasp's shaft. Jim and I are carrying on with tank-sinking until the shaft is sunk."

"I hope it turns out all right," smiled Kidman.

"Right! Why man we'll strike chlorides any day! We have only to prove the mine and companies will rush us."

"Sounds like a dream."

"It's not. And we'll let you into it!"

Poole's eyes were watching the cattle.

"We want ready money quickly, we have not sufficient bullocks to complete this contract. We'll sell you a fourteenth share in the mine for ten working bullocks or sixty pounds."

"Right. You can have the bullocks."

Both men laughed relievedly.

"That lets us out," exclaimed James. "We can see money all around us and yet are short of ten bullocks to make a start."

They selected their ten bullocks, then he loaned them another ten as an added help. And rode away with the fourteenth share, whimsically smiling at his mining venture.

He arrived at Silverton to meet the first call of six pounds to help sink Rasp's shaft. He sold a few bullocks to Sackville and paid the call, never dreaming that his six pounds was going to help prove one of the richest mines in the world.

Sackville was doing very well.

119

"I'll be wanting stock in fairly large numbers soon, Sid," he said. "Return to the district and keep me supplied. We can work up a big thing here; this silver boom has come to stay. Why, they're even talking of a telegraph line to Silverton!"

"A telegraph line!"

"Yes, that makes you think!"

"More than all the silver in the world. If they build a telegraph to this wilderness, it means that a man can get in touch with city markets from here, and also to outback stations wherever the telegraph runs."

"Yes."

"That is the best news that I could wish to hear."

"H'm. Well, you had better return and dig in, otherwise you will lose whatever object you have in mind."

"I'll be back soon after I've sold my bullocks in Adelaide."

He drove his bullocks across the border at an uninhabited spot soon to be the railway town of Cockburn, then down through South Australia to Adelaide.

He struck a famished market and sold the cattle at a profit of £1000. In high delight he hurried to the Scotch lassie at Kapunda. He told her they were going to be married. Smilingly she agreed.

Now, he wanted to dispose of his mining-share profitably. He met a sharebroker who offered to find a buyer.

Kidman returned a few months later with another mob of cattle to learn that his share had been sold to Bowes Kelly for £150. But the sharebroker was in difficulties and could only pay him £100. However, that meant a clear seventy pounds profit. Young Kidman was quite satisfied with his first and only mining venture.

Bowes Kelly was soon to be known to all the mining world. If Kidman had held that one fourteenth share it would have made him a millionaire.

Back at Menindee, then down the Darling to Wentworth, over the Victorian border, and across the northern end of Victoria buying horses. "Useful sorts." He struck the Murrumbidgee at its junction with the Murray and rode up into New South Wales until he struck the Lachlan; then up this river

300 miles by track to Condobolin, then on until he struck the Bogan above Dandaloo, 100 road miles. Following the Bogan north to Brewarrina (200 road miles) he turned south-west down the Darling back to the Barrier over 500 road miles. Then lightheartedly he faced the Wild Dog Track. At Adelaide the bottom had dropped out of the market. Horses were unsaleable.

Kidman returned to Kapunda and his sweetheart's sympathy. She was a little girl with a quick way of thinking. She told him a story about Bruce and a spider; of a man who climbed and fell only to climb again.

"You do seem to make things easy, Bell," he smiled.

"The market will rise again," she replied. "Every market does."

"Of course. I'll make a fortune yet."

"Fortunes are made every day by those who keep on trying. One day holds as many opportunities as another, and there are plenty of days coming."

"Fail to-day and soar to-morrow! And what if a man makes a fortune and loses it?" he laughed.

"Try another day, and soar again!"

"Make a see-saw of life!"

"Yes, if you are not made to climb a steady path there is no need for a man to become disheartened just because he has lost a fortune. There are plenty of sunshiny days, make another fortune on another day."

"You make it easy, Bell," he laughed. "My wealth is only in a few horses worth some hundreds of pounds—if only they were saleable. And yet from ruin I feel as if I had only to reach out for fortune."

He reached for the paper, opened it and read a notice:

Tenders are invited to contract in the running of a mail-coach from Terowie in South Australia approximately 350 miles north-east across the New South Wales border to Wilcannia.

He sprang up, staring. In a flash he had remembered Wagner of Cobb and Co.

"I'll tender!" he exclaimed. "If successful I can use the horses in running the mails."

He trained to Adelaide, and tendered successfully. Growing ambitious to build up a series of big mail contracts, he trotted his horses up to the Burra and there George Rayner met him.

"Good day."

"Good day."

"Your name Kidman?"

"Yes."

"You have secured the contract to run the mail from Terowie to Wilcannia?"

"Yes."

"Well, I'm after it. I'll give you £1200 for the contract, £600 down and £600 in six months' time?"

"It's yours."

"Right. Come and sign up."

Elated, Kidman turned his horses towards the border. At a stroke of the pen he had made as much as he had given for the mob. And he still owned the mob.

Rayner had been far sighted too. Those new silver discoveries across the border spelt money. At a profit he sold the contract to Hill and Company. When Rasp's Broken Hill shaft struck chlorides the great rush started and the passenger coaches of this firm brought them in thousands of pounds per month.

Young Kidman crossed the border and hurried his horses right back to Wilcannia, hearing that tank-sinking contractors had come in force to the district. He sold half his horses profitably there, then rode through the first rabbit plague. Millions of them, carpeting the earth with moving grey.

"By crikey!" he thought, "if all these rabbits have bred up from the five that came out in the First Fleet they'll eat out the continent if they're not checked."

The pastoralists were to learn that rabbits came in "waves". That although droughts, floods, disease, bush-fires, and other natural causes checked them again and again, unfortunately sufficient were always left to breed up. The country might appear free of rabbits for years, then a cycle of intense breeding would be followed by waves of rabbits. During the early settlement days the rabbits had followed the early pioneers into Victoria. Spreading as they multiplied, they crossed the Murray and invaded South Australia in 1878. Other waves from southern New South Wales periodically advanced farther and farther north. Their advance guard had, in 1886, reached the Warrego and Queensland border. Those in South Australia obtained a good hold, multiplied with good seasons, then the first wave emigrated towards the west. That 1500-mile invasion into Western Australia was wonderful: across the great Nullarbor Plains, waterless in places for over 800 miles. The invaders, however, did not enter Western Australia in force until 1895. Nothing seemed able to stop the pest which was to cost Australia hundreds of millions of pounds. Man could not stop it; nor mountain nor river, nor plain nor desert.

Sid Kidman rode along, wondering at these ominous battalions.

A brightly painted sulky, heavily loaded, drawn by two outstepping horses in new harness, came swiftly along the road. Both men pulled up for a yarn. They discussed the rabbits:

"Bad for the country," said Kidman.

"I'm not so sure. Good for us anyway," was the reply.

"How?"

"I'm a rabbit-trapper. And if rabbits keep as thick as now we'll have more money than the squatters soon."

"Rabbits are a good price then?"

"Wonderful. When they first came Weinteriga was giving a shilling a head, but that would break the Bank of England."

"It would. You would soon have all the bank's money if that price kept up."

"It won't. But this rabbiting is going to grow into a big new industry. You mark my words."

The rabbiter was a true prophet. But the rabbit plagues proved paralysing. In the lesser rainfall areas at least they were to ruin, or reduce the stock-carrying capacity of many millions of acres by thirty per cent.

Young Kidman had to drive the other half of his horses into Queensland where he sold them well. He had travelled 1600 miles to a highly profitable finish. But for every pound he had already made he was to make a thousand from the knowledge he had gained of the Three Rivers.

He continued travelling, buying horses in Queensland, New South Wales, Victoria, and bringing them into South Australia, now, with its growing agricultural districts, a hungry market. With far-seeing delight he saw throughout the north-west the boring for artesian water. Private bores were to bring up gushes of water which would flood the land with wealth.

By 1884 the New South Wales Government had set out to sink bores along roads and stock-routes. With splendid success; routes hitherto impassable through lack of water were now opened up. When Kidman saw the dry track from Wanaaring to Milparinka thus made passable to man and beast he laughed from sheer pleasure. It was a great omen for the country of the Three Rivers away to the north and west.

"Let there be water!" he said to Nelson. "And they tap, tap, tap the earth and get it. A miracle!"

Later the Queensland and South Australian Governments were to start boring for water. Their success was to mean fortune for thousands of individuals besides a young drover named Kidman.

He was growing with Australia. As the nation was growing and developing its resources so was the young man growing and developing. And on the right lines: he was beginning to be known as a "solid" man. Already people were remarking: "This young Kidman seems a fair-dealing young chap!"

"Yes, never falls down on a deal. Is as good as his word." In a country where all was movement particularly towards the bush, and where news was passed on by word of mouth, men sooner or later became known individually. Kidman paid on the spot, or to the time stipulated; kept every promise; took no mean advantage. Stockowners began to save the pick of their horses for "young Sid Kidman".

One evening he pulled up at a large station. The monthly mail had just arrived. At the homestead people on the veranda were clustered around an illustrated Sydney paper; down at the men's quarters a group were peering over each other's shoulders at a paper. Someone shouted to him; it must be great news. The papers were describing the departure of the Sudan Contingent from Sydney on 3 March 1885. The first time that Australian troops had left for service overseas. The leaving of the contingent was the sole topic of conversation at the station, as it was, mainly, throughout Australia.

"Whoever would have dreamt that we would be concerned in a war overseas!" remarked the overseer thoughtfully. "We are not so isolated as we thought we were."

"It beats me," said the cook, "I thought we was like a speck in the ocean. Looks like as if the currents touch us too!"

Sid Kidman rode away thoughtfully into Queensland. Somehow he had never connected Australia with the affairs of the older world.

On the Paroo he bought a mob of cattle, drove them to Adelaide and lost £400 on the deal. He smiled. It was not that he had misjudged the market. He had been out of the "telegraph country" and much can happen to a distant market when you are months out of touch. He had not gauged correctly. He had not sufficiently allowed for time; for a growing market constantly influenced by its varying needs; by the operations of other dealers; by the constantly changing influences upon each other of the different colonies; by increasing herds; by railway lines creeping out to tap the back country; by activity in road-building, and faster and easier transport of mobs to market.

He simply had to learn still more about markets. With a smile and a joke to the Scotch lassie he rode away again. And everywhere he told all and sundry of "Kidman's great horse-sales" that would be a yearly feature in Kapunda. The pick of Australian horses would be sold there.

16

On Time with the Mails

It was on the mail-coach from Broken Hill on the rocky road to the new Terowie tin-field that young Kidman met Jimmy Nicholas—a very earnest Nicholas with something on his mind.

"You are Sid Kidman, the horse-dealer?"

"Yes."

"You know the country pretty well?"

"Yes."

They were sitting on the box-seat beside the driver. The coach rumbled and swayed along to the song of the driver, the chatter of the passengers balancing up on the roof and those crowded inside. They would be sore and bruised and tired before the long day's stage was finished. Nicholas was covertly taking Kidman's measure. That young man appeared as if nothing in particular interested him. He was now a past-master in dissembling. A strong, sunburned man, his casual glance a scrutiny.

Nicholas was sure that this was the man who could co-operate immediately and efficiently. But would he? He leaned impressively towards him. "You know the country," he said, "but there is something you don't know." He waved towards the rugged hills. "Wild, isn't it? Just hills and rocks, mulga, and dead-finish, gum-tree creeks and cockatoos. A few silver camps twenty miles apart. Prospectors here and there. A rush to this new Broken Hill. You can hardly say this locality is in New South Wales, though it is. Just an isolated spot poked right away in somebody's backyard, and is nobody's business, so to speak. Despite this big silver-rush, it won't be noticed 'down inside' for quite a while. And that gives us our chance. Now, look here" (he stared at Kidman) "in Rasp's Shaft they have struck chlorides! They've gone through feet and feet of chlorides; they've struck kaolins. They are sinking straight into a mountain of silver!"

"Well?"

"Well man! Don't you see! This new Broken Hill Proprietary Company is going to be a great success. That camp is going to grow into a Silver City. Quick! Fortunes will be made. In this isolation a city is going to spring up."

"Well?"

Nicholas stared straight out over the horses ... "Oh, nothing. I thought it might interest you."

"Mining is not in my line."

"I know. It was something else I was thinking of."

"What?"

"Transport."

"Now you're talking."

Nicholas earnestly touched his arm. "Lines of coaches to carry the thousands and thousands of passengers that are soon coming. Government subsidies for mails!"

"Why don't you do it?"

"Do you think I'd be talking if I could do it! Pat O'Neill and I have a small coach contract to Wentworth. To branch out into a great carrying business would need horses—hundreds of them!"

Kidman laughed. "I see. I'll supply the horses if you secure the contracts!"

Nicholas seized his hand. Thus started a mail and passenger carrying service second only to the famous Cobb and Co. Young Kidman started immediately to engage the right men to help in his share of the work. As he rode he thought deeply. He had guaranteed a big undertaking, calling for organization and time. Meanwhile he had his horse, cattle, and (recently) sheep-buying connexion to keep up. Then, he was anxious to start his Kapunda horse-sales. He intended to get married; he was determined to be a squatter; and now he had to get many hundreds of coaching horses. He wondered if ever a time would come when man would invent flying-machines and so cover great distances quickly.

Curiously enough, the very man he was now seeking, Mulga Bill, was wondering the same thing. Bill, dreamy eyed, sat on a box in a station kitchen, his grizzled face clearly showing he was thinking deeply.

"What's the pain in your head, Bill?" inquired the cook.

"A bloke in Sydney, called Hargrave, reckons he can make a machine that will fly in the air."

"Bah!" exclaimed the cook; "these cranks should be carted to the asylum."

"It does seem queer, but Hargrave is a heady man; there's something in it! Mark my words, our grandkids will see flying ships in the air!"

The cook gazed pityingly at Bill. "Mulga," he said gently, "you an' me have as much chance of producin' grandkids as we have of layin' emu eggs."

Kidman engaged Mulga Bill to establish the first "changing" stage on the first coach-route. Then he rode fast to Silverton. He induced brother Sackville to come into partnership with the coaching enterprise; and to definitely join his brother in stock-dealing; to make the Broken Hill a half-way base to Adelaide; Sackville to transact all stock business during his frequent absences. He got brother Charlie also to help, not only in the droving but in the organization of the coach work.

Nicholas secured several contracts quickly, and Sid and Charlie found themselves in a whirl of rapid travelling; securing and handling the teams and building the relay houses at every twenty-five miles of each coach-route. Broken Hill boomed. The Broken Hill Proprietary Company, destined to grow into the history of the nation, was floated in 1885. Thousands began to pour into the Barrier.

In the midst of it all Sid Kidman found time to get married and build a little home in Kapunda. Then for the first time he lived in a house since he ran away from home. Sometimes he would wake in the night and miss the stars. He would lie there, realizing the difference between the quietness of a house at night and the night of the bush. After he had built his home he had no money left. So he saddled Prince, smiled farewell, whistled to Nelson, and rode away through the north-west corner of New South Wales into Queensland, just west of the Warrego. Every here and there for many miles along the border were camps and teams in the bush, the ring of their axes echoing far away out in the timber. A border barrier against the rabbits was being erected, and tens of thousands of posts were wanted. A huge undertaking that proved a failure, although later, when made a dog-proof fence, it saved the nation untold money. This fence was an attempt to stop the rabbit invasion entering Queensland from New South Wales and South Australia. That was 1886. The fence was going to take years to complete, and huge sums were to be spent in upkeep.

Sid Kidman, with a mob of horses, returned to Broken Hill after the first coach contract from Broken Hill sixty miles north to Eurowie had started. Their next route was from Wentworth on the Victorian border to Balranald, approximately 120 miles. Coaches and relay teams, drivers and change men were already engaged. Nicholas secured further contracts, and young Sid Kidman found how busy life could be. Again and again he found time to drove a mob down past Kapunda and see the little bride. Her unfailing encouragement was worth more than gold.

The coaches were the Yankee thorough-brace type, first brought from America by Cobb and Co. to pioneer the Victorian routes. Now, however, splendid coaches were being made in Deniliquin (New South Wales) and at Charleville (Queensland). The coach-body rode on a thorough-brace, which gave it a swinging backward and forward motion. These two braces (springs) were several thick strips of exceptionally heavy harness leather, the ends being clamped and bolted. Ordinary steel springs would often have been overloaded and broken. The thorough-brace was practically unbreakable, while imparting to the coach "cushion" spring enough to give passengers some degree of comfort. On these unmade roads, they needed all they could get. The driver on the box-seat was high above the horses, his feet firmly down in the "toe" of the coach, a foot-brake beside him.

The coaching days in Australia, under newly pioneered conditions, developed drivers who seemed born to the era, born to handle teams of half broken-in horses over fast stages on rough roads, across country liable both to droughts and floods. In the opening of each new route Kidman got his thrill in the action that followed the planning and organizing. The starting of the only half-tamed team; the race to be on time with the mails, resulting occasionally in a hairbreadth escape. One particular day the coach stood fronting the mail change, the two broken-in polers already harnessed. The mail and luggage had been roped on, otherwise nervous passengers might not have climbed aboard. In the dusty yard, Kidman, Nicholas, big Bill Cranston the driver, and Mulga Bill were struggling to harness four recently handled colts.

"It's all right with me," shouted Cranston as he manhandled a rearing chestnut, "but what about the passengers?"

"They'll be all right," called Sid Kidman, "they won't do any harm."

"Which! the horses or the passengers?"

"Oh, they're all right, Bill. They'll be tame as ewe lambs by the time you've galloped them a few miles."

"Well, if you can harness them up I'll drive them." They did so, then let down the sliprails, and hung on while manoeuvring the wild-eyed colts to the coach. The passengers stood in an eloquent silence. They slipped the trace-chains on in a twinkling and Big Bill leapt to the box and the reins.

"All aboard!" shouted Kidman as they clung to the horses' heads. Hesitatingly the passengers obeyed.

"Hurry! hurry! We can't hold them much longer."

"Let 'em go then!" said one passenger.

"Hop aboard!" shouted Nicholas. "You'll be left!"

"I know I will!"

"But your luggage is aboard, man!"

"It can stay there!"

"Look out! They're off!" As the horse holders leapt aside the leaders reared, plunged, then the team was away, with Kidman leaping for the boot of the coach. Cranston clenched the reins in knotted hands, his feet braced against the footboard, holding back with all his strength. The colts went mad. Sparks flew from hoofs as wheels flashed around; and the passengers clung to the coach and hope.

"Thank God I'm insured!" sighed a stout commercial. "If my wife could only see me now!"

"She'd be seeing that insurance money," laughed a bushman.

"She'll be handling it soon," answered the commercial. A lurch, then sway of the coach threw the passengers in a heap.

"Sorry if I bumped you, lady," laughed the bushman, "but it's a rough night at sea."

The woman sighed. A young girl was hanging on with both hands, her eyes big and bright, her hat all mixed up with her hair. This was her first coach trip. With a thunder of hoofs and wheels, then a screeching of brakes, they took a hairpin-bend at the gallop. The girl found herself on the coach floor minus her hat.

Through the rumble and rattle came the shouts of the driver roaring on the leaders now negotiating a dangerous gully. With a rattling thunder they sped over a culvert, the horses leaping from the vibration at their heels. It was exhilarating on the box-seat, clinging there while the bush sped by, the big vehicle swaying and rocking to the hiss of flying gravel, the quick ducking of heads as low branches swished by, the breath-holding second as the wheels grazed a tree, the skill and nerve of the sweating driver. Below them a frightening picture of energy. Flying manes and tails, glassy eyes, lathering bodies, flying hoofs. If the harness should break—the coach overturn——

At eight miles the team steadied down, with his nursed strength on brake and reins the driver pulled them up. They stopped with heaving flanks, trembling as they pressed close together. The passengers emptied themselves out of the coach. The body leader started kicking and the team reared and plunged and lashed back, a hoof landed "Smack!" upon a wheeler's forehead and he dropped. Despite the pulling and shouts of the driver the team plunged forward jerking the coach on top of the fallen horse. Men were clinging to the horses' heads, but the more nervous passengers hung back from the entangled, squealing mass.

"Grab their heads!" shouted Cranston. "Give them a hand, quick!" He wound the reins around his arms and hung on. They swung two horses to the ground and knelt on their heads as passengers rushed to lend their weight. Then Cranston leapt down to straighten out the tangle. With amateur and nervous hands undoing the traces, a winker slipped off a horse and away he galloped, taking his collar with him. They rolled the coach off the crippled horse, pulled him clear from the track, then harnessed the remaining four. With men clinging to their heads, the driver leapt for the box, shouting "Ladies first!" as he grabbed the reins, "and hurry!" But the horses were winded. They started with a plunge, but soon steadied down. The passengers felt for their pipes. The mail would be on time.

17

The Coaching Days

As time went on, the Kidman brothers and Nicholas linked up with town after town, until their coaches connected western New South Wales right through from Hungerford, on the Queensland border, to Wentworth, on the Victorian border, thence west, and across the South Australian border to Morgan, where train connected with Adelaide. The coach trip from the Queensland border to Morgan in South Australia was 700 miles. To feed this line they pushed out auxiliary routes to important towns east and south-west, and to developing pastoral townships and mining-camps to the north.

The coaches travelled day and night, 150 miles every twenty-four hours while on the stage. Occasionally, through sickness, accident, or unforeseen occurrence the one driver would have to take the mail right on. In the rush work at the starting of each new line, Sid Kidman, freshly arrived from outback with horses, would occasionally drive. Seldom, however, at night, for his trained habit of falling asleep at a moment's notice had now grown dangerous. He fell asleep once in broad daylight and dropped the reins. What the passengers said kept him awake afterwards. He was bowling along with a spirited six-in-hand, a warm day, drowsy air scented by flowering trees. He fell quietly asleep, the near-side leader's and near-side wheeler's reins slid from his hand. Two passengers beside him stopped talking. Gently, the man nearest Kidman nudged him. He was awake on the instant. The horses were trotting along nicely, with two reins dangling down their rumps on to the pole. From inside the coach came the chatter of women; but there was silence beside him and on the roof behind. Gently he gathered the remaining reins in his hand, gently but with delicate agility he slid down to the footboard and gathered the fallen reins from behind the horses' tails. Almost immediately he was up on the box again wearing a bright smile.

"Near go that time," he observed.

"Near go!" exclaimed a passenger. "What——"

Then the passengers said things all together.

Old George Raynor had the dangerous habit of falling asleep when driving at night, but possessed a sub-conscious power always awake. He would fall asleep with the reins clenched in his big hand, but those fingers never unclenched. Also, let the slightest unusual tug come, just a tremor where tremor should not be, the slightest change in the rhythm of hoofs or wheels—and he was awake on the instant, shouting reproof to a stumbler, encouragement at the beginning of a hard pull, reproof to a shyer, or with his foot already on the brake if rounding a nasty curve or dipping down into a gully.

Billy White was another who while he slept drove by instinct. With Mrs Downs, of Wilcannia, a solitary passenger, the coach rolled along one cloudy night. Near daybreak an extra bump woke the dozing lady, startled to see a shadow somersaulting past the half-open coach door. Billy landed neatly with the reins still in his hands. Quickly he brought the team to a stop, hopped up on the seat and yawningly started again.

The drivers were expert in crossing flooded creeks on pitch-dark nights, making an uncannily accurate estimation of the depth of the water swirling past among the trees. Theirs had to be the instinct too of realizing whether the ford would be swilled away or merely deepened, or washed to some different position. A ticklish job in the driving rain under an icy wind, the dull lamps making the darkness worse confounded. The passengers would be sitting quietly, apprehensive, perhaps, if they guessed what was about to happen. The shrouded figure out in the night high up on the box-seat had to get the coach through if humanly possible. There came his voice cheerily hoarse. Then the gathering up of the reins sending a confident tremor to every horse's mouth. The whip slung out gently to crack reassuringly, then the reins tightened as with urging shout the team smartly gathered speed. Then the rush down the bank and the plunge into black waters with cracking whip and shouts and thrashing reins as the leaders out of depth swam for shadowed trees opposite. Then two more horses swimming, the coach deep in water as the two leaders got their feet and strained forward while the polers swam and black water hissed into the coach, to the consternation of the passengers. The sigh of relief as a tremor tells that the coach-wheels are climbing up or are on "bottom"; the splashing out of the water as the leaders struggle up the opposite bank. The coach has "got through", until the next creek anyway. The mail must get through on time! Occasionally a river or creek in a raging banker would defeat the little time-tables of man. Even then the coach may carry passengers who *must* get through.

A night of thunder and lightning, sheets of wind-driven rain, the team ploughing along. Huddled up on the box are the driver, Kidman, a trooper, and black tracker.

"We *can't* get through," growled the driver. "It is impossible. You know Bunker Creek! It flows like a mill-race and swirls out the crossing every flood. It will be a banker now. Impossible."

"I *must* get through!" said the policeman.

Below them was the blackness of the Bunker, lightning burnished its sullen flood like dull, moving copper. Through the blackness came a hiss of waters swirling past branches.

"You see for yourself!" growled the driver.

"Try it!" snapped the trooper.

He had touched the psychological chord at the precise moment, that "pride of the road" that will never stand the slur. He would not *try* to get through!

"Have it your own way then!" shouted the driver. "But don't blame me!" He flung out the whip, shook the reins, and shouted furious encouragement. The horses gathered themselves up and plunged ahead. "Watch out inside!" he roared. "Watch out inside there! Are you awake?"

Then they were into it with a splash and a sinking, a flailing whip, shaking reins, wild shouts. And the waters engulfed them, black icy waters swirling over the vanishing leaders. The four horses behind entangled by the drowning bodies plunged frantically with entangling harness as the current slewed the coach downstream. Luckily the inside passengers had held the door open and now they jumped out in to the water and clawed back to the bank. Struggling for a foot grip on the pole while clinging to the mane and harness, the four men in front battled to cut the wheelers free. Half-drowned, the men and the four horses floundered back to the bank. Shivering in the pelting rain, they stared at foam scuds hurrying past.

"I *must* get through!" hissed the policeman. He looked at the black tracker; then began to strip.

"Don't be a fool!" urged the driver. "You've felt the strength of the current; you've seen it wreck a coach; you've seen two horses drown."

"I *must* get through!" reiterated the policeman.

They entered the water together, the ghostly white form with the tracker beside him, black as the night. They could see the shoulders of the policeman forging out there just a while with the foam scuds slurring over him, but the tracker swimming by his side was invisible. Then the darkness swallowed them both.

"Jolly game men," said Kidman. "The men they are after haven't a chance against men like that."

"If they're not both drowned!" growled the driver.

On another night drive, black and cold, a swim made Kidman an enemy for life—just because he laughed. On the stage from

136

Bourke to Wilcannia, the coach carried a lady of aristocratic proportions and tendencies, and dressed *not* for a coach journey. They dashed into the Talleywalker with a shout and splash. Suddenly the lady found herself upright in brown, cold, swishy water. She held her breath and dress as, to the driver's shouts, the leaders swam until, getting their feet, they plunged through the shallower water. After the plunge up the opposite bank came the "Whoa!" of the driver, the stamping, then panting of the horses.

"Are you wet, lady?" called the driver. She descended in a dripping silence, came to the front of the coach, and glared up under its watery headlights. Kidman laughed sympathetically, but was taken in the wrong way. What the lady stuttered had best be left unrecorded. And she abashed the traveller who volunteered to lend her his spare suit. But she had to accept or be frozen. They placed a headlamp behind a damp tree and there the unfortunate woman stripped and donned the traveller's suit. But she never forgave Kidman.

During the long trips, travelling night and day on some routes for hundreds of miles the passengers sang, played cards, or swapped yarns to while away the time.

Good drivers meant everything to any coaching enterprise. To keep unwavering control over a smart team, and to get the best out of a tired team on a bad road, meant getting in on time with the mails. The main control was by reins and the whip not necessarily to be used physically on the horses. Many teams were of five, though Jimmy Nicholas and others had driven their eight-in-hand. Some men were "stylish" drivers. Andy Blake was a dandy among this lot. Some men drove more by voice than whip and vice versa. Bill Cranston was noted as one of the most powerful men on the road. That, coupled with his being a careful driver, earned him more than his share of half-broken-in teams, with resulting thrills. At one mail change, he stared dubiously at the men manhandling a team of raw colts into harness. But he took the ribbons and they plunged away. Thundering down the Mootiwingee gorge half-mad but under control for all that the king-strap broke and the king-bolt jerked out. The pole and two front wheels shot away with the bolting team, and Cranston shot out with them, clinging to the reins while the coach front crashed down with a jar that sent the passengers flying. Cranston was dragged along the ground but, regaining his feet, held back on the reins while plunging forward like a leaping kangaroo. Then the leaders got away with the bars, leaving him hanging on to the two wheelers' reins. He slewed these around and back to the crippled coach, where a little group of disconsolate passengers stood sympathizing with each other's bruises.

It was all in the game in the coaching days.

18

His First Station

Despite the rapidly increasing turnover, the partnership did not make big money. It nearly all went in the rapidly expanding costs: opening up new coach-routes; buying ever larger mobs of stock for Sac's business and for city markets. At times the partners wondered how they were going to meet expenses. Yet, always the money came. Sometimes it looked as if the business was running away with them, like a bolting coach.

"You'll be the ruin of us yet," stormed Sac when Sid came smiling in with 10,000 sheep. "How in the name of Kingdom Come are we to sell a mob like that?"

"We'll sell them all right, Sac. If we only clear a shilling a head we'll make 10,000 shillings."

"Yes, and if we only sell half we'll lose our entire capital! You stop this stock gambling, or you'll smash all of us. You hear me?"

"I hear you, Sac. I'll go very steady in future."

At which Sac would glare. As the silver towns died out after their little day he transferred business to Broken Hill, which undoubtedly was going to last. But he was to receive many a shock—to fairly dance with dismay—when young Sid would come riding in with news of the purchase of 3000 head of cattle, or 10,000, 20,000, or 30,000 sheep.

But for Sackville's judgment, his coolness, his ceaseless watching of the Adelaide and (later) Melbourne and Sydney markets, his young brother possibly might have crashed them. On the other hand, the younger brother's buying had in it a stroke of genius; it was only ever altering circumstances in the cities that prevented them again and again making a fortune on a single deal. In those days, out in the farther back, many a good bargain was made in both stock and stations through no news coming through. But though several times disaster loomed close, they neither crashed nor made the fortune.

With 5000 head of sheep from the Upper Darling, Sid Kidman was passing by Wilcannia to meet Thackaringa Billy coming with another 5000 from the Warrego. With a smile at the corners of his mouth, Sid was reflecting on what Sac would say when he found this mob of 10,000 so soon thrust upon him. One of his men rode up.

"I would like to go into Wilcannia to-night, boss."

"Why?"

"To buy a pair of boots."

The man was burning for a bender. If he entered town it meant that Kidman would be short of a man in the morning.

"What size boots do you take?"

"Eights".

Kidman kicked off his boots.

"There you are! Brand new eights, ready broken in. You can have them for ten shillings. Now you needn't go into town."

Glumly the man picked up the boots. Somehow the edge seemed off his thirst.

The next day, leaving his mob to be droved after him, Kidman rode fast and towards sundown caught up with Thackaringa Billy's mob.

"Are you going to box the mob?" inquired Thackaringa.

"No, they travel easier in separate mobs, and I don't want to 'flood' Sac with the lot at once."

"Are you going on ahead into town, then?"

"No, I'll come along with you."

Thackaringa's eyes seemed almost to smile.

"How do you think Sac will take this mob?" he drawled.

"There's no telling," smiled Kidman. "Jolly hard, I suppose; it's only two months since I brought him the last mob. It all depends on the market. Perhaps he will be annoyed. But we'll sell them; we always do."

"Plenty of people say you will come a crash, Sid."

"Of course. But those men don't realize that the country is growing, population increasing, townships growing into towns, towns into cities. And all have to be fed, on a continually growing market."

Several days later as they neared "the Hill", Thackaringa remarked: "Hills look bare."

"Yes, the axe soon clears them. Where they are building the town was a dense mulga flat that you could hardly ride through. Now you wouldn't know the place."

"In a few years the hills will be bare for miles," said Thackaringa, "and the flats too. Axe and firestick will see to that."

In Broken Hill Sid Kidman faced the wrath of Sac. After which, smiling somewhat ruefully, he retired to his hotel. The fast growing town was roaring day and night. It is difficult for us now to imagine the whirl of life that ushered in the first ten years of the "Silver City". Sid Kidman found every hotel, every boarding-house, every hash-house, every room crowded. Thousands of men under frontier conditions forming a rush town where Fortune might come knocking at any man's door. "Flash" men shod their horses with silver shoes; more than one pipe was lit with a ten-pound note.

They put Kidman in a room with two young chaps who were "cleaning up" for a dance.

"Aren't you going to have a bath?" asked one as he polished his boots.

"No, I'm not," growled his mate. "I had a bath a month ago, and I can last another week this weather."

"Water scarce?" drawled Kidman.

"Yes—expensive too."

A fact, a tragic fact, for years; as I with thousands of others know only too well. Typhoid ravaged the town until long after it had grown into a city.

It was on a coach trip that the realization of Kidman's life's dream began. He met William Coombs. Coombs had just returned from Central Australia.

"I hear that the north-to-south railway line is pushing on," said Kidman.

"Yes. But the line is an enormous undertaking for South Australia with its population of 300,000. To build a 2000-mile railway through uninhabited country!"

"They'll get it through by degrees. We're growing."

"H'm. I've just bought a place out there, Owen Springs, from Sir Thomas Elder; some 2200 square miles in the very centre of Australia. It's close to the Macdonnell Ranges, about 600 miles north of Hergott Springs railhead. Has 2500 horses on it and a few cattle. I hardly know what to do about it. Very few men have even been there."

"That is where some new pioneering is going on; taking cattle through the Macdonnells into the Northern Territory?"

"Yes. The first cattle to enter the Territory were from the Queensland side in 1872. Now they're poking in up through South Australia. The Macdonnells is pretty wild country."

"I'll give you £1000 for a half-share," offered Kidman. "I'll go straight out there; muster, and see exactly what is on the run; bring down a mob for sale; and periodically visit the place."

"Right!" agreed Coombs. "That takes a weight off my mind. I've got rather many irons in the fire. You will find that you have undertaken a tough job."

"I'll love it!" said Kidman gleefully.

He hurried back to Kapunda and told the wife. She looked into his face a moment:

"So you have started at last!" she said slowly.

"At last!"

"Well, I am glad you are married."

"So am I. But why?"

"Because if you had not been, you would have settled down

on some outback station and been satisfied for life. Now you must keep returning to civilization to see me, not to mention attending to your stock sales."

"You're not coming up there to live then!"

"I am not! You are to keep returning here and mix with other men in cities and towns. That is the way you will grow."

He put his arm around her: "If every man had a wife like you, the world would not be big enough to hold us."

With Abe Shannon for company he took the northern train to Hergott Springs (now Marree). From that quaint little train he gazed out on to the northern South Australian bush. So different from the bush he had hitherto seen. Here, as soon as they passed Goyder's line of rainfall they were in the lesser rainfall country. The timber was sparse and small, mostly mallee, mulga, and acacias. The Flinders Range along which the line ran for nearly 300 miles, was stark but glowing at times with gorgeous colour. Then they puffed out on to the gibber plain country, stretching north, east, and west to the hazy horizon. Occasionally they crossed some large, dry creek, lined with coolabahs or gums. Relics, these creeks, of ages past when rivers flowed through this land. A sparsely peopled land of brilliant sunlight, vanishing mirage, and bright bluish-grey sky. Pioneered largely by Sir Thomas Elder, who befriended so many explorers, the land so far taken up was in huge cattle stations, or just squatted upon by venturesome wanderers of Harry Raines's type. Nearing Hergott Springs, Kidman pointed to a distant sand-ridge.

"Would you think we were in Australia, Abe? Just look at those jolly tinkers."

Away on the skyline, like a string of crawling spiders, moved many camels.

"They're the boys to travel without water," said Shannon.

"They are, and carry big loads too. I don't believe we could open up the country farther north, Abe, certainly not to the north-east, if it was not for camels. This country will owe the old 'Humpy' a debt of gratitude before the north-east is developed."

"They've done a lot as it is," said Abe. "Nearly all the explorers in the Centre and on the Western Australian side have used and are using them. They did great work with the Overland Telegraph Line in 1870–3, and have helped open up many a station. Giles and Gosse and Warburton and Lindsay and others could not possibly have travelled without them."

"They could not. And the stations out here where there are no roads could not have managed. Where the country is sandy and waterholes forty, sixty, or more miles apart no team could travel."

"It is surprising how they have increased," said Abe. "Taken to the saltbush and acacia as if born to it. The old Humpy will make a meal from nearly every bush we grow, and fatten on it, and breed. I wonder who brought the first camel to Australia?"

"I don't know who. But the first camel to come to South Australia came to Adelaide from Teneriffe in 1840. Two mates died on the voyage. At Mount Poole station they told me that the camels for the Burke and Wills expedition came from Peshawar, brought out by the Governor of Victoria. But all these in northern South Australia were bred up from Thomas Elder's Beltana station that we've just passed through. He imported 100 camels in 1866."

"Who is your school-teacher?" inquired Abe wonderingly.

"A wonderful teacher," smiled Kidman. "You've met her at Kapunda! But I take a particular interest in camels. They are in my line—stock. And I may have to deal in the jolly tinkers soon."

Hergott Springs was the beginning of a township. The camps were at the springs. As many as forty teams have watered there. But in recent years, alas, the drifting sands have swallowed the springs. This camp was out on an ironstone plain with a sombre range in the west behind it. The little township presently to come was to be of strategical importance in the wilderness, for it was now railhead base to which came the cattle down the great Birdsville track from south-western Queensland.

Sid Kidman fully grasped this significance.

"Take your time, Abe," he drawled, "and buy a likely looking plant of horses and saddlery. We've got a long ride ahead. I'm putting in a few days here to have a look around."

He sought each teamster, pastoralist, Afghan, and traveller in the camp. And soon learnt what each man knew of the country north-west, east, and north-east. The country west was uninhabited for 900 miles. This was the end of the Birdsville track. At this depot the big mobs from a hardly known area would be trucked for civilization. From here the drovers would face the long track back almost due north, keeping east of Lake Eyre while jogging on up through the South Australian "corner" into Queensland to meet the Three Rivers coming down from the north and north-east. Some drovers would carry on up to the very Gulf; there lift another mob and slowly bring them down the Birdsville track again.

The man who was familiar with this geography would have a tremendous advantage over his fellow dealers who knew only the coastal and inner country of the eastern states.

Footsore, thirsty, hungry, to this camp on a gibber plain the herds would come. Now, if a man only had a station handy, a place with water and plenty of saltbush, he could water and feed and fatten many a mob at their journey's end—add pounds of money to them before sending them on their long train ride to market.

In conversation with some sunbrowned men he thought he had located the place—Mundowdna. He had. He rode there, it was only fourteen miles away and situated nearly midway between Hergott Springs and Farina, the next little railway camp to the south. It proved to be 1000 square miles of country under thick saltbush, bluebush, and cottonbush, with cane-grass, buffalo grass and Mitchell, and clumps of mulga with sand-hill wattle and coolabah. Sandy country carrying thirst quenching parakeelia, and plenty of saltbush. Its Dingo Creek was well defined with permanent soakages alive with top-knot pigeons and waxbills, cockatoos and galahs. Half-way up rocky Wirringinna hill was a wonderful spring capable of watering 800 head of cattle. But elsewhere on the run lack of water was the trouble. Still, the feed was there, and a priceless strategical position.

He rode back to Hergott. Mundowdna could wait, its advantages unrealized, until the day when he would be in a position to buy it. He had connected up his Three Rivers and droving-route now with a railway system, a priceless resting and fattening depot, and a city market. With a brain seething with plans and dreams he started on the 600-mile ride north-west. They skirted the grim shore of Lake Eyre South and jogged on into the harsh, wild north. And a tough land it was in those days. They crossed what was later to be the South Australian border and pushed on towards the very heart of Central Australia. And every day their quest was water!

19

His First Stampede

At last they rode on to Birts Plain. Covered with grass, it spread into distance, a pleasing sight. Kangaroos formed grey dots here and there. The Macdonnell Ranges filled the distant horizon.

Owen Springs station was in the very shadow of the Macdonnells. The homestead and outbuildings were rude shacks with the barest of rude bush furniture; the bunks of cowhide.

Kidman glanced distastefully at the bottles and tins lying about and the squawking crows around the unclean killing-yards. Black-bearded men, each with a revolver in his belt, eyed the new boss coldly. Aborigines, unclothed and scantily clothed, were lounging about; smoke from gunyah fires drifted above some old-man saltbush quite close to the homestead. Evidently a crowd of roughnecks. Well, there was no replacing them for a long time; he wanted work done in a hurry.

He swung into the job with a smiling vim that had a trace of the iron in it and soon had most of the men working willingly enough. This area of 2200 square miles practically meant "the world". There were no fences, therefore, really, no boundaries. The horses could run wherever they liked; their grazing limited only by the distance from a waterhole. These were far apart. Often musterers in hiding would watch the almost wild horses come trotting down a gorge to circle upon a patch of creek sand. Then with heads down and pounding hoofs they would paw the sand away, snort at the damp sand, then paw again, even to a depth of four feet, and thirstily drink the soakage water that trickled through. As they drank their fill they backed out while others shouldered into their place. But let the echo of a hoof sound from up the gorge and they were away like the wind. At dawn they would come out from the ranges to feed on the plains till some alarm sent them galloping for the gorges of the Macdonnells.

The problem of outwitting and galloping them to the distant stockyard was a job that taxed the minds and bodies of the musterers. A job to delight in. The waiting among the silent foot-hills until a steely dawn showed the shadowy mobs coming out on the plains to feed. Then the mounting, the spurt straight at them with whips cracking in the wild gallop to keep the flying animals headed for the stockyard.

Sentinelled up on the ranges, or pressed low to the mulga as the horses thundered past, the wild blacks gazed at these invaders of their prehistoric domain.

Mob after mob were thus yarded, to be shepherded on the plain by day, and yarded again at night. They proved to be a fine stamp of medium draughts that freedom and rough country had trained to gallop almost as fast as lightly built horses. And there were considerably more than 2500. Few had known a branding-iron, much less bridle and saddle. As the weeks went swiftly by, Kidman felt more and more pleased with his bargain.

With 500 marketable sorts mustered and drafted, he prepared to sell stock from his very own station. The packhorses with the cook and black boy horse-tailer driving forty spare riding-horses made an early morning start. With the men mounted and spread well out from the yard, the sliprails were let down. The horses crowded out, the leaders fanning out immediately at the gallop. But riders closed around their flanks and rear, the mob closed up behind a horseman in the lead. Staunch stockhorses those men were riding, cunning old stagers that knew every inch of the game.

With flying manes and tails the unwilling mob were guided the way they did not wish to go, leaving their beloved ranges behind them. Pounding over the spinifex, thudding through the Mitchell grass to the crackling of sticks and flying gravel, the mob galloped on. In ten miles the horsemen, now pressed close around them, had steadied them down. At a steady trot they pressed on. Amongst the moving mob was constant inner movement as with eager whinnyings mate sought mate. A chestnut surged up from the tail to near the lead as his whinny drew answer from a mate. A bay worked across from the right flank to the left, greeting his mates with eager snort and whinny.

These horses were the pick of separate little mobs that had roamed their own feeding-grounds. Now, all boxed together but freed from the restraint of the yard, they sought their friendships exactly as humans would have done. And, like humans too, little bands of friendly rogues worked out to the wings seeking a chance to gallop for it. Again and again, with sudden shout and crack of whip at the gallop, the man on either wing would swerve down on rogues who with outstretched necks were preparing for a flyaway gallop. The men drove them fast and far that day to tire them.

That night they camped warily, as they would each night, for horses are harder to drove than cattle. Horses are restless all night; are temperamental; you never know when you have them. They camped by a waterhole away from the mulga. A shadowy night, a half moon obscured by slowly drifting clouds, the muddy waterhole a film of silvered copper, queer shadows on the red ground from the drifting clouds. The utter stillness of a Centralian night. Far away, once only, the smothered howl of a dingo. The horses lifted prick ears, eyes momentarily shining. Away from the mob the glowing coals of the fire, the huddled forms of men sleeping with "one ear awake" among the pack-saddles. Ready booted and spurred, those sleepers. The night horses, saddled and bridled, standing close by. Wonderful horses are night horses. Born to see in the night, trained to know and do instantly what the rider would wish to do while sensing exactly what the mob would do. Ready to gallop on the instant, to turn and swerve and wheel and jump. A slowly moving shadow was the "watch" as he rode around.

Three men were on watch to-night, quietly riding round and round the outskirts of the mob. Anything might startle the horses; the screech of a night bird, the fall of a branch, the rattle of a saddle-flap as a horse shook itself. The mob was restless; a few lying down, but nearly all clustered in mateship groups. Now and again the swish of a tail, the stamp of a hoof. Now and again one, two, and three would quietly poke out towards a flank, but always the shadow of the watch would come gliding towards them and poke them quietly back.

At midnight the watch changed over. All was well. The night was darker. And in the stillness a darker shadow came elusively gliding on noiseless feet; a shadow that seemed to be and yet not to be. The thing glided right in amongst the mob. A horse turned suddenly to see a big beak and two phosphorescent eyes within an inch of its nose. Instantly the horse snorted and backed—the clout of the emu's kick was like a hammer blow swallowed in a burst of thunder as the mob were off. Smothered shouts of the watch, a leap for night horses that already were on the move, a flying gallop for the wave of thunder that was bearing straight down on the mulga.

The watch in the lead and flanks lowered their heads, gripped with their knees and rode for life. No hope of turning the mob; no hope of doing a thing except ride for life until the mob steadied down. Those racing behind were clinging to horses whose eyes were blazing as, with bits between their teeth, they put every ounce into it and almost shrank in stature under bunching muscles strained to the limit of speed. God help the rider who could not cling with perfect balance of body. With a crash they hit the mulga. Then the breathless thrill of men crouched low over galloping bodies that leapt and dodged and swerved and jumped as branches swished, while knees quivered as trunks sped by and lowlying limbs grazed the shivering back. With hands twisted in the manes and every sense tingling they raced, trusting in God and luck. Black as pitch in the mulga. Roots cracked like pistol-shots when horses crashed with broken leg or neck. Then a rush of open air with silvered sky and ...

"Thank God!" for the open plain again.

In seven miles the night horses won out, they got to the lead, they steadied the mob, then rung them and held them until daylight.

When Kidman rode back into the mulga he found the losses surprisingly few. A few horses lying huddled and still, more unfortunate ones lying or standing with broken legs. Of the men, not one had gone down. It would be an anxious trip now right to Adelaide. When a mob has once stampeded, whether horse or cattle, they are liable to "rush" again and yet again. It was Kidman's first stampede. He was to ride in many more, and much larger ones. But the mad thrill of each breathless ride would never grow old.

He got his mob to Adelaide and sold them handsomely on a rising market.

Two years later he was sole owner of Owen Springs. To him that station was just "it".

20

Spying Out a Continent

As time went on, Sid Kidman found that owning a station did not necessarily mean riches. His life was cast in the lesser rainfall areas. Station life there, in any colony, was essentially a frontier life. Rough country, rough conditions, pioneer transport; some stations in the lesser developed colonies 1000 miles distant from railway; 500, 600, and 700 miles were ordinary distances.

Kidman realized this tremendous difficulty for the pastoralists of the undeveloped areas—the hoof the only transport to market. Even good country so isolated could hardly pay; for transport is vital to settlement.

It took time, labour, money, and thought to drove a mob of fats 700 to over 1000 miles. By that time the fats were poor and worth fifty per cent less. Then must follow a long train journey to market where they would arrive in still poorer condition. In the case of four-year-old beasts it thus meant that the owner, after spending four years in getting them prime, and another year, possibly, "on the road" to market, would receive a price which hardly paid droving expenses. On this apparently insuperable difficulty Kidman spent years of thought. How to bring cattle from 1000 miles away and yet land them in market in prime condition was the vital question.

In the still undeveloped and unfenced northern South Australia, Northern Territory, Western Australia, north and south-western Queensland, the stock had "the world" to roam in. Homesteads were of roughly gathered stone or pisé, of axe hewn slabs or sheets of bark, or later of iron and rough bush timber. Many a homestead then (as many still are in the most isolated areas of Australia), was of bark and slabs. Station stores arrived every six to twelve months by horse, bullock, or camel-team. Up north during the wet season, the slow-wheeled transport would invariably be held up. Not so much because of water (except along the sub-tropical coasts) but because of bog. In the arid areas, failure of the yearly "wet" held up transport because of lack of water for the transport animals. That was why camels in these areas were fast pushing the horse-teams off the roads. This aroused bitter antagonisms between the teamsters and the Afghan camel-drivers now fast growing a "little Afghanistan" at Hergott Springs. So the majority of stations, particularly in Central Australia and the Territory, waged a continuous fight for existence.

West of Owen Springs for 400 miles to the Western Australian border was country unoccupied except by a few aboriginal tribes. It consisted of broken ranges running west with plain and patches of semi-desert, spinifex, and mulga. West of that border for 500 miles was the unoccupied desert country of Western Australia. The greater part of this 900 miles is still unoccupied to-day. The crossing of those western wastes had been achieved during the seventies only after failures and hardships during repeated attempts by such men as Forrest, Gosse, Giles, Tietkins (Kidman's friend the overseer of Corona), Warburton and Lewis.

North of Owen Springs for 1000 miles was country holding a few pioneer stations. A thousand miles south was Adelaide. In between was lesser rainfall country to within 200 miles of the rich southern coast. That country held only an occasional station such as his own.

Kidman conceived a far seeing, a very careful scheme. But the result was to bring only partial success. The span of one man's lifetime was not long enough to enable him to overcome the tremendous difficulties in this country; the many problems peculiarly its own, each of which had to be solved before success could even be glimpsed.

With his big dream, his "greater chain" down along the Three Rivers to the east was to become a great success. He now dreamt of forming a lesser chain of stations down through the centre of the continent. By linking one station with another, he dreamt he could defeat droughts. He believed that the Northern Territory and Central Australia would be developed, though in lesser degree than other States. A man who owned a chain of stations down through the Centre could buy stock from anywhere north and bring them down through the chain, each station forming a link where they could rest and water and keep their condition until they reached Mundowdna. Fattened there, they could then be trucked at Hergott Springs or Farina for Adelaide. Such a scheme, thoroughly organized, would mean that a man could supply the South Australian market. And the man who picked each link in such a chain strategically, would hold his advantage even after the country was developed.

East of Owen Springs were several stations to the dry Todd River. East of the Todd was the Simpson Desert—which up to this day no man has crossed. East of this desert, and 300 miles from Owen Springs, was the Northern Territory-Queensland border, over which was the country of the Georgina, Diamantina, and Cooper. And leading from it was the Birdsville track. Down this country of the Three Rivers was to be his main chain comprising two lines of stations running to the New South Wales border. The eastern line would run over the border straight down to Broken Hill, where a railway was soon to be. From this main chain he would be able to send stock to Sydney, Melbourne, Adelaide, or Brisbane. The western line of this chain, on striking the New South Wales border, would turn a little west of south and, while continuing to hug the border, would carry on through the north of South Australia, joining up with the Birdsville track on its way to Hergott Springs railway.

Between this main chain and his central chain would be the

Simpson Desert and, south of the desert the worst of the salt-lakes country to Lake Eyre. Though this big desolate area divided States, its geographical position (once he was established) would bar opposition to him from man. Road, telegraph, and train were fast developing away along the coastal and richer inland country. In 1887 the South Australian railways linked up with the Victorian at Serviceton; and in the same year the South Australian line from the Burra to Cockburn on the New South Wales border near Broken Hill was completed. A year later, the New South Wales and Queensland railways met at Wallangarra. On completion of the Hawkesbury River bridge in 1889 it was then possible to travel by train from Adelaide via Melbourne and Sydney to Brisbane: 1788 miles in a few days. Thus four of the five coastal cities were linked up. Lines were creeping inland in each State. But Kidman's country was many hundreds of miles farther out than any of these lines.

The traversing of this country of the Central Territory, South Australia, south-western Queensland, the Barkly Tableland, the Barrier, the Gulf country, northern Queensland, not to mention the three "corners" and the happy little visits to Kapunda ate up an awful lot of time. So that business now calling him fairly often to a capital could be quickly seen to, so far as coastal travelling was concerned, while now from any capital he could take a train into the country, to its terminus, buy horses and ride straight out to the farther back.

All this development was linking up with the young man's plans and dreams. His inland trips kept him in a fever of constant and quick travelling. Probably only a master of horses dealing in horses could have done it. He covered distances which would be surprising even in these days of the motor car.

Old Prince and Nelson were now past strenuous work, so he pensioned them off, Prince in a sweet Kapunda paddock, and Nelson at the little Kapunda home. The cockatoo made noisy advances of friendship, which Nelson scorned to notice. On warm mornings he would walk down the paddock to have a yarn with Prince who often would walk to meet him, the cockatoo comically following the dog. When the master came home both horse and dog would come hurrying up in greeting to the screech of the cockatoo. To replace Prince he bought a fine upstanding chestnut which was to be a loyal companion for many years. But it never crept so deeply into his heart as Prince had done. His travelling dog was now Needle and this faithful friend came to be as dear as Nelson. But his affairs were growing to such an extent that he more and more employed drovers.

As each drover arrived at headquarters with his mob, he was expected to be able to give full particulars of the country through which he had travelled, the quality of feed available and where, the capacity and positions of the watering-places, the numbers and condition of stock on the properties through which he had passed. And Kidman retained in his extraordinary memory all this information. Frequently he knew more about certain properties than the owners themselves.

He never liked sheep (no cattleman ever does), although in later years they proved good friends to him.

Kidman had long since noted that invariably there is a "drought on" in some position of Australia, sometimes several at once, and hardly noticed by the remainder of the continent. Even in a bad drought there are large scattered areas holding good grasses and water. He tried to anticipate these "local droughts", studying their cycles and geography. Thus he would buy a mob of cattle from a drought-stricken area, push them across a 100- or 200-mile dry stretch, and into country he knew contained good feed. He would lose some, but in the good country the remainder would fatten. A few months later one of his drovers would arrive to drove them to market.

And he would watch the thunder-storms! That is exactly what the blacks do, the kangaroos do, the cattle in the unfenced areas do—they "follow the thunder-storms".

Throughout inland Australia thunder-storms fairly often "follow one another" in a sequence. A week after such a storm grass springs up where rain has fallen. The claypans hold water for a time, and so there is drinking-water.

If Kidman heard of thunder-storms recently fallen out in the arid parts, he would hurry to the driest stations nearest this area, buy a mob of cattle and push them straight out in the path of the distant storms. That storm area would be a narrow strip 100 or more miles away, probably in unoccupied country. He often had the information from his friends the blacks, from an Afghan camel-driver, or a wandering dingo-poisoner. He had to locate the path of that storm and get his cattle there.

Sometimes in the sandy country he took risks; but never in this did he make a bad mistake. Then, he would get to know of markets in the back country. Stations in the Gulf or the Territory would often give five or six pounds for breeding-cows when coastal markets would hesitate to give two pounds. Thus he often sold a mob of breeders to far out stations, returning to the coast with a mob of fat bullocks.

In all these ways he spied out the links in his future chains of stations, the patches of good country, the frontages to rivers and creeks, the lagoons and waterholes, the flood-water country and saltbush plains. He localized and planned his stock-routes to help feed the capital cities, and longed for the day when he would possess the capital to start. But try as he would, scheme and plan and work with one eye on the country and the other on the city, he simply could not buy a big mob cheaply, fatten them, and land them on a hungry market at a soaring price. He only wanted just that one big start. It was many years in coming.

Latterly, during his visits to town, he became very interested in little groups of people who appeared in the streets banging a big drum, clashing tambourines, and singing hymns. He used to follow them up, throwing coins into the ring to the cheerful exhortations of the man in the centre. Perhaps the hostility and rowdyism that the Salvation Army had to suffer in its early days out here first aroused his sympathy and interest. Whether or no, he admired the people and their work all the rest of his life. The surest place to find Sid Kidman, when in town on a Saturday night, was among the crowd around the "Sallies".

Sackville Kidman was a steady, thoughtful man who planned well and thoroughly; a step at a time. While considering any undertaking he eliminated, as far as possible, all risks beforehand. There was nothing of the meteor about Sac; he was the steady builder up. A man who always kept his promise, he was liked and respected far and wide. So many enterprises now on hand which ranged over such great distances needed the steady thinking of the elder brother. One slip, either of the droving, the coaching, the station buying, the dealing, the shipping, and the four men would crash. Thinking these thoughts he drove to inspect a big mob that young Sid had just brought in from Queensland.

"My—heavens! ..."

Sid quietly sat his horse, awaiting the brother's outburst. It came. Sackville could swear fluently and expressively when he chose. He did so now.

"Don't swear, Sac. Don't swear!"

"Don't swear be damned——"

"What's wrong with them, Sac?" drawled Sid softly.

"What's wrong with them!" Sac roared to the agent. "He brings me 4000 scrubbers at a fiver a head an' expects me to sell them when a good bullock is worth only seven pounds."

Then to Sid: "You go away on your own and no one knows where you've gone until you come back with a mob of rumpers like these."

"They're not scrubbers, Sac. There's some good sorts among them."

"You empty-headed fool. You'll break us yet!" roared Sac.

"We'll pull through all right, Sac."

"Pull through! You'll have us carrying our swags!"

"And we can do that too! I've done it before."

"Then you can do it on your own."

But the younger brother, in forcing the elder's hand, was merely fighting for the fortune he felt was ahead, forcing both his brother and himself to the limit mentally as well as physically. With quick thinking and quick work on the wires, Sac was able to dispose of this mob at a small profit. And the brother was out on the roads again with the capital to buy another mob. Mob after mob, quickly bought and quickly disposed of, even though at a bare profit, was making their name as stock-buyers known far and wide.

21

Learning Geography

From a long trip to the Gulf of Carpentaria he rode into Longreach in central Queensland. Surprised at the number of horses and camps outside the town, he was not backward in asking old Jack Hall.

"What's doing, Jack?"

"Don't you know?" the teamster replied. "A gold-rush to the Kimberleys."

"The Kimberleys?"

"Away towards the north-western coast of Western Australia."

"Crikey! That is a long way to rush!"

"Twelve hundred miles as the crow flies. No towns in between after passing the border. Nearly all 'nigger country' too."

"What started the rush?"

"Don't know rightly; news is slow in dribbling through. It's got to come all around the Australian coast and then spread inland. We've known the news a long while but no particulars. The first party struck the gold more than a year ago. The men leaving here now are only the tail-end of the rush."

"I hope the poor chaps find plenty. They deserve it."

"Too right they do. Come far?"

"Only from Longreach this stage."

"How's the water?"

"Good."

"Grass?"

"Good."

Old Jack Hall was known nearly to the Gulf. He was noted for detailed accuracy in giving directions across 100 miles of trackless bush:

"Keep due north five miles, then keep two little black hills close to your right until you see a table-top mountain in the distance. Pass it on your left and five miles farther on you'll come to a heavy clump of gidgee. Pass them close on your right, then a mile farther on you'll see a line of creek trees, etc."

The man who followed old Jack's directions could not possibly get lost.

Kidman thus witnessed one of the most remarkable "rushes" in Australian mining history. Victorian parties rode over 3000 miles before they reached the scene of discovery. All parties from the east had to cross the wild Northern Territory into the rugged and even wilder Kimberleys, with packhorses, drays, camels, and on foot; some actually pushing their food and tools on wheelbarrows. How many perished by the way will never be known. Fast fading from living memory are the thousand stories of endurance, and of men sticking to sick mates to the bitter end. At the rainbow's end too was disappointment, for the field proved not nearly so rich as rumour stated. But Hall and his party in 1886 had set a mighty wheel rolling, made the real start of gold discovery in Western Australia. For, a little later, from Hall's Creek was to start a rush to the south, another 2000 miles over unknown country; some of it desert.

Kidman, however, carried on, droving his stock down through southern Queensland while marvelling at this last mad venture of the prospectors, little dreaming that their discoveries were to affect his fate. Though he never followed mining, it indirectly influenced his entire career.

Hearing of a mob for sale at Springvale station, he rode there and met the pioneer pastoralist Millson with whom he formed a lasting friendship. He secured the mob and started them south-west towards Bedourie. A tiny frontier outpost, Bedourie boasted hotel and store and police station, as well as the big trees of the Georgina near by. It owed its existence to the great Birdsville track. Straight down through Bedourie came all the cattle from the Gulf, from the Barkly Tableland, and from northern Queensland stations. Kidman camped his mob just outside the township and rode across to a camp under a coolabah-tree. There was old Simpson, hoary old pioneer.

"Come and have a drink of tea, Sid," growled the old man. "You're after a yarn, I suppose."

"Of course. What's the news, Bill?"

"None. There's plenty of mobs on the road. There's been no rain for a year. There's a lot of new country being opened up nor'-west on the Barkly Tableland, rolling plains it is far as the eye can see with hardly a tree. Good country. But they'll have to find water, and then they'll be up against the transport problem. The police found a new chum perished down the Birdsville track a fortnight ago; and two men perished on the Cooper a month before that. There's some big scale cattle-duffing going on in parts; and horse-thieving is a regular science. I'm going north to lift a mob from Coorabulka for Normanton. But there's no news."

A lad hesitantly approached the old man.

"Could I have a washing-dish, Mr Simpson?"

"A washing-dish! You'll want a tooth-brush next! A King William Street squatter, you are.

"These new chums," he apologized, "worry the life out of a man. Fancy asking for a washing-dish when there's no water to wash in! Help yourself to some tea and brownie, Sid, while I fix this cove up. Then he can feed the niggers while we go up to the pub for a yarn. I'll want the drink."

"Plenty of time," smiled Kidman. "Treat the young fellow kindly, Bill. We've all got to learn."

"I've been a mother to him these last six weeks," snorted Bill. "But what can you do with a boy who ties a horse up by its tail!" He took a little square of canvas from a pack-bag, dug a hole in the ground and pushed the canvas into it, thus making a sort of dish. In this he mixed up flour into johnny-cakes and spread them on the coals. After which he poured in a sparing drop of water, and washed his fingers.

"There's your washing dish," he growled. "When you've finished with it shove it back in the pack-bag. And don't let those niggers get at the Epsom-salt."

"What do they want salts for?" inquired Kidman.

"They think it's cough mixture."

"That's not as rough a cure as one they have at Coongy," laughed Kidman. "A big black stockman came to the homestead one day complaining of a pain in his stomach. They gave him 'dynamite pills', gun-powder mixed up with fat."

"Cure him?"

"Yes, he never complained again."

"Just as well he didn't breathe on the fire. I had a nigger once," went on Bill, "had something wrong with his guts. We gave him half a pannikin of kerosene, thought it might oil him up or shift something anyway. He coughed and spat and spluttered all over the lamp and the whole place went up. We never saw that nigger any more."

As they strolled across to the pub, old Bill growled.

"My throat's like leather dusted with ashes. That Bedourie shower yesterday was a beauty. There must have been thousands of tons of dust flying through the air. I could drink a brewery and still need a gargle."

"It was jolly dusty," agreed Kidman. "Couldn't see the mob all day."

"I couldn't see the township," growled Bill, "let alone a mob of cattle. No wonder they call this the place where the crows fly backwards to keep the dust out of their eyes."

When Kidman said "So long" to the old pioneer it was to be for the last time. Old Bill and his new-chum mate were drowned when crossing a flooded Gulf stream. The old man who from boyhood had learnt that every drop of water is precious, was to perish in it.

*

Months later, when Sid Kidman drove up to the little Kapunda home he was greeted by the cockatoo shrieking from the garden gate.

"Hullo, father! Hullo, father!"

"Sounds ominous," he murmured.

It was. A baby girl.

22

Telegraph and Train

Broken Hill now had a population of 15,000; it was to reach 35,000. The great Broken Hill Proprietary Company was emerging triumphant from the feverish stage of mining speculation.

South Australia had built its line to Cockburn, and the Silverton Tramways Company completed the remaining thirty-five miles to Broken Hill in 1888. In that year Broken Hill produced over £1,000,000 worth of metals. Thus the foresight of South Australians drew to their State the trade of a prosperous city.

And Sid Kidman slowly found fortune coming his way. The coaching enterprises were prospering. Sackville was established in Broken Hill on a large scale, the town providing a rapidly growing market for the mobs of cattle and sheep Sid was now pouring in. The railway now saved the young drover the long, slow, and expensive trip to Adelaide, doing away with the almost waterless portion of the track across the border. Also, should Sid glut the Broken Hill market, Sac could rail the surplus to Adelaide, even to Melbourne.

"If only we could get Forders," said Sid for the tenth time.

"I've tried and tried, as you know," answered Sac. "They won't sell; don't want to sell."

Forders was a small selection of fifteen square miles on the border, a "strategic gem" so far as the Kidman enterprises were concerned. It always had good grass and water and was in the very position where tired cattle could be rested and fattened before being sold in the Broken Hill market, or trained for the Adelaide market. This small area could be made the Mundowdna of their New South Wales activities. But the brothers who owned it were content. Forders was not for sale. Sid Kidman had to wait years before he secured it.

"Grass," he drawled to Sac, "is money. You find the markets, I'll find the grass." He now knew monthly of the stock movements from many stations, and the progress of the mobs coming down any stock-route. He knew the city markets day by day and what each could consume weekly. And he could calculate the dates on which various mobs should reach their respective markets. More, he could do this months ahead. When he saw a scarcity coming he would, by telegraph if possible, supply the deficiency, or ride night and day to any stations in closest proximity to that market. And his mob would arrive at that market to the very day of the scarcity.

Kidman took increasing advantage of the railway lines now pushed out into each State, and of the telegraph lines now tapping the inlands. So, at last, he began to climb. He bought a note-book in which to note his numerous deals. Business involving many thousands of pounds, movements of big herds, payments to many men, were recorded in that little black book. The time was to come when all these, and a paternal government's interest in his financial affairs, would demand an office in Adelaide.

But Kidman's head for many years yet was his pigeon-holed office and a map of inland Australia combined. On any day he could tell, without referring to any documents, where his drovers would be camped that night on any route in any State, what their mobs were, and when they should reach their destination.

In Broken Hill at the conclusion of a trip Sid Kidman was discussing business with Nicholas when Sac said:

"Look here, we must keep an eye on Western Australia."

"Why?"

"Gold. Ever since that Kimberley rush, rumours of gold have been coming from the West. The papers are writing now of a discovery at some place called Yilgarn and Pilbara. A rich field in the west would mean a rush from the other States. And they want cattle."

"We'll supply them," said Sid brightly.

"How? When they reach Adelaide, you have still got nearly 2000 miles to drove them, half of which is waterless."

"Well, we'll ship them."

"That is what I was thinking of. I wonder if it could be done."

"If there is going to be a gold-rush in the West," broke in Nicholas, "I am going straight across to open a line of coaches. There will be a fortune in it."

"That is a good idea. We had better watch the West."

"You bet I will," said Nicholas. "By the way, Sid, my congratulations."

"What for?"

"Another girl."

"Yes. The prettiest girl in Australia."

"Born in a golden age, let us hope," laughed Nicholas. "By the way, talking about gold, we had better watch nearer home as well. What are these rumours of an opal-rush out on Momba run, Sid?"

"It might mean something big," answered Sid. "They've just found a patch of opal at a place they call White Cliffs, about sixty miles north-west of Wilcannia. I remember opal being found on Momba station in 1884, just when the big Broken Hill mine was forming. Nothing much was done with the opal; there was no one to buy it. Now they seem to be selling it like hot cakes to foreign buyers."

"The place might grow into a town," said Nicholas, "if so we'll run a coach there quick and lively."

"They will find difficulty in locating drinking-water in that country."

"Miners will overcome any difficulty if mineral or gems are there."

"Let us hope they find a regular market for the opal," said Sackville. "It will mean transport opportunities and another stock market for us."

And so it proved. The famous opal-field was to support a population varying between 2000 and 3000 for over twenty years. It became the most famous light-opal field in the world, as Lightning Ridge was the best black-opal field. And Australia was to receive a lasting advertisement by the sale of the "fire" stones overseas.

In 1888, the Pilbara goldfield in Western Australia was officially proclaimed. A few years later the world was to be startled by the Golden West.

23

Droving Days

Riding to Weinteriga, Kidman camped there a night and was cheerily greeted by "the boys".

"Come and get your legs under the table Sid, before the crowd rolls in," called old Parky. "You're comin' on in the world, Sid. Comin' on. Have you heard the weights for the Cup?"

"No," smiled Kidman.

"Any news from the Cliffs?" inquired the overseer.

"Yes. Plenty of excitement. Some big patches of opal being found. A thousand men are there now, but they are having a desperate struggle for water."

"I've a good mind to save up my cheque," declared a young station-hand, "and have a go at this opal-gouging."

He did. And he became an "Opal King". From being a station-hand at one pound per week he spent thousands travelling the world, and was invited to a king's levee.

"I'd like to know the weights for the Cup," persisted old Parky. "Don't any of youse blokes read the papers?"

"You know they're read a dozen times over," said old Don. "The weights aren't out yet."

"There are some late papers in my saddle-bag," said Kidman. And a man was out of the door like a shot.

Old Parky was "mad" on racehorses, but he was a sorry man to-night. His lifelong friend old Don, the rouseabout, was going to Wilcannia to-morrow on holiday. Parky hated to be parted from old Don when Don was going on a "bender". They always "holidayed" together. But they played up so when in town that the manager told them next time they went holidaying together they could stay "holidaying". The one thing that stopped Parky from defying the manager was that he had saved a year's cheque to have one grand "splash" on the Cup. But he was worried at old Don going on holiday—"with nobody to look after him".

"He'll get into all sorts of trouble," said Parky in an aside to Kidman. "Those town blokes will take him down right and left. If it wasn't for the Cup, I'd tell the boss to go to hell."

"But if you went with Don you'd go broke," answered Kidman, "and would have no money to put on the Cup. The boss is really doing you a good turn."

The boys came striding noisily in, all talking about "the Cup".

"I've backed every racehorse in Australia," declared Parky in his squeaky voice. "Give me a racehorse an' th' world's mine. You can keep your wimmin, an' your wine."

"That's why you're a station cook at thirty bob a week," remarked a rouseabout.

"Yeh. An' if I was a rouseabout I'd cut me throat."

"That's what mine feels like," growled the overseer. "Isn't that billy boiled yet!"

Parky grabbed the tea canister in a huff as a stockman remarked, "Strewth! I see Carbine's been given ten stone five in the Cup."

Parky screwed around from the fireplace. "He's right, then!" he exclaimed. "Carbine would win if he carried a ton." He grabbed the billycan in one hand and the stew-pot with the other.

"Be on it! Carbine will win the Cup!" he shouted as he planked stew-pot and billycan on the table.

They found hot water in the billycan and a handful of tea in the stew.

Next morning old Don was very excited, fussing around rolling his swag, forgetting his shaving strop and mislaying his pipe. The first holiday for twelve months; a cheque burning a hole in his pocket. He hated going without Parky. The enviously solicitous Parky tried to help him in the packing, throwing in now and then a word of advice.

"You'd better take your water-bag, Don, it's a long hot walk into town."

"Do you mean to insult me!" snarled Don. "Want to spoil my thirst? I'm drinking beer at every pub going into town, and I'm drinking water coming back!"

Kidman gave old Don a lift into Wilcannia, then decided to ride on into Queensland and buy cattle for the rush rapidly developing at White Cliffs. Six months later when returning with a mob of bullocks he met old Jack Hall camped at Beetoota.

"Where is your team, Jack?"

"All over the place. What with the camels and no feed a man can hardly make a living. The camels have just about driven the teams right off the roads in these parts."

"Stations in the real sand country could never carry on, Jack, if it was not for the camels."

"Yes, I know. But the 'Ghans are not content with sticking to the sand country; they are spreading out all over the place."

"Oh, well, when the rains come you'll be able to get on the roads again."

"Yes, and then the blooming rabbits will come again."

Kidman laughed. "You're a pessimist, Jack."

"Maybe. But really, Sid, it's surprising what damage those furry little pests have done. They've honeycombed the sand-ridges with burrows. Country that was tiptop a few years ago now wouldn't feed a bandicoot."

"They'll go, and the feed will spring up again."

"I'm not so sure," replied old Jack slowly. "I've had a look at some saltbush they've been eating—and they eat down to the very roots."

"That's bad. I've noticed the same thing myself. Well, my black boy says the billy is boiling. Come along."

"That is not the worst about the rabbits, Sid!" persisted Jack.

"Well!"

"They're even ring-barking the young mulga."

"That's bad, Jack."

"It is. What they can't eat they kill."

After lunch, old Jack took a carefully wrapped paper from his pocket. Gently he unwrapped it and showed to Kidman a beautiful horse upon a fruit-tin label. "Isn't he a beauty!"

"It's not a bad picture," drawled Kidman.

"Picture! Don't you recognize him?"

"No."

"Why, that's Carbine!"

"Carbine?"

"Great Gee-roosalem! That is Carbine, the horse that won the Melbourne Cup."

Kidman laughed. "Someone has been pulling your leg, Jack. That is only a fruit-tin label."

Jack would not be convinced for quite a while. Very crestfallen, he put the label in the fire.

"If only I had yoked in my team the cow that told me that was Carbine," he swore, "I'd cut ribbons off his hide! I've showed that label to a dozen blokes and I wondered why they laughed."

"So Carbine won the Cup," mused Kidman.

"Of course he did. Don't you read the papers? And you a horse-dealer, too!"

"I don't know a thing about racehorses," admitted Kidman. "I was wondering if an old station cook I knew really did put his year's wages on Carbine!"

"If he didn't, he's a sorry man now," gasped old Jack.

Coming down from Queensland now, young Kidman found that Customs officers were stationed at Birdsville, at Beetoota just by the South Australian–Queensland "corner", at Oontoo (Innamincka) on the South Australian border, and at Warri, on the New South Wales border. These barred the stock-route entrances into South Australia and New South Wales. It was useless to try getting through elsewhere. Besides—there was no water! The fences, too, were well patrolled. Some good stories could be told of those border patrols.

There was a pound per head duty on cattle taken from Queensland across the border. So that any owner, drover, or stock-dealer crossing the border with 1000 head would have first to pay £1000. The main gates through the border fence into New South Wales were the Warri and the Adelaide gates. And the man with a big mob of cattle found either a costly gate to go through.

Some months later at Broken Hill, Sac said to him: "You know Comongin station in Queensland, on the Bulloo River?"

"Yes."

"Well, McLean and Barker have not been very successful with the cattle they send to Sydney for sale. They have asked me whether we would consider marketing the cattle on shares."

"Of course we will."

"Well then, go up and lift a mob."

That same day Sid Kidman was on the roads. It was only a 500-mile trip to Comongin. *En route* he called in at Norley station. Bryerty the manager was away, and the book-keeper was ill.

"Camp a night with me," he urged. "Every soul is away and I've got the blues. Keep me company, and go on in the morning."

That evening, while yarning to the book-keeper, he picked up an old Sydney newspaper and read an advertisement:

"To be sold on the 31st, two blocks of country on the Lower Bulloo——"

The very blocks he wanted—adjoining the border fence. One was the block he had ridden over as a lad, the first flood-water country he had ever seen. The 31st was only a few days from now. Straight bush to Charleville from here meant 140 miles—a two days' ride. Train from Charleville to Sydney three days. He could just do it.

"Can you let me have some fresh horses?"

"Yes. What is the hurry?"

"I must be in Sydney within a week."

172

He was. With several hours to spare, he swung into the selling office as another hand reached for the door.

"Charlie!"

"Sid!"

"What are you doing here?"

"Came down to buy two flood-country blocks on the Lower Bulloo."

"So did I."

They laughed, and went inside.

They bought the blocks, Sid Kidman took the first train back to Charleville. Heavy rain had fallen, rumour was that the outside rivers were in flood. Making west with his horses he swam the Ward and the Paroo, returned to Norley station, picked up his own plant, and ploughed through the flooded country north to Comongin. Once there, with the help of the station-hands, he mustered 500 head; then with several half-castes started droving them south to Broken Hill.

For 200 miles the country was under water or mud. The Bulloo had spilled her yellow stream into every channel-way, every lagoon and billabong until the swamps were lakes. She had rolled on then, spilling out into the flat country until she filled the Bulloo Lakes on the border, and began spilling out into New South Wales.

The drovers had a rough time with the cattle, often to their knees in water, creeping cautiously along on the higher ground between channels of the river, often finding it difficult to find a dry ridge to camp on at night. While travelling through Bulloo Downs station, deep channels held them up for some days.

Kidman pitched camp, lit a roaring fire, then started baking a big supply of johnny-cakes.

"Jacky," he said to a half-caste, "swim your horse across that channel there, then ride on until you come to the twelve-mile channel. See how deep it is, and whether we can swim the cattle across."

"A'right, boss."

Half an hour later, and the half-caste's horse came floundering back through the channel.

"Boss, boss, me see 'em man on island, him walk about alla same bullock, longa hands and knees, 'im eatem grass!"

Quickly they saddled horses and swam across. On a sand-hill island was a poor fellow huddled up with his head in a bush. Kidman thought him dead. He was a breathing skeleton, in a frightful state. They held him to a horse, swam him back to the fire, and washed him. Rolled in blankets with fires all around him, he gradually came back to life. He could not eat, but thankfully sipped hot tea. He had been caught on that sand-ridge for forty days and nights. He had worked as an office man for Gibbs Bright and Company in Sydney, had bought several horses, and ridden into the bush, seeking experience and a droving job. He camped on a sand-ridge one night. Rain fell. Thunder and vivid lightning stampeded his horses. He slept at last, but rushing waters awoke him before the dawn. In the morning he found himself marooned. He could not swim. His name was Greenwood. That very day he had written a despairing note, asking whoever found his body to communicate with his people. But from the very first, he had had a strange presentiment that he would be rescued on a Thursday—he had been marooned on a Thursday, and he fully believed that at the eleventh hour on a Thursday he would be rescued.

Finding that his case was beyond hope of recovery in a rough drover's camp, Kidman took him through flooded country to Bulloo Downs homestead, where George Griffen, the book-keeper, nursed him back to health.

As a story of endurance and faith throughout forty days and nights, the man's own diary is of interest:

April 2nd—Walked about twenty miles and camped.

April 3rd—Heavy rain and no track. Camped on a sand-hill with black boy from Bulloo Downs.

April 4th—Walked about five miles. Raining.

April 5th—Saturday, camped, raining.

April 6th—Walked about fifteen miles to fence on river all through grass swamp.

April 7th—Came to gate on wire fence and camped. Waited for black boy, who said he would put me across creek as he came back. No tucker or matches, all lost, got wet in swamp.

April 8th—Got across creek but found there was a deeper one to cross, so camped on a sand-hill between two creeks.

April 9th—Tried all day but could not get across.

April 10th—Tried to cross back but could not as water had risen, and am very weak. The black boy told me creeks were only knee-deep. No sign of him.

April 11th—No sign of him and very hungry. Don't know what to do.

April 12th—Rigged flag—pole on sand-hill. Am awfully tired and hungry.

April 13th—No sign of any one. I am on an island about 200 yards by 100. Caught a fish and ate it raw and some weeds. There were live horses on hill but they have gone away.

April 14th—Water not going down. Caught two fish. Eat a lot of trefoil grass. Cannot walk far.

April 15th—Looks very like rain. Caught one small fish—no sign of any one. Don't know what to do.

April 16th—Very cold and cloudy. Water rising—water as far as you can see. Am very weak to-day. The native dogs were very bad, but they have gone away—I hope so.

April 17th—Have suffered all night with cold. It rained a little. Caught three fish and ate a lot of weeds. If I had a fire would not care. Cannot stand up for long at a time.

April 18th—Very cloudy but not so cold. Can see a lot of cattle on plain. Caught three small fish. Ate a bit of trefoil, water still rising.

April 19th—Very cold and raining. Could not catch a fish. Don't think there is much chance for me. All my clothes are gone (what with rain and scrub)—I cannot get warm.

April 20th—Quite a change in weather—caught four
fish. Feel better. Cannot walk fifty yards without
wanting to sit down, water still rising.

April 21st—Perchance this should be useful to anybody I
have kept a true account. I get up at sunrise and
drink a pint of water and then eat trefoil and a weed
with a woolly flower on it. I eat as much as I can,
then try to catch some fish which I skin and take all
the bones out. What I have caught have been about
six inches long. Then I go on watch on top of hill.
Then eat more weeds. Then bed at sundown. Have
done fifteen days on this food to-day. This and the
mosquitoes are very bad.

April 22nd—Fine day, water still rising. Could not get
any grass or weeds; all covered with water. Caught
five fish—can hardly walk to top of sand-hill.

April 23rd—Water at a standstill. Caught seven fish. If I
could get to river [Bulloo] could catch plenty I think.
Fine day but cloudy. Mice are a nuisance. They gnaw
everything.

April 24th—Water going down. Shifted camp today.
Caught five fish. I get weaker every day. Hope
someone will come this way soon.

April 25th—Fine day, water going down, but slowly.
Caught one good sized fish, about $1^1/2$ lb.

April 26th—Am very sick to-day. Could not go fishing to-
day.

April 27th—Am very bad with dysentery. Begin to lose
hope—I've been here so long now.

April 28th—Found teal's nest of eggs, good luck. Caught
two fish. I can never walk from here, I am sure, as I
am too weak.

April 29th—Caught three fish. Rained during night and blew
very hard. Month to-day since I left Thargomindah.

April 30th—Bad luck; lost my fish hook. Don't know
what I shall do now. No sign of any one. Have a
blanket for flag.

May 1st—*Had a feed of weeds etc. No sign of any one.*

May 2nd—*Getting weaker. Eat same. Can do nothing but wait.*

May 3rd—*Horses came back to-day. Round where they had crossed. See cattle on other side of creek.*

May 4th—*Found two duck eggs. Could not sleep all night for pain. Looks very like rain.*

May 5th—*Raining and cold. Eat what weeds I could get—cannot last long like this.*

May 6th—*Very heavy rain last night, water still going down. Eat same as before.*

May 7th—*Fine day but cloudy. Eat same as before. No sign of anybody.*

May 8th—*No news, eat same as before.*

May 9th—*Cold and windy. Water rising. Found one egg (duck's).*

May 10th—*Cold but fine. Can see a lot of cattle, but no sign of any one.*

May 11th—*Fine day but very cold. Cannot get warm—water still rising. Eat same as before.*

May 12th—*Am very weak to-day. Water still rising.*

May 13th—*Fine day. Water at a standstill—no sign of any one. Eat same.*

May 14th—*Fine day. Am getting weaker. Hopes for to-morrow (Thursday) as it was the day I met the black boy Dick.*

May 15th—*Water coming down slowly. No sign of any one. Eat same.*

May 16th—*Beautiful day. I cannot walk to top of hill so cannot hoist blanket. For the first time am very low spirited.*

May 17th—*Very cold and like rain. Cannot do anything.*

May 18th—*Fine day. Am very weak. Begin to think this is not the right track, but it seems both a sheep- and cattle-camp.*

May 19th—*No news. Eat same.*

May 20th—*No sign of any one. Don't know what to do.*

*May 21st—I think I can make up my mind to die here, as
I can hardly stand. I have done all I could. Can hear
bells and dogs barking but am too weak to cooee.
On May 22nd—Found by Mr Kidman and black boy and
taken to Bulloo Downs.*

24

Westralian Gold Buys Queensland Cattle

In 1891 gold had been found in the Murchison River, Western Australia. In 1892 Arthur Bayley and John Ford, after many hardships amongst the mulga and spinifex, sandy plain and rocky ridge, camped one evening at a native well, Coolgardie. Next morning they picked up gold. In trembling excitement they "specked" piece after piece. A month later they found their famous reef, and broke off the gold in bucketfuls. The news spread like wildfire; a stream of men came pouring out of Perth. In 1893 Flannigan and Hannan under romantic circumstances found Kalgoorlie. The reign of the Golden West had started in earnest. The Bardoc and Siberia rush quickly followed. In 1894 Hall and Spearman located the Mount Jackson field. Old Tom found the rich Kanowna alluvial field.

A great rush set in from the eastern States. Steamers were packed. There was no railway communication with the west then.

This great stream of men suddenly pouring into the huge, undeveloped west wanted—meat. And transport! Nicholas and Charlie Kidman left to pioneer the coach-routes. Cobb and Co.

were already there. Shrewd, quick, energetic, and with their New South Wales experience at their finger-tips, Kidman and Nicholas soon had lines running from Esperance Bay on the coast straight north through Norseman, Coolgardie, Kalgoorlie, Broad Arrow, Menzies, Leonora to Lake Way, a 600-mile coach line. With a branch line to Sandstone, a packhorse line from Southern Cross to Coolgardie, and lesser lines as towns sprang up.

Under such circumstances, in undeveloped country swarming with eager, footsore men, where gold was soon being dug up in tons, the coaching venture could not but prove a success, even though carried on under great difficulties and expense. To help keep this transport running the Western Australian Government allowed them £500 a year for water. The combined coach-route mail subsidies eventually yielded £40,000 per year. They drew fourpence per ounce for carrying gold. On one trip, with six fine greys in the coach, they came dashing into Kalgoorlie with £60,000 worth of gold from Leonora. The coaches on every line were stormed by passengers who often outbid one another for a seat.

Meanwhile, Sid Kidman was travelling three States by train and horse buying cattle, buying through telegraph too, getting them on the roads to the nearest railhead. Sac organized from Broken Hill, keeping the New South Wales enterprises running smoothly. Much of the work was done by a constant stream of telegrams between the travelling brother, the stationary Sackville, and city agents.

From Port Adelaide the cattle were shipped to Fremantle in a pioneer attempt to supply the gold population with meat. Of the first two steamer loads, in the old *Asphodel* and *Lissdale*, approximately half of the cattle were lost. Afterwards, better organization gained by experience, reduced losses to a minimum. Sid Kidman bought cattle, sheep, and pigs at Gunnedah in New South Wales and shipped them from Newcastle to Western Australia. He kept moving because others were moving too. But the super-knowledge of the man in the stock resources of his own country proved too overwhelming an advantage against rival organizations. In Western Australia, the firm of Emmanual Brothers and Forrest co-operated with the Kidman venture. Thus Sid Kidman found himself in a partnership with "Big John" Forrest, the explorer admired so much by the mule-camp man who had befriended him with his one-eyed horse. And so, by having plans already laid for this business, the brothers escaped the disastrous depression which overtook the eastern States from 1891–3.

For a decade, many millions of borrowed money had entered Victoria from England. Much of it was misspent; the market became flooded with landbills. Banks began to crash, the trouble spread to other colonies. But the great gold boom saved Western Australia.

Throughout all this added activity, Sid Kidman never for a moment relinquished his grip on his "spider web" stock-routes coming down from the north. On that frail and hard-won connexion depended his dream. Coach lines and shipments of cattle were only helpful routes to an end. So from those far-scattered northern stations he continued buying cattle and sheep but now by telegraph, telegraphing transport arrangements to drovers.

His old comrades of the roads; men he had studied; men he knew so well; most of whom had been bosses when he was a station rouseabout—these boss drovers suddenly found themselves working for "Sid Kidman". Coming down the Barcoo, the Thomson, the Cooper, with his mobs for Broken Hill; coming down the Georgina and Diamantina with his mobs for the Birdsville track to train at Hergott Springs for Adelaide; coming down the Paroo, the Warrego to train at Bourke for Sydney; or entraining at Charleville with a mob for Brisbane.

In 1896 he bought his first Queensland station, Annandale, situated on the extreme south-western corner of Queensland, the farthest-out station in Queensland, the South Australian border fence adjoining its southern end, the Northern Territory fence adjoining its western side. A compact 1300 square miles of sand-hill country, then well grassed, it had a seventy-mile frontage to the Georgina River. What had attracted Sid Kidman more than anything was the beautiful flood-water lake Moncooney, which was a vast "clover" patch when dry, as was the smaller lake Titherapatchie. He bought it through John Barker, of Adelaide, for £5000. It was stocked with between 4000 and 5000 cattle and 500 horses.

That large belt of dry country purchased so cheaply he hoped to make bloom, for he dreamt of artesian bores. Out in the "dry belt" a few both private and government "gushers" had now been struck.

Kidman determined to run a mail coach connecting Hergott Springs to Birdsville, 300 miles. He must find a use for the trained horses now being released from the New South Wales coach-routes, for now other men were bidding for contracts and securing renewals. Along other routes, developing railway lines made coaches unnecessary. Then too, Nicholas, who was really the coachman, was concentrating all his energies in Western Australia. Where too, rapidly expanding railway lines would presently do away with coaches.

The loss of the coaching business brought little regret to Kidman; it represented merely a partial means to an end. As did his present idea of opening a coach-route to connect the lonely, south-western Queensland droving town with the South Australian railway. Birdsville and Hergott Springs were both "keys" in the great stock-route. And the man who experienced the difficulties of a coach-route with the knowledge gained of water and grass for hundreds of horses, could use the knowledge when bringing thousands of head of cattle across this poorly watered area of the track.

He organized the route successfully. Probably there are few, if any, drier or sandier routes in the world.

At this time the stock market collapsed, and station men were battling against ruin. Fat bullocks could be bought for thirty-five shillings per head. A line of 7000 big-framed bullocks from Tinnenburra station were boiled down and realized only eighteen shillings and fourpence per head. Mobs of sheep sold at as low as sixpence per head. No wonder graziers were bewildered.

In November 1897 Kidman brothers bought from the bank, Tickalara station in south-western Queensland, almost adjoining the New South Wales border. It was a strategic property on which stock coming down from Queensland could be rested before the next stage into New South Wales, and the Broken Hill market.

The buying of these places, the appointing of managers, the quick organization of mustering-camps to muster mobs of fats for the drovers who would get them on the roads for market, meant time and rapid travelling. Each mob shifted from any station was immediately helping to pay for the property.

After a rapid business trip to Adelaide, Kidman called in at the Kapunda home on a "flying" visit, then rode north; took up a block of 2096 square miles of country adjoining the Northern Territory border; stocked it with horses from Owen Springs, and called it Eringa. In later years, he amalgamated it with Macumba and Hamilton stations, making a block of 47,888 square miles, which was to form the backbone of his Central Australian-South Australian chain.

For the next three years he was kept busy supervising and stocking, at the same time travelling far and wide to keep his stock-dealing connexion with the city markets constantly moving and on the increase. In 1898 he found time to buy a share in Austral Downs. This station in the Northern Territory, adjoining the Queensland border towards the Gulf was the northern end of his proposed main chain. In that year, too, he bought Carapundy station, 326 square miles in north-west New South Wales.

A start immediately having been made to pay off each station by a sale of fats from it, the remainder was quickly paid from profits on the sale of mobs from other stations. Organization was now beginning to tell. Kidman could see his main chain of south-western Queensland stations beginning to form.

Just when fortune for the brothers was coming fast, Sackville died in November 1899. When everything was squared up, to the widow's lot fell the Broken Hill business. Sid

Kidman retained most of the pastoral properties. He started alone again. Besides losing a brother he had lost a staunch adviser and friend. More thoughtfully he carried on with his work and ambitions.

In 1900 Sid Kidman's disgust was great when he found he had to start an office. Though he could keep every detail of this far-flung business in his head, various government departments demanded such things as returns, etc. The country was "growing". And with it his business was growing so fast he could not keep account of everything in the little black note-book.

With a sigh of relief he thanked the wife when she came quietly to the rescue. She had already marked out Andrew Thompson. A quiet old gentleman, trustworthy, good with the pen, he was installed as office man at the home in Kapunda.

25

Forging Chains of Stations

Sid Kidman, dealing alone again, next bought Carcoory station 1000 square miles, carrying 4000 head of cattle, and adjoining Annandale. He paid Ronald McGregor £5500 for it. Carcoory was mostly plain country of saltbush and Mitchell-grass, just the ordinary far-out country upon which a rough homestead is built near a convenient waterhole, with a few head of stock put upon it, and a track marked to the nearest civilization. It takes time and battling and the development of the country to develop such places. Carcoory was situated between the Diamantina and the Georgina rivers, sixty miles north of Birdsville. The country then was very dry, more ominous still—the waterholes were low. But then, had conditions been more favourable, he could not have bought the station so cheaply. Stock too were very cheap. With a quiet delight he worked in the taking over of the station, seeing it a stepping-stone to others along his beloved Three Rivers. Leaving Arthur Barlett, manager of Annandale, in charge, he rode north, seeking cattle to buy. As he roamed he had visions of his mobs lowing over the sand-ridges of Dubbo Downs, the dunes and lignum of Annandale, the saltbush plains of Carcoory. From these mobs would be bred the sires and dams of his great herds. He pulled up under a gidgee-tree, staring out at brilliant sunlight, bathing grey-topped ridges, flats of saltbush, mulga, and needlewood.

He had made a real start. He was forty-two years of age and felt wonderful. He had a wife and a nice home and a growing family. The big horse beneath him was powerful and willing and full of life, and he had plenty such. Needle, standing prick-eared there, would give his life for him. This country was young; he was young; the stock was young; all life stretched before him.

During this trip, he "specked" 2000 head of good store cattle and 1000 head of especially fine breeding-cows on a station belonging to the Rocklands Pastoral Company.

"They'll fatten on the saltbush quickly at a big profit," he thought. "If I can get them cheaply I may have just enough money left to buy them."

He did, at the company's headquarters, during his return trip when passing through Melbourne. Two thousand bullocks at twenty-five shillings per head, 1000 cows at one pound per head. Very cheap. He had to bargain very hard, although they knew that the south-west was ominously dry. It was the very last of his money. He wired a drover to lift the cattle and take them west to Carcoory. Then he boarded the train for Adelaide, feeling a bit tired, looking forward perhaps more than ever before to the Kapunda home and the little Scotch wife.

A great welcome awaited him at home: by wife and children, Prince and Nelson, and the cockatoo.

"So you have started with your big stations at last!" said the wife, with a smile.

"Yes, and you jolly well watch them grow."

"And how long are you going to stay home this time?"

"Oh, a long time, Bell. Nearly a month."

"It is about time you came home. The children will actually begin to know you."

He smiled. He loved the youngsters.

"The girls will soon be young ladies; they are inches taller each time I see them. The next thing I'll know is that they are leaving school. I've got to think of their future, Bell. And I've got to start those Kapunda horse-sales soon. You will see me home a lot oftener then."

"And now that you are home, I want you to come to church next Sunday."

He looked startled. "Sunday," he said slowly, "I was thinking of doing a bit to the garden fence——"

"You can do that this afternoon. I've got the palings and hammer and nails all ready. Promise now, church on Sunday morning!"

Not too enthusiastically, he promised. He had a yarn with Prince and Nelson, scratched the insistent cockatoo, then mended the fence while carrying on a conversation with the children. He listened to all their woes and joys, then spoke learnedly on the virtues of soap and of learning things in school. Diplomatically they changed the subject.

In the evening while the wife was knitting he sat there, enjoying the quiet comfort of home life. A knock came at the door, the wife sighed.

"I was waiting for you to finish your dreaming," she said, "then I thought you might talk to me. Now whoever this is will keep you discussing cattle all night." She put the knitting on the chair and answered the door. Charlie Coles, old Dan, and Abe Shannon, with half a dozen of the boys strode in.

"Heard you were home, Sid, so called in for a yarn," Charlie announced breezily.

"Jolly good idea," answered Sid. "Sit down, boys; sit down."

The wife was right. Cattle, horses, sheep, camels, donkeys, dogs, country, water, was talked until far into the night.

When Sunday came he escorted her to church, though not with the same easy grace with which he attended a cattle-sale. Walking home later along the pretty road, she was pleased to observe him almost beaming.

"I'm glad I went to church, Bell," he acknowledged.

"I am very glad you liked it. Now, wasn't it a nice sermon?"

"I didn't hear much of it," he replied thoughtfully. "I was sitting next to Abe Shannon. I bought those cattle from him; I've been after those cattle for a long time."

187

In 1900 the Northern Territory was peopled by wild aborigines and dotted with huge cattle stations. There were about a dozen mining-camps in the north, worked mainly by Chinese. The white population in this great area only numbered a few hundreds. These pioneers besides experiencing a desperate struggle, were isolated and practically unknown to the rest of Australia.

Sid Kidman was thinking of this great country as, camped under a bauhinia-tree, he made johnny-cakes on the coals. A still, cloudless Central Australian night. Somewhere out there, horse-bells tinkled. Needle sat by the fire, in anticipation watching the master making charcoal tarts. A little aboriginal boy squatted there, his eyes rolling as he listened to the night.

"No more fright, Jacky," said Kidman reassuringly. "Soon fellow now we catch him station; plenty white feller man; no more wild blackman!"

The boy smiled seriously, much less certain of his safety than was his master.

Sid Kidman, on one of his usual cattle-buying trips, was only going half-way through Central Australia. But he wished to know the country and the conditions right through to the coast. He had planned, six months before, for a particular drover to meet him on one of the frontier stations. He would beat time by sending this drover to find out what he wanted to know. Meanwhile, he would, if possible, find out what no other man knew. Whether, from the eastern limits of the Macdonnells it was possible to ride south-east to the Georgina in south-western Queensland. If so, he would know the usefulness or otherwise of a large area of unknown country. And he might find an entirely new route for stock. A few days later he met his drover, Dick Townshend.

"How are you, Dick?"

"Real well."

"How's the country?"

"Good."

"Your horses?"

"Good."

"Well, I want you to take your plant and go up to Wave Hill station. Buy cattle there, if you see anything good, and drove them north to Wyndham on the Cambridge Gulf. They occasionally ship cattle from there to Java. There must be a track of some sort from the Territory leading to it. On the way through the Territory call in at Victoria River Downs and see what you can buy. I'll arrange with the Emmanual Brothers in Western Australia to ship the cattle from Wyndham to Fremantle, for sale in Perth."

"A rough trip for the cattle, boss. I suppose about 2000 miles by sea, all down along the north-western then western Australian coast. That on top of a droving trip! The cattle will be poor by the time they reach Fremantle."

"Yes, Dick. But the Emmanuals will have paddock country near Perth. We will fatten them before putting them on the market."

"I see. Meanwhile keep the goldfields going by cattle shipped from the eastern States along the southern coast."

"Yes. But Western Australia will soon be able to supply its own cattle. That is why I am moving towards this end."

"Right, boss. When do I start?"

"Soon as you're ready."

"That will be in three days."

"Right. And—keep your eyes skinned!"

Townshend, with a smile, nodded. He now knew that his real job was to report in detail on the country, routes and possible routes, water locations, on the occupied and the unoccupied country he passed through.

He started three days later, as if an overland trip of 1000 miles through wild country was the routine of life. It was, to a number of Kidman's men. The result of that trip was to be far-reaching; in fact, its true significance is only appearing now. Besides the shipment of beef to England, it was to mean the building of meat-works, the formation of several great English companies, and indirectly a probable streamship line.

After seeing Townshend off, Kidman bought several mobs from the isolated stations, made arrangements for his drovers to "pick them up" in six months' time, then rode east in his attempt to penetrate through to south-western Queensland. His tiny black boy stuck to him though speechless with fear: he felt he was between the devil and the sea. After leaving a tangle of ranges south of Arltunga, Kidman got into the Simpson Desert. A small desert, but very real. A barrier of giant red sand-ridges; utter desolation, with not one drop of water.

Accepting the inevitable he turned back, returning by the usual track down through the Centre, and so into South Australia. There, in his own country, black boy Jacky came to life again. The attempted trip had not been in vain; Kidman had proved it impossible to reach his Three Rivers from that position in the Centre. That, for him, was a geographical fact of great importance. All cattle from the Territory (excepting the north from just below Austral Downs) seeking markets in the south would have to go right through his contemplated Centre-South Australian chain of stations. And the north-to-south railway must creep up along that very line. It was now at Oodnadatta, only about 130 miles south of the line that the Commonwealth was to proclaim as the northern border of South Australia. Since January 1891, work on the line had ceased. But if Federation was achieved and the Commonwealth eventually carried that line up through Central Australia, then it must pass through his contemplated chain. The sooner he started to form that chain the better.

Kidman had learned something else also. If he could take up the whole western boundary of the Georgina, he would have no neighbours!

26

Rain is Money

Some time later Kidman, fresh from Brisbane, met Isadore Emmanual in Adelaide.

Emmanual was pleased: "Those 1500 cattle Townshend shipped down from the Northern Territory arrived in surprisingly good condition. We have done very well out of them."

"That's fine."

"There is a big proposition up there."

"What is it?"

"Victoria River Downs, 9000 square miles of country. Townshend says the number of cattle on it is anywhere from 80,000 to 120,000 head. They are never completely mustered or branded. The country is well watered, but rough and wild. Plenty of blacks; they harass the place a little. We can get it, Kidman, with its subsidiary stations, Carlton Hill and Napier (about 12,500 square miles altogether) very cheap."

"How much?"

"£27,500. Goldsbrough Mort and Company have given me the offer. On terms too. £1000 for the offer for three months."

"Take it," said Kidman. "We can give them £10,000 down, and pay off the rest by selling a few mobs of cattle. I'll just about be able to finance my share."

"A four-sixteenth," said Emmanual.

"Right. I can do it."

"I don't suppose there is any other country in the world," said Emmanual, "where men can buy a kingdom stocked with 100,000 head of cattle for £27,000."

"There is a catch in it somewhere," answered Kidman grimly. "But if it is only distance and transport and inaccessibility, we can overcome all that in time."

The station was bought by the Emmanual Brothers, four shares each. Sid Kidman four shares, W. F. Buchanan, J. H. Richards, and Charlie Kidman one share each. Sid Kidman soon bought his brother's share. Dick Townshend was appointed manager. A gigantic venture. Under Townshend's managership it had to work out its own destiny, 2000 miles away. Emmanual hurried back to his own many interests in Western Australia. Kidman took the train to Kapunda. The "chariot" was waiting for him. Poddy little Oscar and Pompey recognized the master instantly, and Fred had to keep a tight hand on the reins. The master had hardly time to leap in to the seat before they were off. At any other time the two little fat ponies would trot leisurely along. But with the master in the chariot ... That was how he caught his trains.

"Well, how long this time?" asked Bell when the excitement was all over.

"Oh, a good while, I think; three or four weeks anyway. It's good to sit in this old chair, Bell."

"It will take you a long time to wear it out."

"Yes," he smiled, "I wish my saddles would last as long. I say, Bell, this little old country of ours is moving along."

"In what way particularly?"

"Well, this is 1900, and all's well. We are a Commonwealth now, and will be officially on 1 June 1901. Historic date, Bell. We've got Australian Bushmen contingents fighting overseas in South Africa, and this year we are sending a naval contingent to China. Next year we hold our first Federal Parliament too. We will no longer be colonies; we will be States merged in one Commonwealth. We have provided old-age pensions this year, and lead the world in kindliness to the old and infirm. Our inventors too, Bell. Lawrence Hargrave's box kite looks a real step to these flying machines they dream of. That American chap, Wilbur Wright, has asked Hargrave if he can use his patents. So we might see flying machines yet, Bell. Our railways are pushing out all over the continent; telegraph and telephones and cables have connected and are still spreading; our population has increased to 3,750,000. We are growing up, Bell."

"Now, I suppose all this means that you are growing too. What have you done now?"

"Bought a four-sixteenth share in Victoria River Downs."

"Where on earth is that?"

"Away out in wild country, about eighty mile inland from the mouth of the Victoria River, Northern Territory."

"It sounds big."

"It is!" he said enthusiastically. "A hundred thousand cattle, 12,500 square miles of country!"

She sighed. "You have a little plot here in Kapunda worth all that—if you only knew it."

"It is what I have always known," he answered softly. "I love to come back to it."

In 1901 Sid Kidman took train to Hergott Springs, then rode north to the Queensland border. He passed through the border fence with a smile. All customs dues were abolished on 1 January 1901. He took his time in closing the gate. "I'd like to know how many thousands you've cost the cattlemen," he smiled. "You'll let my cattle through duty free after this."

He rode on to Birdsville. The customs officers had mostly departed. So ended a picturesque chapter in the story of the border fences. The border patrols would ride no more.

He rode on to Carcoory, hearing that Dubbo Downs station was for sale—cheap. It was with misgiving that he saw the barrenness of Carcoory, the outside waterholes all dried up. With the manager he rode rapidly over the station, seeing that the cattle were distributed proportionately over the remaining feed and permanent water, making sure that the station was in working order to fight this threatened drought. Then he rode west to Dubbo Downs. It was a station of 800 square miles on Eyre Creek, an eastern tributary of the Mulligan. As it adjoined Annandale, he could shift the herds from one station to another, should necessity arise. He bought Dubbo Downs for £2100; much of it had been partially ruined by rabbits. Between the station and the border fence is a long succession of claypans and sand-ridges, where the rabbits were well "dug in".

On all sides there was talk of drought in the south-west. He forced this worry from him, knowing that this was the reason he had been able to buy these stations and cattle cheaply. Besides, if in this country a man was to be frightened by every threat of drought he would never get on. He was working now on his faith in the Three Rivers. That if it did not rain over the country itself, it must rain sometime away to the far north, the north-east, or north-west. That would bring the Three Rivers down, independent of local rain. He was counting on the eventual certainty of rain here, or on the watersheds of those rivers. Good rain in any one of those quarters would save everything.

To see conditions he rode north 300 miles. The country was in an awful state. Then 150 miles north-west and crossing the Territory border pulled up at Avon Downs station. The country was better there, though isolated to the south and south-west by lack of water. None but a clever drover would be able to shift stock from there until rains came. The station was on the Rankine River, one of the headwaters of the Georgina.

On this station he "specked" 1200 "stores", bullocks that in twelve months or less would fill out and grow rolling fat. He bought these at three pounds ten shillings a head, half cash and the remainder in under twelve months. He arranged with drover Gleeson to lift the cattle in approximately twelve months' time and bring them leisurely down the Birdsville track via Carcoory, then to be droved through the South Australian "corner" to railhead at Hergott Springs (Marree).

Feeling a bit weary, though full of optimism, he started on the 550 miles ride to Longreach. After crossing the dry belt, and getting on to the great Queensland downs, the country looked much better. From Longreach he travelled north to Hughenden, then west to Richmond. There he bought 150 good bulls on behalf of Victoria River Downs, and saw them start west on their long trek to the Northern Territory station. To dodge dry conditions the drover had to take them north and through the Gulf country, then west to Anthony's Lagoon, striking north-west then for the Victoria. It was an eighteen months' trip. Some of the bulls were taken by crocodiles when swimming the northern rivers. Occasionally men and horses, as well as bulls, had to fight for their lives.

Kidman returned to Longreach, and from there trained to the coast. From the train he admired the changes in the country; always for the better; so different to the lesser rainfall areas. He longed to own some of those beautiful stations. But then, had his life been cast in these rich lands he could never have hoped to own a chain of stations.

He returned to Kapunda. This time his homecoming was busy indeed. He had to start the organization of his horse-sales, after all these years. If the initial sale was a success, a sale would be held each year. The fame of those sales was destined to grow until the name of Kapunda was known in India, in the Dutch East Indies, and in other parts of the world where horses are imported.

The great drought of 1902–3 blighted south-western and central Queensland country. Carcoory was struck first. In an endeavour to save stock the manager started on the road the 2000 bullocks Kidman had bought from the Rocklands Pastoral Company. The drover headed them towards Kelpie, which in normal times was a big waterhole on Haddon Downs. It was dry, and every hoof perished. Then he sent 1000 head of breeding cows towards Pandi Pandi, hoping for grass and water there. Every hoof perished. Then the drought claimed victims from the herds on Carcoory, Annandale, Dubbo Downs, and from nearly every station north and south for 1000 miles. There was no getaway for the herds; no escape. Numbers of men, after a lifetime's struggle, found themselves ruined. Around

Birdsville the only wild life was crows and dingoes. On a perishing horse, Kidman rode up to Carcoory. His face was powdered with dust. A few men were slouching listlessly about the homestead.

"How many cattle have you got?" demanded Kidman.

"We had two," answered one, "but neither belongs to you. We have killed one, and are going to kill the other—the last!"

"What are you doing here?"

"Oh, we are keeping a few spare horses together."

"Well, the only thing I can do is to pay you off to-night. What water remains?"

"None for stock. The last drinking-water is in the well in the creek and it will be dry in a week."

He walked into the store. Its empty shelves held a few pounds of flour, half a canister of tea, and a sugarbag swarming with ants. "What are you doing?" he asked a man sitting there.

"Storekeeping."

"What! Storekeeping on an empty bag of sugar?"

He paid the men off, not without a little argument from the cook's wife. She was a city girl and wore a silk frock with enough flour and dough on it to make a damper. She stuck up for her husband's job, but Kidman said, "If I don't pay him off now he'll get nothing. The only money I have in the world is the little I have with me. When I pay you off, I'll be completely broke."

Fred Brooks (killed later by the blacks in Central Australia) had ridden across from Dubbo Downs to meet him. "Fred," said Kidman, "run in what horses you can find and yoke them to the wagon. There is a little chaff left. Load up anything that is of value and take it to Annandale. I am going to close this place up."

Next day he was left alone. The mockery of it. Big black clouds rolling up while he stood without a shilling in the world. Around him the desolate expanse of Carcoory. The homestead abandoned. On all his stations he must have lost 35,000 head. On a coolabah nearly killed by the drought crows squawked, fullbellied. Black dots, too, across the creek, and everywhere.

Crows feasting on his bullocks while he didn't have the price of a meal. And these black clouds rolling up—the silver lining—too late.

Suddenly he heard the crack of a whip. He felt the blood leave his face. Those Rocklands bullocks! Those 2000 head at twenty-five shillings per head; those thousand cows at one pound per head. £3500, all gone in crows' feed. And here was the drover coming for his money, his twenty-five pounds per week from the time he had left Carcoory until he should return.

How slow the sun was in going down. Like the big black clouds that had come too late. A bird called cheerily away down among the creek trees. He listened with a bitter smile. He had not thought there was a real bird left alive in the land. Only the blasted crows. It must get its water from the well; it was cheery because it knew of coming rain, the breaking of the drought.

Again he heard the crack of a whip. Strange! No real drover ever returns empty handed to the crack of the whip.

And again the crack of a whip! Then he heard the lowing of thirsty cattle. He stared amazed. He heard a cheery shout.

Cattle! Coming to camp at the waterhole—the hole full of carcasses—the hole that would be full of water before midnight by the look of these clouds ... Yes ... Thunder! Low and rumbling: and a flash of lightning. What on earth could these cattle be? How could cattle travel in a drought like this? Perhaps it was his drover returning with a mob he had picked up from some other luckier station. Two jobs at once! Some men were born lucky.

But it could not be. He had come from the south and the south was a desert; what cattle were alive there could hardly stand on their legs.

He walked down to the creek. Away on the opposite side appeared the lead of the mob, stringing out as they came seeking water at the long dried hole. A few spots of rain fell spattering on their backs. The boss drover rode down the steep bank above the hole, disappeared, then reappeared above the bank clinging to his horse's mane. As he rode forward Kidman breathed with intense relief.

It was not *his* drover.

"Good day."

"Good day."

"You are Mr Kidman?"

"Yes.

"I've brought your cattle."

"What?"

"I've brought your cattle. I'm drover Gleeson with 1200 Avon Downs bullocks for delivery to you via Carcoory. Don't you remember me?"

Kidman stared across at those bullocks, drops of rain splashing on his face. Those Avon Downs bullocks! He had momentarily forgotten them. He felt a lump in his throat.

"You are jolly welcome," he then said with a laugh. "Have you ever heard of a silver lining?"

"Well, yes. But I don't quite understand what you mean."

"The storm comes up; and you come with it; and grass means fortune. What are the bullocks like?"

"Good. They'll be prime in another month if this rain comes."

"That's great."

"But Mr Kidman"—and the drover stared uneasily at the sky—"if the rain does not fall ... well, I seem to have reached my limit. The cattle have not had a drink for fifty hours, I have not seen a blade of grass, not even a fallen leaf, for three days!"

A thunder-clap shook the skies, it went rocketing and rolling, recoiled to roll away again, growling and rumbling. Dust splashed up from quickening raindrops.

"There'll be surface water in half an hour," laughed Kidman. "And plenty of feed in a week. But how on earth have you kept them alive?"

"The drought was not nearly so bad up where I lifted the beasts. I just poked them along steadily then when I neared the bad country I held them on feed a couple of months, until a storm broke farther south. I hurried them across a fortnight later and got on to the storm feed; then held them there until another storm broke. I followed the storms down. Looks like as if they are the beginning of the break of the drought."

"They are!" said Kidman. "Look! Away to the east, black with falling rain! God be praised."

The cook in his wagonette came slowly around the flanks of the mob. "Better go up to the house and light your fire," shouted Kidman, "it will rain soon—it is raining now! Come," he said to the drover, "let's have a look at them—quick, before sunset has gone!" Laughing like a schoolboy he strode ahead of the horse down towards the cattle.

When green feed carpeted the earth he drove those cattle to Marree, then trucked them to Adelaide where they realized twelve pounds five shillings per head. He paid all his obligations; put £6000 in the bank; then hurried to Kapunda and the sympathy and encouragement of a little Scotch wife.

27

Making a Fortune

At Kapunda he now built a fine new home. He could afford it. And an office too; for it was overwhelmingly obvious that "Sid Kidman" would become an organization. From now on Wally Will was his Kapunda agent.

Kidman had kept the belief alive that he was going to make Kapunda the horse-buying centre of Australia. He already had agents scouring four States buying horses, business he arranged by wire. And he was organizing for the very pick of Australian horses to be concentrated yearly at Kapunda.

Kidman again left home to inspect Annandale, Kaliduwary, and Dubbo Downs. Where before had been desert the feed was two feet high. He felt his spirits rising with the new life arising from the country. His heart sang with the birds busy now in nest-building. He smiled as the breeze rippled the grass. Lagoons over a 1000-mile long stretch of country were sweet with water, alive with wild fowl. Every waterhole was full, some rivers were still running. Life, life everywhere. And he felt full of life, and had a wealth of experience to guide him. That was what counted—experience. He had won experience and £25,000 with it. He had lost the money only to gain a greater fortune in experience. That was the sum total of life—

experience. His bank was in his head. He would gain yet more experience, and grow stronger and stronger.

He was happy in his camps at sundown. He noticed that the little bush rats that built castles of sticks were now seldom seen; he wondered if it were the cats that were eating them out. Broods of domestic cats gone wild were increasing all over the land. Many a day he saw a pathetic little bundle of feathers beneath a nesting-tree. He felt sorry for the birds. But the cats were not an unmixed evil; they must eat untold numbers of young rabbits. Like many others, he was to learn that swarms of cats would have no more effect in keeping the rabbits down than a few fly-catchers would wipe out a plague of flies. When the cycle of a rabbit plague was to come, nothing would stop it.

Meanwhile Kidman would restock his stations as quickly as possible. He travelled fast through south-western Queensland into the Gulf country, then west through the Barkly Tableland of the Northern Territory. On that vast tableland with its treeless downs grazed huge herds of cattle on mighty stations of 6000, 7000, 8000 square miles in area. On these unfortunately poorly watered but otherwise natural grazing-grounds so distant from markets he would buy, for immediate, three months, and six months delivery every hoof of cattle he could. Terms: a deposit on each mob from his £6000, the balance at three, six, or more months after delivery.

The drought had not been nearly so bad on those distant tablelands. He was certain too that the drought had not wiped out (as was generally supposed) south-western Queensland either. The herds were too big, the unfenced country too vast, Many of the great stations did not know within some thousands of head what their own country carried, let alone the whole land. From his own knowledge of the herds, he knew that, taking losses in the Press as correct, there must still be tens of thousands of cattle alive in the south-west alone. Queensland had lost 1,000,000 cattle out of 4,000,000 in the drought just broken. The remaining 3,000,000 would now fatten rapidly. The owners would be eager to sell to make room for oncoming stock. A travelling buyer out in those distant areas where so few called would be welcome. Especially Kidman, for his name was "good" now far and wide.

Yes, there would be isolated stations in the drought area that had missed it. His experience would guide him to them. Then, there were the great stations of the Territory that had missed the drought, out-of-the-way country that he knew well. The field would be left almost entirely to him; other cattle-buyers would operate mostly in the coastal, central, and near western districts.

At Dubbo Downs he saw many cattle feeding in the knee-high grass across the river. He turned to the manager:

"Whose are those cattle, Jim?"

"A few might be yours. They're Sandringham's, Glengyle's, Cluny's, everyone's."

"Well, I'm going to have a look at them."

"Impossible. The river is high, running swiftly."

"That won't stop me." He walked to the river and began to strip.

Unwillingly the manager stripped. It was a tough swim, but they crossed safely. Very soon, Kidman saw that all the young cattle in sight had been freshly branded—with a distant station's brand.

"You are a jolly good sort of manager letting them take all those big cleanskins," he said with a frown.

The manager mumbled a gruff reply. They swam back over the river. Kidman ordered a quick muster. But they only got a few cleanskins, the other station had "got in first".

At coffee time of nights Kidman strolled across to the kitchen when the big bell summoned all hands. He believed in feeding his men well; was the first to raise the standard of rations in the far back country. And he liked to listen in and add his quota of yarns to the romances invariably told at "smoke ohs" and "coffee time". Each man squatting around the kitchen, a pannikin of coffee in one hand, a lump of brownie in the other. The day's work done, it was the ideal time to "swap yarns". The cook told tales of "Billy the Rager", of "The Whistling Canary", of "Mick the Bone Crusher". Then he turned to giant snakes, finally drifting on to tortoises. And his tortoises grew and grew. After the last monster, old George the boundary-rider sipped his coffee reflectively.

"Yes," he remarked in the silence, "tortoises grow to a fair size down here, but not so big as they was in the old days. I remember, near where Innamincka station is now, I come to the waterhole at dark and dipped a billy of water. There was an old dray lying there but I took no notice. When I was turning in though I thought:

" 'Now how the blazes did a dray get there? There's no one travelling in this country!' So I strolls across to have a look, an' just when I puts my hand on it it slips into the water."

With Jacky as horse boy Kidman rode swiftly through the Camooweal district, then to Lake Nash station and there bought 1500 fat bullocks at four pounds ten shillings per head. These, and other mobs he bought, were to be called for by drovers on an agreed upon date. At Carrandotta station he bought big mobs of sheep and cattle. At Guthrie station he bought 10,000 sheep at seven shillings per head, raced to the nearest telegraph station and sold them over the wires at one pound per head, making £6500. For months he travelled with Jacky.

That darkie, though considering himself a full-blown stockman, now, was a terror for boiled lollies. It was Kidman's delight to ride unconcernedly past any roadside store until the youngster threatened to burst into tears. Jacky's great ambition was to own a pair of boots. Kidman bought him a pair at a wayside store. Jacky that day wore those boots proudly. Next day he was barefooted again:

"Why don't you wear your boots, Jacky?"

"Those boots belonga me no plurry good, boss. He bitem my plurry toe."

Kidman bought thousands of head of cattle from Rocklands and Alroy, Herbert Vale and Alexandria Downs. At Alroy a big mob of good cows in calf attracted him, the very thing to restock Dubbo Downs. He bought them cheaply and put them on the road immediately. Returning through Queensland he bought Brighton and Chatsworth bullocks, then turned his horses' heads towards Cloncurry. By now, his first mobs would be nearing their trucking destinations. It was time for him to get in touch with the big markets and arrange sales. He had bought 20,000 cattle, at an average of £4 per head (£80,000) and £10,000 worth of sheep; and had left his bare fare to Adelaide.

Those cattle and sheep were his assets. The cattle were already in good condition; the sheep too. And all were travelling in charge of good drovers over country on which there now was an abundance of feed. Feeling supremely confident, he took the train to Brisbane. He had only been in town a few hours when a stock agent called.

"Heard you were in town, Kidman."

"Who told you?"

"Oh, a little bird."

"Did the little bird say I am going straight on to Sydney tonight?"

"No, but I guessed you might be. I can sell you 600 head of prime cattle already on the Birdsville track."

Instantly Kidman thought of Bill Naughton's mob he had met on the road in charge of Blake Miller. He knew they *were* prime.

"Yes, and I daresay if I took them they would turn out to be old pikers."

"No, on my word! Four and five year old bullocks. Cheap too."

"What do you call cheap?"

"Ten pounds a head."

"That is not cheap!"

"You know it is, man. They're prime and already half-way down the Birdsville track."

"Is Blake Miller in charge?"

"Yes he is. How did you know?"

"A little bird told me."

"What the little bird doesn't tell you isn't worth knowing."

"I'll give you eight pounds ten shillings a head, delivered at Marree, on a month's sale."

"Heavens man, don't be hard!"

"I'm not hard. You're trying to sell cattle; I'm trying to buy them."

"Well then, we'll make it eight pounds ten shillings a head where they stand."

"Not on your life. You pay the drover to Marree."

"Oh, all right. What with droughts and cattle-buyers an honest agent finds it hard to keep the wolf from the door."

"That's why I notice them all buying these new-fangled motor cars," smiled Kidman. "Come now, won't your client be pleased at the sale?"

"Yes. As a matter of fact he was prepared to take seven pounds fifteen shillings a head."

"Ah. So you've beaten me out of £450."

"If I thought I was smart enough to beat *you*," replied the agent composedly, "I'd dash out and buy myself a Rolls Royce."

Thus Kidman bought another 600 head of cattle, incurring a further liability of £5100, payable in a month's time. But he thought he knew where he could place those cattle, swiftly he had calculated the possible date of their arrival at Adelaide. He went straight to the telegraph office and wired an Adelaide agent. The result was that the cattle were sold on the track for twelve pounds ten shillings per head before the month was up.

In George Street, Sydney, he heard a voice behind him:

"Hullo, Kidman, where have you been?" There was G. S. Yuill.

"Oh, out in the south-west, buying cattle."

"Get any?"

"A few. Twenty thousand."

"What! Twenty thousand!"

"Yes."

"Come along, old man. I've got some friends who want to talk to you."

They offered to join in with him on a half-share basis.

"No," he replied. "But if you like to give me a premium of £10,000 for a half-share of the cattle, you can come in. (You will make another £10,000.) Then I'll put a similar amount over it and go straight back to Queensland and buy big to supply the meat companies."

"Ten thousand pounds is a very big premium."

"Not when there is £100,000 to be made. If you won't agree to that then I am off to Melbourne to-night and home."

Negotiations fell through—fortunately for Kidman.

As the cattle arrived at their respective destinations, mob after mob were sold on a rising market. It was ten months from the start of the trip until the last mob was sold.

Kidman cleared £40,000.

28

Links of Land to Form a Chain

Feeling like a millionaire he basked at home under the care of the nice Scotch wife. He mended all the fences and made a cage for the cockatoo through which the bird soon chewed a hole to walk out of. He listened to the Salvation Army of Saturday nights while following them from corner to corner with his pockets full of shillings. His wife mustered him for church on Sundays, and carefully laid the foundations in his mind for a big new house.

But presently he showed signs of restlessness. Forty thousand pounds and his experience! Each day at intervals while pottering about the home he would stand and gaze towards the north. He could see the great south-west, its grey-black plains, its serried sand-ridges, its old-man tablelands and worn down hills, its gibber plains burnished copper-red spreading hazily into mirage. And running right down through it the Three Rivers in snaky lines, 1000 miles long, of dull green gum and coolabah lining the dry grey-brown watercourses, their countless channels flanked by lignum. Then he saw the yellow-brown floods come slowly creeping on heralded by their shrieking flocks of wild fowl; saw the earth come to life under saltbush, the desert ablaze under flowers; heard the chant of full-bellied blacks deep in the mulga; saw himself riding along the Cooper with little black boy Jacky.

He wanted to go back. And that chain of stations! Breathlessly he thought of it—£40,000! He could buy a lot of stations now, so many were in the hands of the banks; others were held by men who, disheartened by the recurring struggle, awaited a buyer. And here was he, only wanting the land, he who could stock any land swiftly and cheaply, for he knew almost the entire stock of the continent; he knew how to get it, and where. Although the country had bloomed again, he knew there must come in its cycle another drought. But by then he should have his chain of stations. And with that chain he would fight any drought link by link, preparing throughout the good seasons and beating this treacherous bush that smiled her brightest while gradually working up to a drought.

"Aren't you going to invest your money, and settle down comfortably?" asked the wife. She could read him through and through.

"Bell, I couldn't settle down, as you call it; I'd pine away like an old piker."

His eyes were bright, his mouth grim set. Then he kissed her. "I couldn't stay at home, Bell. Stagnation is harmful to any man or country, in good times or bad."

So he went off again out into Queensland and the Diamantina. The country was a flower garden; the saltbush and the gidgee fresh to welcome him; 'roos and emus stalked the land, big and fat. He met numerous blackfellow friends, they and their lubras and piccaninnies, all in fat good humour. But there were many that he did not see.

"They are dying out," he mused; "they are not like the grass and birds and animals that spring up renewed after a drought. I wonder why? There are comparatively few white men in this country; there is plenty of game in good seasons; introduced disease has not been nearly so bad in this particular area as in others—yet the blacks die fast."

Quickly Kidman set about restocking Annandale and Dubbo Downs. The sooner new herds were built up again the stronger would he be when dry times came. He bought Pandi, a small place just over the Queensland border in the South Australian "corner".

Monkira station he secured cheaply. It was a big flood area of 2500 square miles fronting the Diamantina and was to prove a strong link in his chain. He spent £7000 on one bore alone; it repaid with flowing water worth thousands of pounds per year. Shrewd development work eventually made this station nearly drought-proof. It grew the fattest of all his bullocks—one dressed in Adelaide sold at 1990 lb. giving 240 lb. of caul fat, said to be the heaviest bullock ever slaughtered. Another huge beast the drover had the greatest difficulty in getting to railhead. But it proved too heavy to stand up on the 400-mile rail journey and died in the truck.

In Sydney Kidman met Mr Ivey, a manager of the Bank of New South Wales.

"Hullo, Kidman. I've been told to keep a look out for you."

"What have I done?"

"Goodness knows, and he won't tell! But you bought Carrandotta cattle from the bank a few months back."

"They're paid for," smiled Kidman.

"I know they are. If they weren't, I wouldn't be looking for you now. How about buying the station?"

"What price?"

He named a prohibitive figure.

Kidman shook his head. "Just at present," he drawled, "I've invested every shilling. It will be months before I have any cattle coming in for sale. Until then I can't consider the offer." But he wanted this 4000 square miles of good country on the Georgina River and shrewdly suspected that by waiting a little he would get it—at a much reduced price. Meanwhile he quietly ascertained what stock were on the property and what numbers were in suitable condition for sale. Found out also that there was a mob of bullocks on the road to market and 300 bales of wool in transit to London for sale. Hence, when some months later

Pitt, Son, and Badgery offered it him on a walk-in-walk-out basis, he bought for £65,000. Fortune stood to him. The mob of bullocks was trucked at Bourke for Sydney five days after he bought the place and realized almost a record price, and the wool sold excellently in London.

There were then between 5000 and 7000 head of cattle on Carrandotta, at Walgra substation. Years before it had carried over 100,000 sheep, about 26,000 cattle, and 2000 horses. A series of drought seasons had cut these figures to 18,000 sheep, 5000 odd cattle, and about 800 horses.

In due time, with his wife and Mel Shannon and Julius Grunike, Sid Kidman headed for Hughenden. From there he drove by buggy to inspect Carrandotta. He was immediately struck by the spick-and-span appearance of the homestead; he could not find a tin, a piece of paper, or an empty match-box thrown anywhere about the place. Well pleased with his inspection he remarked, "You'll soon build up again."

"Like wildfire," replied Edge, "a few good seasons is all we want."

As was his custom, in the course of an ordinary conversation he tested the knowledge of the manager as to the stock and property under his charge. Many times employees and others did not realize they were thus under cross examination. On this occasion he was soon confident of the capabilities of Edge.

"Good. There's the jolly dinner-bell."

They walked back to the homestead—and a huge pile of telegrams. As he opened each telegram he handed it to Edge to read, who was amazed at the extent of the business, the information of which this man was carrying in his head.

"I don't know what I would do without telegrams," he remarked to Edge, "letters would never catch me travelling as I do."

"They save you writing letters."

"I seldom write letters, my daughters help me write them when I'm at home, otherwise I would never get through."

At last Edge, fidgety for some time, said respectfully but

firmly: "Don't do that sir, I can't stand papers or empty match-boxes blowing about the place!"

Kidman gazed at Edge, then at the litter of crumpled envelopes on the floor. He bent down and began picking them up.

"Neither can I, Edge. I shan't do it again."

Edge held out a letter. "Here is a letter received from the Bank of New South Wales showing that you have squared up for the station up to date of my last return, 31 January."

"I don't want to see that. How much is owing?"

Edge told him. He pulled out his cheque-book.

"I'll give you a cheque now. Pay it off. The bank," he continued, "were giving you so much per year. I will give you a £100 a year more, and a bonus when the place pays."

"That is very considerate of you."

"Well, I will be only too pleased to pay it, if you earn the money."

"How about the books?"

"I don't want any books, I want the place to pay."

But Edge insisted on records being kept, on everything being up to date in black and white.

"Have it your own way," agreed Kidman. "So long as you make it pay!"

"And my instructions for running the place?"

"There are none. You know your job. Always treat the employees well, though; feed them well, and if the men do a bit more than usual, give them a bonus. But allow no waste. I'm never afraid of what a man eats, but I am of what he wastes."

"There never is waste on this place," declared Edge. "And the men will appreciate that bonus."

Kidman stayed only a couple of days. On getting into the buggy, Edge remarked:

"Well, you haven't seen much of the place."

"I've seen as much as I wanted to—there are no empty tins lying about."

"H'm."

211

"Well, Edge, you have no boss now; no bank inspectors; no anybody—only me. I won't trouble you—make the place pay. Good-bye."

"Good-bye."

He never visited the station again while he owned it. The Carrandotta herds, with good seasons, built up with remarkable speed. A time soon came when Edge marked 20,000 lambs for the year's increase. Soon, 60,000 Carrandotta sheep had travelled to South Australia for sale. Between 1903 and 1914, when Kidman sold the station at a big profit, Edge had marketed over 130,000 sheep and 30,000 head of cattle, besides yearly increasing consignments of wool. That wool was sometimes up to twelve months in reaching Sydney; by wagon 500 miles to Winton, then the rail journey to Townsville, then steamer to Sydney.

Carrandotta paid for itself very quickly; then immediately became a fighting link in the chain.

In 1904 Kidman bought Bulloo Down, Sandringham, Glengyle, Peake, and Coongy stations. Bulloo Downs was an old love since the days when he met Mudmaps. Mudmaps had kept his word; through the years he had advised him. Now the station was drifting. The once great property was no longer the "show" station of Queensland. When he and Mudmaps first rode across it, it had carried 43,000 head of cattle, sending a mob of 300 fats to Adelaide every fortnight, which at that time meant a droving trip of 600 miles to railhead. Probably the station at that time cleared £40,000 a year. Possibly overstocking and rabbits combined had greatly reduced the carrying capacity of this station.

After returning to Adelaide with his wife he trained to Broken Hill where he secured horses and a buggy and left to take delivery of Bulloo Downs, picking up Jack Watts at Tickalara on his way. Sid Kidman felt sure that the country would "come back". The reserve price was £40,000. There were no bidders and he offered Powers Rutherford and Company £20,000, an offer eventually accepted. There were 3000 cattle on it. With the little Scotch wife in the buggy he drove to Bulloo Downs to take delivery, calling in at Tickalara station *en route* to give Galloping Jack Watts the job as manager. Galloping Jack was one of the most famous horsemen of the day. One of the lightest riders Kidman had ever seen, he stuck on a horse like a postage stamp. This once great station was strategically situated to help supply either Brisbane, Sydney, or Adelaide markets. Kidman dreamt of restoring it to its former glory.

Sandringham station, a 4000-mile block of country adjoining Dubbo Downs and Glengyle, now came on the market. He bought it. Its western boundary ran out on to the Territory border, west of that was No Man's Land. The Georgina ran through its eastern area. Some of it flood-water country, and "the world" to roam in for the cattle, limited only by the supply of water! He would seek deep in the earth for water for the future herds of Sandringham.

His foresight and information as usual proved thoroughly accurate. The station was efficiently mustered and he sold 1000 heifers at nine pounds per head, and 400 yearlings at six pounds per head to Nocatunga station, also three mobs each of 400 fat cattle, one each to Sydney, Melbourne, and Adelaide. The prices realized by the sale of these cattle more than paid the purchase money for the whole property.

Thus he had overcome one of the greatest difficulties of the men in such distant areas as, for instance, the Barkly Tableland. From there, a mob might have to travel 1000 or more miles to market, and take six months, probably more, to reach rail transport. The mob would then be footsore and poor in condition, and when they reached market be barely saleable.

But Sid Kidman could now buy a mob from the Tableland, walk them to Sandringham and allow them twelve months there to refatten if necessary.

One day he was angry indeed. He walked into the store and there was the station cockatoo enjoying itself in the flour-bin. He chased it out. Screeching, with crest erect and wings flapping flour, it cursed him hoarsely. That bird was the stockmen's pet and its education had been sadly misdirected. It swore with a vim that lighted the devil in its glistening eyes. Kidman gave it his boot and it turned a somersault as it hastily reached a small tree beside the store. Up this it climbed, sidled on to its favourite branch, and from there screeched a tirade of invective.

"Hi, you fellows!" called Kidman to the stockmen, "if I catch this cockatoo spoiling my flour again, I'll shoot the wretched thing!"

When he finally rode away a consultation was held and a plan evolved to educate the bird against the doom that surely hung over it.

Kidman's next purchase was Glengyle station. He had long wanted it, with its 6183 square miles; its deep, permanent holes on the Georgina; its plains and hills and flats of lignum and saltbush. Strategically, it adjoined Sandringham, Kaliduwary, Dubbo Downs and Annandale.

He had jumped at the chance of buying Coongy, 1600 miles of "strategic" country adjoining Innamincka station in the South Australian-Queensland "corner". Coongy was not the great station it had been when he rode over it as a youth. Dry times, dust-storms and rabbits had wellnigh ruined it; besides causing havoc with the saltbush the rabbits had killed all the white wood, apple-bush, and butter-bush. Coongy was owned by Norman Wilson's Estate. Sid Kidman made an offer of £5000, which was not accepted. They considered they had at least 2000 head of cattle on the run and would not accept less than three pounds five shillings per head. Kidman eagerly accepted this price; privately he doubted whether there were more than 1000 cattle on the station. The run was mustered within six months and only 920 head of cattle and horses could be delivered. Sid Kidman thus secured Coongy for £2990.

Now he had linked up south-western Queensland stations with northern South Australia.

Peake station was a link in his Central Australian-South Australian chain. A large block 200 miles south-east of Eringa, its eastern boundary was Lake Eyre. With Kempe as partner they bought it, with 800 cattle, from John Bagot for £9000.

When Kempe died Kidman purchased his share. The north-to-south railway line, ever creeping towards the centre of the continent at Alice Springs, now ran up through this property for about seventy miles, the railhead having reached Oodnadatta in January 1891. This station was to prove a weak link, to swallow a lot of time, money and labour.

29

The Rain-Maker Earns His Buggy

A cycle of good seasons had come. Kidman's cattle increased and multiplied, grew fat and were sold in the usual station routine. The mobs he continually bought from other stations brought swift profits. He had long since schooled himself never to waste regret over a loss. He would never come home to the wife and tell her of one. If asked, he might say, "Oh, I lost a little on those jolly beggars," and then go on playing with the youngsters. But he was pleased at success.

"I'm beginning to move," he drawled one evening. "Just glance at these figures, Bell. The boy on the one-eyed horse never dreamt he would buy all these cattle in a year."

He handed her a typed sheet. It was a list of nineteen mobs of cattle he had bought from as many different stations in 1904. It totalled 23,516 head for which he had paid £132,129.

She studied it awhile before handing it back. "You have done well," she said, "the girls are just leaving school and you have always promised me you would go home and see where our people lived."

He sat back thoughtfully. "You want a trip home," he mused.

"Yes, and so do you."

"Well, it pays any one to travel," he drawled. "It would just finish off the girls' education too."

"Yes; you are making money now and I want the girls to have the very best that life has to offer. You remember what education has done for you!" she reminded him.

He sat thinking awhile, remembering how years ago the Scotch lassie had so shrewdly "educated" him on his rush trips to Kapunda.

"The girls are ready to go overseas now," she said. "And Walter will grow up. So you had better put a little bit by for him too."

"I suppose so," he murmured and returned to his figures. He found solace in the thought that Victoria River Downs was now paying its way. The great station had been expensive to run. Supplies had to come from Port Darwin by lugger, then eighty miles up the savagely beautiful river to the station depot. Several drafts of horses had to be kept for mustering the half-wild cattle. Horse-shoes were used literally in tons because the country in places was a maze of rocky ranges. That station wore out more horse-shoes than any other station in Australia. In the rough work, saddlery and plant of all descriptions had constantly to be replenished. Townshend selected a team of daredevil riders and set in to muster the place. He could never do it, it was far too large, too intersected by waterways and ranges.

But eventually he was branding 20,000 calves a year; in several seasons he branded 25,000. It was rough on horseflesh, rough on men. Still, the men at least loved the life. It was active and varied enough to keep them from going stale. Entirely cut off from the outside world each wet season, they made the most of the bright, sunlit months of the "dry". Riding for weeks, sometimes for months, at a time, in the mustering-camps away from the head station, there was occasionally the chance of a little excitement from the blacks. The fine, active, big warriors who roamed those ranges were willing for a bit of spear-throwing should opportunity favour them. Again, on occasion, the musterers had to swim or raft across rivers and the crocodiles that are so plentiful there invariably lent an interest to the crossings.

The blacks speared numerous cattle; but the herds were so vast that no one troubled overmuch. The trouble was in attempting to muster these cattle when they imagined every sound was a blackfellow.

One year when the Perth market was over supplied it was decided to drove Victoria River Downs cattle to Queensland, New South Wales, and South Australia, and sell them as stores. They started 5000 bullocks from the station, and 3360 of these were delivered at Coongy after travelling 1700 miles. The droving cost a shilling per head per 100 miles—seventeen and sixpence per head delivered to Coongy. Twelve hundred of these were droved on from Coongy to Muswellbrook in New South Wales, a further 700 miles. A record droving trip of 2400 miles.

Kidman inspected Norley Downs station in south-western Queensland; a beautiful station with the homestead on the banks of a picturesque billabong. Then carrying 4000 cattle and 500 horses, the price was £25,000. He knew that it could be improved to carry far more stock; he had ridden through it in his droving days when it carried 40,000 head of cattle. The rabbits had nearly eaten it out.

At the moment, however, Kidman was engaged in a business deal with a blackfellow. Not the wild man of the Victoria River, nor yet a warrior of the north-western Kimberleys. This was old Tindah, the "rain-maker", with his mate, Paddy.

"Mine word. I bin sit down look out longa you three pfella day!" declared Tindah.

"It's no good me coming here, Tindah," replied Kidman. "This station no good; no grass, no water; poor pfella cattle everywhere! You pfellas no good now; too fat, too lazy; all a time sit down! Me have to get him some old pfella make him rain 'proper'!"

"My word boss this pfella country all right!" protested Tindah. "By-em-by I make 'em big pfella flood!"

"Well, why don't you make 'em rain now?"

"No time, boss! All a time muster cattle; work all a day! Too much plurry work!"

"Well, you need not muster any more. You make 'em rain instead! How much you want 'em make big pfella flood, make plenty feed jump up alonga poor pfella bullock?"

Tindah knotted his shaggy brows while glaring wisely at Paddy. After due consideration he turned to Kidman.

"Hundred quid!"

"Phew! One hundred pounds! That is a lot of money." Kidman turned to his mate standing by.

"How much would you want to make a big pfella flood, Paddy?"

"Two pfella shillin' !" answered Paddy briskly.

Kidman laughed heartily. "I'll tell you what I'll do," he said, "I'll give you a couple of horses and the best buggy on the place if you make a big pfella flood."

These terms were agreed to, Galloping Jack standing grimly by. He was going to be general manager, managing both Bulloo Downs and Norley. He was not at all looking forward to the nights of howling and tin banging that were sure to follow the rain-maker's efforts.

"How many days will it take you to make 'em rain?" inquired Kidman.

"Mine think it two pfella week," frowned Tindah.

"Are you sure you can make 'em in two pfella week?"

After a doubtful glance towards Paddy, Tindah growled reflectively: "P'raps three pfella week."

"Are you sure you can make 'em in three pfella week?"

"Sure pfella!"

"Do you want any one to help you?"

"Yes. Wantem Davey and Jackie."

"Are you sure that will be enough?"

Tindah scratched his head, then worked the problem out on his fingers. "Mine thinkit better have Dick too."

"All right. We will go over to the store and draw your rations."

At the store, Kidman ordered rations for three weeks. The storekeeper issued the jam, tea, sugar, and flour. To each item Tindah promptly added, "Want 'em 'nother tin jam, 'nother packet tea,"—and got it. As each request was satisfied he suddenly thought of something else, particularly in the pipe and tobacco line. When all seemed settled he demanded:

"Want 'em one pfella tent so can make 'em rain inside!"

"Keep out of the wet," said Watts. When the tent was supplied, "Want 'em two pfella tomahawk!" demanded Tindah. These were immediately supplied and he seemed exhausted but at the last moment thought of buckets for carrying water.

"And that's about all the rain he will make," declared Watts. "What he can dip out of a waterhole in a bucket."

Kidman laughed, but gave them the buckets, saying: "All right, Tindah, now go off and make 'em rain big pfella flood!"

As the rain-makers with their assistants went staggering away to camp, Watts said, "There go some fairly efficient musterers off duty for three weeks. If they make rain, I will eat grass."

"Their intentions are good," smiled Kidman. "But by the look of the sky they have no hope of winning that buggy."

Gravely the rain-makers retired to the tribe to discuss the vital details. Their reputation was at stake, for Tindah had guaranteed a flood and he was the recognized rain-maker for 100 miles around.

For sundry days and nights afterwards howls and smokes and banging of tins announced that the rain-makers were at work.

All up along the Three Rivers, Kidman was looked upon as a "good mark" by every tribal rain-maker. It was known that even for a slight shower he would give a bullock, sundry bags of flour, tea, sugar, tobacco and tomahawks. While for a really decent rain his price was phenomenal.

Kidman bought Norley. And Tindah "made" rain. By a strange coincidence, to the day three weeks after that bargain had been made rain fell heavily, resulting in such a flood that the river came down a banker.

On Kidman's next visit to the station Tindah was waiting for him.

"My word, me good pfella make 'em big pfella flood. What about that buggy!"

"It is yours, Tindah," laughed Kidman. "But you make too much big pfella flood, drown him bullock! Why you no stop him!"

"No can stop him," replied Tindah gravely, "all right make 'em tumble down, no stop 'em."

Kidman turned to Watts. "Which is the best buggy you've got on the place, Jack?"

"There is one in the shed with green wheels that will do them."

"Is that the best buggy?"

"No, but it is quite good enough. The best one is that expensive American specially built buggy with the red wheels."

"We will give him that; I promised him the best buggy."

They walked across to the buggy sheds and Kidman pointed out the spick-and-span buggy with its bright red wheels.

"You take that pfella buggy there, Tindah."

But Tindah stood frowning. "That pfella no good longa me," he mumbled.

"Why?" inquired Kidman in surprise.

"He make 'em too much plurry tunder an' lightnin' jump up!"

Tindah's superstitious soul stood in awe of the red wheels. But he accepted with delight the old green buggy.

When Kidman owned Norley station he quickly set about introducing new stud stock. This station later bred Bullawarra who became a famous steeplechaser, eventually winning the Australian Steeplechase carrying twelve stone eleven pounds. Kidman was never a racing enthusiast. Many of his men, however, were, and he was always pleased when any one of his station-bred horses won a city race. He was a firm believer in introducing the best of blood stock to improve the breed of all stock.

30

From Station-Hand to Station-Owner

In 1905 Kidman bought Thargomindah station. Both it and
Norley in south-western Queensland were to prove strong links
in his main chain, the south-western Queensland-New South
Wales chain.

He visited Sandringham. Letting his horse go, he walked
into the store just in time to see a bedraggled cockatoo
emerging from the flour-bin. "You jolly tinker," he raved. "I'll
fix you this time!"

He hurried to the manager's quarters, seized a gun and came
striding out as the cockatoo, sensing the menace, hurriedly
climbed the little tree. He gained a branch as Kidman raised the
gun. "Don't shoot poor Cocky, Mr Man!" screeched the bird.
"Don't shoot poor Cocky!" Kidman dropped the gun and stared
amazed at the raised crest, the quivering wings, the bright eyes of
the bird as it screeched imploringly: "Don't shoot poor Cocky,
Mr Man!"

Kicking the gun aside Kidman went to the stockmen busy
around the camel-packs. "If you jolly fellows don't keep that
bird out of the flour-bin I'll wring its wretched neck!"

He rode down through Dubbo Downs, Kaliduwary, and Annandale to see that all was well, then through Birdsville and along the famous track to the border, continuing thence through the sand-ridge and gibber plain country to Hergott Springs, where he heard that dingoes had practically wiped out the sheep on Mundowdna. Wondering if this would mean anything to him he bought Macumba station near Oodnadatta.

The north-to-south railway had reached Oodnadatta in 1891, where work on it had ceased. Now this line on its way to Alice Springs must run through or past Macumba station. Whether or no, it might be turned into a base to receive cattle coming down to present railhead from the Territory. And when developed it should prove a link in his secondary (Central Australian-South Australian) chain.

Macumba was nearly 2000 square miles of wild, unimproved country. It was in the dry belt but the Macumba, and part of the Alberga and the Hamilton ran through it; while in exceptional floods it received part of the waters of the Finke as that old-time watercourse rolled on towards Lake Eyre. These were all dry creeks and rivers, so for permanent water he intended to put down bores.

Years before, in his droving days, he had spied out the Macumba country. Cave had just taken it up. Kidman sent 3000 bullocks there on agistment to a flooded area of beautiful feed. He thought the bullocks would stay contentedly there. Months later, he arrived at Macumba waterhole. The "homestead" was a tent and a bullock-dray loaded with rations, guarded by two old black gins and a blackfellow. The men were all away. When they returned from the bush a week later all hands rode out to muster Kidman's cattle. But they had gone. A thousand had drifted out into the big sand-hills in the never-never country and there perished. These bullocks had smelt light rains far out in the desert lands, which had lured them like a will-o'-the-wisp. When they got out where the rains had fallen there was no water, and they couldn't return.

That has been the fate of countless beasts in that queer, grim little area where the sun shines down upon the black-shadowed canyons among the sand-hills.

Eventually 1000 of the cattle were recovered. Some had travelled north towards Huckitta Springs. Kidman took up another 1000 square miles; he could have taken thousands more had he wanted them. He built a homestead by Macumba waterhole and installed Herb Foulis as manager. It is a tough job, developing the frontier stations.

At Marree, he was offered Mundowdna for £4000. One thousand square miles, unstocked. The Whites had battled hard to make a sheep station of it but the dingoes won. Mundowdna was a key station, geographically and strategically. It was within eighteen miles of the north-to-south railway. To this station could be droved the cattle coming south from his Central Australian and south-western Queensland stations, and there rested and fattened for market. And so could his south-western Queensland cattle coming down the Birdsville track. Then, trucked as required from Farina, they would arrive fresh in the Adelaide markets. Also, Marree was the end of the great Birdsville track for all cattle consigned to Adelaide from south-western and northern Queensland. Many mobs of cattle, other than his own, would be constantly arriving, footsore and poor. To truck them over 400 miles in such condition would inevitably mean loss.

But if Kidman could buy them at a price, he could put them on Mundowdna, fatten them, and truck them when the market called. And many a travelling mob was in that way diverted to its hard-won waters and saltbush pastures.

Delighted with his purchase, Kidman gave the managership to John Brooke, a great bushman who had been manager for Jimmy Tyson. But with characteristic caution Kidman said:

"Come and give it a trial, and I will give you what you ask if you are worth it. Every man must prove his worth first to me."

With two boys, Jacky and Hooligan, he rode north. Jacky was black as the ace of spades. Kidman got him when his parents died at Cowarie. "Kidman's Jacky" was to be a travelling companion on many long trips. Hooligan was a white lad, with a bright smile and freckles crowned by a shock of red hair.

Kidman, as he became firmly established, constantly sent city lads to his stations.

"They'll never do you any good," a squatter told him. "You will spend years training them, then just when they grow to be of use, they'll leave you."

"No matter," replied Kidman. "Any man of mine who can better himself elsewhere has my good wishes. I always better myself when I see an opportunity. No doubt some of these lads will leave me when they grow up; but there are stickers among them, or I am no judge of boys or men. Anyway, the country wants these boys from the city; if I don't profit by them, the country will."

Young Hooligan was his latest recruit and a source of great amusement to Jacky, whose height was about four feet nothing. He would chuckle at Hooligan sitting so grimly and sorely the horse beside him. The one thing that Jacky held against his adored master was that he did not smoke. Jacky, even long after he grew up into "flash" years, could never understand a bushman who neither smoked, swore, drank, or arose with the birds at dawn.

With them on this trip rode an Englishman touring the world and very sensibly seeing Australia by travelling through it.

On the Birdsville stock-route they met a battler driving a little mob of horses. Both patties pulled up.

"Good day," said Kidman.

"Good day."

"What are you doing with the horses?"

"Going to sell them."

"Has there been any rain up the road?"

"We had a fall at Annandale of eighty points while I was there, but it looked to be heavier north."

"What was the feed like on Glengyle?"

"Bit of dry feed about, but the surface waters were drying up."

"How much are you asking for the horses?"

"Fourteen pound a head."

"You are asking a pretty good price!"

"They are mostly broken-in horses."

"Well, I will give your price, but you will have to deliver them to John Brooke at Mundowdna."

"What about payment?"

"Are you going to Adelaide?"

"Yes."

"All right; I'll give you an order on Coles and Thomas to pay you."

"Right. That's easy."

When out of hearing, the Englishman remarked:

"You bought those horses without question."

"No, I gave a little too much for them."

The visitor looked his surprise. Kidman laughed.

"I always pay as good a price as I can to hard-working bush people; it helps them along, and it won't do any harm. That poor chap has worked hard. If he got those horses to market he would not have realized more than twelve pounds a head on them. I may lose a little money, but with 500 of my own horses, I won't notice it." A few evenings later the party camped by a waterhole lined with wattles. While hobbling out the horses two emus came strutting up, inquisitively eyeing the party. Kidman stooped and slipped across to Hooligan with a pair of hobbles. "Quick, Hooligan! that big black one; run and hobble him! We'll put him in with the mob!"

As Hooligan ran in pursuit, Kidman called "Keep around 'em, Hooligan, keep around 'em!" For a time the emus contented themselves with outstalking the stalker—to the intense delight of Jacky and the interest of the English traveller. At last the emus, tiring of the sport, set off over the plain. "Go on, Hooligan," shouted Kidman, "go on! Don't let them beat you!" The gasping lad staggered away after the fast disappearing birds, followed by shrieks of laughter from Jacky. It was after dark when Hooligan came wearily back to the campfire.

"Why didn't you catch him, Hooligan?" inquired Kidman reproachfully.

"I couldn't," replied the exhausted lad. "I don't think he's been broken-in."

Jacky collapsed, shrieking up at the stars.

Many adventures, many queer tangles did Hooligan get into during his "breaking-in" to the bush, but soon he was playing similar jokes on others. And he grew into a good man.

In 1908 Sid Kidman bought Mount Poole station in New South Wales. It was with a thrill of pleasure that he rode across that station. Here were the hills and the plains across which he had ridden as a boy while working for old German Charlie. The quartz-covered hills, Sturt's Depot Glen, Poole's grave— how often he had dreamt by all of these! Here was where he had ridden when seeking the missing cattle. His eyes stared away past Mount Poole towards Mount Sturt; that was when he had ridden with Jack McDermott. And now he owned Mount Poole.

"Historic station, Mr Kidman," volunteered the manager. "One of the first taken up in the Milparinka district."

"Yes," smiled Kidman. He knew more about this station than the manager, probably, would ever know. They walked towards the kitchen, built right against the back of the hill. He took in the kitchen at a glance.

"There's no sauce. And that brownie—you would be lucky if you found a currant in it!"

"Neither sauce nor currants have ever been on the ration list," said the surprised manager.

"They are now then. Feed your men well. Give them all they can eat, and good rations too, but—allow no waste!"

When he was leaving the homestead he turned to the manager:

"There's one thing I want you to do—look after Poole's grave."

"It will be kept in order, Mr Kidman."

"Good. Poole was a good man who gave his life in helping to open up this country. I feel he is a charge on me, now that he is resting on my land."

227

At Tilcha station he met old Jack McDermott, grizzled now and weather-beaten. They shook hands, with a long glance one at the other.

"Many things have happened since you rode across here with me," said McDermott.

"Yes, Jack. The country has grown up. We were all in colonies then, now we are a Commonwealth soon to have a Federal Capital."

"Yes, the country has grown up and you have grown with it. Congratulations. I had the same chances as you. Perhaps more. I am still a station-hand; you are an owner of stations. Ah well, I am glad to see you again. I knew you were coming, news travels fast these days ... it seems only yesterday that I rode out here with the Crozier brothers. We felt as if we were isolated from all the world. It used to take twelve months to get our stores out by team. Now we've only to ride into Broken Hill, step into a train and walk out into a city in less than twenty hours."

"Hark! What's that?" inquired Kidman.

"Oh, the death-wail. Old Topsy has died, poor old girl. She was one of the gins shepherding those sheep the day we rode up to Sturt's tree. Do you remember?"

"Yes, I can see those native shepherds now. What a happy-go-lucky little crowd they were. I would like to see the poor old woman decently buried, Jack."

In the blacks' camp, old Topsy lay dead. Every soul had deserted her, all except her mangy dog. From across her body he crouched up, snarling at the white stockmen coming to bury her.

Old Topsy! A laughing young lubra when the first white men came into her tribal lands. She had seen her tribesmen as proud warriors ranging the lands far and wide; she had sat in the Women's Circle and hushed when the Council of the Old Men sat; she had seen her tribe in its glory; she had lived through its decay. And now, abandoned in death, she lay with her mangy mongrel snarling over her.

"Poor old soul!" said Kidman. "Bury her decently, boys. And don't hurt the dog. Throw a bag over him and smother his teeth when he bites."

31

Overseas

For some time past the little Scotch wife, in her own quiet way, had been bringing pressure to bear on her husband. He was a wealthy man; he had worked hard; he needed a holiday; he should see the world.

Sidney Kidman demurred but eventually consented, not mentioning that he dearly wanted to buy Innamincka station, and thought he could do so if only he could get to London quickly.

His reasoning proved correct. The London people, troubled by huge and recurring losses the cause of which they did not understand, jumped at the opportunity. Kidman bought Innamincka in London for £32,000, with only about 4000 cattle left on it. He handed over the cheque with a quiet smile. His body was in a London office but his mind was away out over the sunlit Cooper. He could see the gnarled old coolabahs and gums; Burke and Wills's death-tree by the homestead; the tree-shaded waterholes—some large enough to float a ship; the plains and tablelands. He felt the silence of that huge station of 7500 square miles. He loved that country. Now he owned it. Something tightened at his heart as he heard the sweet, elusive call of a bellbird; saw Needle trotting at his side.

While wife and daughters enjoyed themselves he saw London in his own quiet way. Much of it was from the top of omnibuses sitting beside the driver. He made friends quickly with the busmen and his sympathy went out to them. They saw their age-old livelihood going; the motor omnibus was coming to destroy it.

His sympathy was all with the men and the horses. Many, he quietly noticed, loved their animals. He offered them a lifework's job in a young, new country.

" 'Ave a pull at me other leg, guv'nor!" replied some.

But others, when convinced that the tall sunburned stranger beside them was really the Cattle King so much written of in their Press, hesitated. The wrench was too great for the majority. Others accepted.

This news was given prominence in the London papers with the result that the wife interviewed him.

"Why, Sid, you must be growing foolish. What do you know about these men? You never saw them until to-day as it were, and yet you are going to take them without knowing anything about them."

"Well, Bell," he smiled, "I took you without knowing very much about you, and I have never regretted it."

Later on in Australia, without exception, those busmen after several years' breaking-in on a station, proved good men.

He was seeing London from a bus one day when a passenger tapped him on the shoulder. "Is that you, Kidman?"

"It's me."

"I'm pleased to see you again. I was manager at Langawirra station when you came out and bought all those sheep."

"Of course you were!" said Kidman heartily. "I bought 10,000 and you gave delivery. The world is small after all."

It was on a bus, too, when feeling a bit lonely he turned to the passenger beside him and started talking Australia and sheep.

"Do you come from Australia?" inquired the man.

"Yes."

"So do I. By the way, there is a well-known identity in

England at present by the name of Kidman. Do you know him, by any chance?"

"Yes, I know him fairly well."

"So do I. I used to be mixed up with him once."

Sidney Kidman did not spoil the joke.

One day he was walking down Piccadilly wearing his felt hat in typical bush fashion when two gentlemen came up to him and one said: "Excuse me, sir, your hat is knocked to one side!"

"Thanks!" smiled Kidman. "But it's all right. I always dent it in there to keep it in its place."

They bowed and passed on.

It was a great treat to him to go out all day and study the shops and the people. Once he got too far east, and into trouble. In the habit of giving money to any he saw in need, he had just given a boy a few pennies when a trolley-man dropped his money-bag and the coins rolled all over the street. Instantly there was a wild scramble. The trolley-man leapt at Kidman. "That is my money you are giving away!" he shouted. In a moment a crowd had closed around them, Kidman was pressed back against a wall, and in the nick of time a policeman came pushing through.

"He snatched my bag!" shouted the trolley-man, "gave me a plug on the jaw when I wasn't looking."

"He does not look a man like that," answered the policeman, after a searching gaze at Kidman. But things looked ugly, and it took the officer all his tact and authority to get Kidman away.

Next day he lunched in a restaurant. Sitting next to him was a "sell" whose belltopper Kidman was quietly admiring. They don't talk freely in England, but Kidman soon struck up a conversation.

"You look like a traveller," he smiled.

"I come from Vladivostok."

Kidman was immediately interested. He had taken a big contract to send some thousands of tons of beef to Vladivostok.

Next day the man called at his hotel and asked for the loan of six pounds.

"You are dressed ten times better than I am, and you look a rich man!" drawled Kidman.

The stranger replied that he was only a clerk, but if he could get his fare to Vladivostok he was certain of a billet. Finally Kidman said, "I don't like lending money to strangers, but I will stretch a point this time," and he gave him the money.

"My wife lives in London," said the man. "I will send the money to repay you in six weeks' time."

But Bell and the daughters laughed. "You will never see your money again," they prophesied.

Six weeks later a lady called. "I have six sovereigns that you lent my husband," she explained. "I want to repay them. Here they are."

Invited as a guest to the home of H. Heber-Percy, one of an old English family of world-famous big-game hunters, he combined pleasure with business. Percy was interested with McCartney, the well-known Queenslander, in Diamantina Lakes station, 2132 square miles, in far-away Queensland. Kidman wanted that station for his Queensland chain. He bought it for £28,500.

Although he was getting no little pleasure out of the trip, and a lot of quiet joy on seeing the happiness of his family, Kidman's heart was in Australia and his mind on that chain of stations. He negotiated a huge deal: disposed of Victoria River Downs station, with the subsidiary stations, Carlton Hill and Napier, to R. T. Smith (a prominent operator in the English meat trade) for £180,000, walk-in-walk-out. Victoria River Downs was refloated into Bovril Australian Estates Ltd with a capital of £250,000. The first directors were Lord Brassey, Sir Edward Wittenoom, Mr C. H. Rason, and Sid Kidman.

The boy with five shillings and a one-eyed horse had become one of the financial figures of the world.

32

Raising £116,000

Back in Australia from the British Isles, Kidman began at once to complete his chain of stations.

"I'll hardly know a fat bullock from a jolly old piker," he drawled to Bell. "This holidaying makes a man rusty."

"Considering you have your head full of refrigerators and transport-ships and freezers and canning and goodness knows what, I think your holiday must have sharpened you."

"We shall see," he smiled. "The Mother Country has looked after Australia well; now it is time we started to help feed the Mother. We'll see what we can do."

"Now just what does that mean?"

"Shipping beef to England. Australia is doing very well in that line, but I believe we could supply the Old Country if we organized properly."

"Oh, well, I suppose you will keep going. If ever you retired you would rust out before you wore out."

"A man *must* work, Bell, every nation must work," he smiled. "Look at the paper here: 'Arrival of the *Yarra* and *Parramatta*, the first vessels built for the Royal Australian Navy.' Keeping abreast of the times, Bell. Men and nations must do it, otherwise go under. I must buy more stations to supply more markets, I must improve my old stations with all sorts of modern equipment to keep them abreast of the times. By doing that I keep my brains active. If I didn't I'd fade away, Bell."

One day he received a wire from Edge at Carrandotta. Count de Sachy wished to sell his adjoining station, Rochdale, very cheaply. Kidman advised Edge to inspect and, if he thought Rochdale good enough, to buy on a fifty-fifty basis and thus make some money for himself.

They bought Rochdale for £1600, mustered the run, and in eighteen months had sold sufficient fats to pay for the station. Then they sold the station for £16,000, walk-in-walk-out.

But the buyer was not satisfied with his muster, declaring that the cattle numbers had been misrepresented. Kidman asked him what value did he allow for the cattle on the run. When the figure was named Kidman said: "All right, I'll take them at that price."

The offer was accepted. The cattle were brought down to the southern markets and realized another £2000 above the purchase price.

The buying of Durham Downs, one of the best fattening properties in south-western Queensland, of 3334 square miles, with Tilboroo, also in Queensland, and Berrawinnia in New South Wales, was again the knowledge of past observation, and being ready at the right moment. Durham Downs could muster 7000 head of cattle. Before the years of overstocking and rabbits, it had carried vastly greater herds. Tilboroo could muster approximately 3000 cattle, 12,000 sheep, Berrawinnia, 12,000 sheep.

The grazing pastures of the three stations were within easy droving distance of one another, and Kidman had realized for twenty years past not only their capabilities, but that the combination was well placed to help feed the big markets east, south-east and south-west. Then owned by one of the banks, the price asked was £105,000. He bought for £100,000. He paid £25,000 down, and another £25,000 within three months. He counted on his mobs of cattle, successively rolling into market within the next six months, to pay off the remaining £50,000. But he misjudged the market. And the bank said:

"You must meet your obligation, Mr Kidman."

Now, he knew that he had a solid friend in the Bank of New South Wales. So, feeling more aggrieved than worried, he made it his business to meet a manager of the bank (Mr Lyons) in Melbourne, and said:

"I owe the London Chartered Bank £50,000. The jolly tinkers want their money and won't give me any more time."

"Give me an order to lift the leases and I will pay it immediately," suggested Lyons.

In twelve months Kidman paid back that £50,000.

Kidman now had a huge telegraph business. Wires came daily from all over Australia; from his managers and drovers; from pastoralists and agents, and from drovers with stock for sale. Telegrams from the Kapunda office sought him throughout the back country. This saved him thousands of miles of travel yearly; his business could never have grown so fast had it not been for the telegraph. And now he had brought out from England another thing of speed, another annihilator of distance and saver of time—a motor car. Kidman was certain that motor transport had come to stay, but would prove for himself whether it was outdistancing the horse and buggy. It would be helpess in the farther out bush, of course; still it might prove useful in country districts where there were roads.

The eldest and youngest of his daughters were to accompany him on a long trip into Queensland. He was nearly ready to start when he heard that Warenda and Tinapagee stations were for sale. Now, his money was again all tied up; he believed in money "working". But he wanted Warenda and Tinapagee.

Warenda station, south-east of Carrandotta, and owned by the Weinholt family, was one of the finest stations in western Queensland. It could be worked in conjunction with his main chain and was also within reach of the main stock-routes to the markets of three States. Tinapagee, 800 miles farther south-east, just across the border in New South Wales, was a large sheep station, and with Berrawinnia was to be the commencement of a group of sheep stations. Though his main interest would always be horses and cattle, he decided that he would reinforce those interests with sheep and wool.

From inquiries he ascertained that the owners asked a tremendous price. Still, one never could tell.

"I'll wire them an offer," he said to Wally Will at Kapunda. "I might find out their lowest price."

So, just before leaving with the girls, he offered £73,000 for Warenda and £43,000 for Tinapagee. He smiled as he thought of the disdainful refusal when the principals received that offer.

The party boarded the train to Farina, the two girls all excitement and jealously guarding their "swags". At Mundowdna a few days were spent overhauling the gear and filling the pack-bags.

At sundown one evening a telegraph boy from Marree rode up with a bundle of telegrams.

Kidman opened the first telegram and consternation spread over his face.

"Not bad news, I hope," murmured John Brooke, who had brought the party to Mundowdna. Kidman handed him the wire; it was from his Kapunda office advising that the agents had accepted his offer both for Warenda and Tinapagee.

To Brooke's questioning eyes he explained: "It means I have to find £116,000. I didn't think for a moment that they would accept the offer. How am I going to find all that money!"

He tore open the other wires—from agents, drovers, managers; market reports, stock movements, rainfalls.

"Let us have something to eat while a man saddles a horse for me right away." A hundred and sixteen thousand pounds! With his capital already invested, how could he find this extra money! He brushed aside the temptation to wire: "Your acceptance came too late." That would break his name. What on earth was he to do?

He mounted and rode fast into Marree. If only he could gain time! Time meant more than money.

The first man he saw in the tiny township was Billy Hayes. Billy was always keen on a deal. Immediately, Kidman thought of the last mob of cows he had bought, 2000 head by wire at two pounds per head.

"I say, Billy, I'm looking for you. A good deal. I've got 2000 cows on the road to Mundowdna. Good sorts in calf. I'll sell you 1000 at three pounds ten shillings per head."

"Three notes!" answered Billy decisively.

"No jolly fear. You've got a buyer already. I see it in your eye."

"Three notes is my price."

"No deal."

"I'll toss you for it!"

"Right."

They tossed, and Billy won. The 1000 cows were his for three pounds per head. Kidman hurried to the telegraph office, well pleased. He had made a start to finance that £116,000. He wired Edge to immediately inspect Warenda and have the report ready for his arrival in Brisbane. Then he wired the manager of Innamincka station to muster every horse for inspection.

Next morning at Mundowdna, just as the party were ready to move off, he handed Brooke a wire to send from Marree. This wire was to Wally Will at Kapunda advising him that he had sold 1000 of the cows and for him to try and sell the balance as he was leaving for Innamincka, Durham Downs, and Norley, and expected to be at Norley in about four weeks' time. But he did not acknowledge receiving the wire about the acceptance of his offer for Warenda and Tinapagee. On receiving this wire Will had no option but to wire the agents saying Kidman was away north and he would not be able to communicate with him for about four weeks.

Meanwhile the party had started on their 1000-mile drive and ride, the girls in continental shirt and riding-breeches the cynosure of the station-hands, the mystification of the blacks. Neither whites nor blacks had seen girls in breeches before. They rode ahead with the black boy, Dougal, Kidman driving behind with the buggy, black boys riding behind with the twenty spares and packhorses. To the girls, fresh from

European cities, this trip was an ever changing joy. This country was so different from any they had seen before.

A bountiful season had filled the scattered waterholes. Fresh young saltbush covered the sandy soil with a grey carpet, while in mounds there stood up the soft grey of the big old-man saltbush. Among the clumps of mulga, grey kangaroos lazily reclined in the shade. Now and again a flock of emus stalked inquisitively towards them, their long-necked heads inquisitively out-thrust. Ground parrots were busy among the grass-seed; swarms of finches and sparrows sped by seeking some midday waterhole. When they reached the real sand country the ridges were a mass of flowers; purples and mauves and yellows, whites and pinks and scarlets upon brick-red or white sand. Almost impossible to realize that in dry times men and horses have perished from thirst upon this very track. Brilliant sunlight and nights of star-gemmed skies. Healthy appetites; deep sleep. And every day riding on into ever changing country.

Kidman acted up to the holiday delight. Hard to realize that the raising of £116,000 was on his mind.

Travelling east of north towards Innamincka, in a few days they ran short of meat, owing to the voracious appetites of the black boys. In brilliant sunlight they saw away over the sand country a mob of cattle slowly emerging from a mirage, the drovers looming like giants on horseback. It was a mob of 500 of Kidman's own cattle. Soon the parties met.

"Pat Kennedy!" called Kidman. "Just the man we want to see. We're out of meat."

"Out of luck, too!" answered Kennedy. "There's not one in the mob fit to kill. They're all 'hammy'."

After a yarn, the Kidman party rode on, disappointment mingling with surprise.

"But, dad," protested Gertrude, "500 cattle and yet not one fit to eat. Why?"

"They are poor 'stores'," explained Kidman, "from Mundowdna, travelling to Innamincka to be fattened for sale. And here is hoping they fatten quickly. At eight pounds per head they would mean £4000 just when I need it."

"Are we likely to meet any other drovers?"

"Not another soul, Gert. This is a lonely track, one of the loneliest in all the world."

When nearing Cooper's Creek they met a mob of blacks whose eyes bulged like walnuts. Kidman pulled up and had a yarn with the old king, whose eyes were everywhere but on Kidman. A tribesman edged up to Dougal.

"What fella him two fella?" he demanded hoarsely, his eyes on the girls.

"Them two fella piccaninnies longa old fella Kidman," grinned Dougal.

"Our trousers are causing a sensation," remarked Gertrude.

But Dougal's daily admiration was for Gertrude's boots. At last, in the hope of keeping his eyes off them, she promised him a similar pair when some day perhaps he might come to Kapunda with the drovers with horses. Immediately, Dougal began planning how he could wheedle a droving job from his boss, John Brooke.

Next morning Gertrude picked a flighty young colt as her riding-horse for the day. She managed it easily enough until a rabbit jumped from a bush almost under the colt's hoofs. He reared aside and crashed down over a root, throwing the girl heavily. Dougal helped her up; she was somewhat dazed.

"Better come along in the buggy, Gert, until you get over the shock," advised Kidman.

Next day they were well into the sand-hills near Lake Hope with two raw young horses in the buggy, the packhorses and spares coming away along behind. Up the sand walls they climbed, Kidman leaning forward with thrashing rein, encouraging voice and whip. The floundering horses battled on and up to roll and slide and plunge down the moving sand on the opposite side. Ridge after ridge they negotiated, the horses working themselves into a panting stubbornness. Taking them gently, with many spells, in the late afternoon they began climbing the last and biggest hill. At the critical moment, when just straining over the top, the buggy capsized and man and girl went flying out over the sand. In an instant

Kidman had sprung to the fallen horses and knelt on their heads.

"Quick, Gert, come and hold their heads while I unhook them. If they break the harness we'll be in a fine mess."

The horses, deep in sand, with the girl lying across their heads, were almost helpless. Rapidly Kidman unhooked the traces, then breathed freely. To be without harness or buggy in this sandy waste with two girls would be no bright matter. Just then the heads of the packhorses appeared coming up over the sand-hill. Soon the black boys had pulled the buggy upright, the frightened horses were harnessed, and they started off again.

"I nearly had my brains kicked out yesterday," called Gertrude over her shoulder, "and to-day they tried to break my neck and smother me."

"You are getting all the adventures," laughed Edna. "The only thrill I've had was a big black savage, all mouth and eyes. I don't know whether he wanted to run away with me or eat me."

At Innamincka the girls created a sensation; but the days following threw the big station into a fever of activity. Some thousands of horses were being tailed out on feed, ready for inspection. Every man on the station mounted, musterers riding north, south, east, and west. The first big mob came cantering in with manes and tails flying, heads erect, all in the pink of condition.

"If I can only draft 500 to average twenty pounds apiece," thought Kidman, "the £10,000 would be another little help. Eringa should muster another 200 at twenty pounds, which would be £4000, altogether £14,000. Then those cows I sold from Marree, £3000. That would make £17,000 so far."

With all that was on his mind he found time to say to the manager:

"That old coolabah-tree where Burke and Wills were buried?"

"It's still up the creek, sir, big and healthy."

"Good. I want you to look after it. Fence it off from stock; and keep it cleared of flood-water timber and drift. I wouldn't like it to be burned down."

"I'll see to it, sir."

They started for the Queensland border and Durham Downs, leaving Innamincka with a cloud of dust above the stockyard and the rumble of hoofs and shouts of men as they drafted 500 picked horses from out 3000 head.

At Durham Downs the pretty homestead was kept beautifully clean by trained black girls. These were all eyes and ready to be smiles as the party of men arrived. But when two, in the nattiest of breeches, dismounted and came smiling towards the station manager's wife the eyes of the house-maids enlarged with a breathless astonishment. Apparently struck dumb they went mechanically about their tasks to stand and stare whenever the girls walked past.

"What a pity they are black," laughed Edna, "what a joke we could have had."

"How many fats have you?" asked Kidman of the manager.

"I might muster 2000 head at a pinch."

"How long?"

"Four weeks."

"Muster that 2000. Send a horseman to Thargomindah to wire Hannigan to take delivery immediately and drove them to Mundowdna."

"Right."

He also took the opportunity of wiring agents that these cattle were on the road to Sydney.

"Two thousand head," he mused, "they'll go down the Innamincka track and follow the Cooper. Brooke will draft them at Mundowdna before trucking them. The Adelaide market by then should be good for twelve pounds per head. That means £24,000, added to £17,000 makes £41,000. That £116,000 is beginning to look small."

Leaving all tracks the party rode 100 miles straight through bush, camping one night on the Wilson River. While saddling up next morning a black stockman rode out from the bush towards Kidman, his face one broad smile.

"Saw your tracks, boss." He looked at the girls with puzzled expression and muttered.

"Good day."

"Good day," they smiled brightly.

"My word, boss, I got plenty fat cattle longa you and me!"

"That good news, Tommy. Where you bin catch him?" replied Kidman in delight.

"Longa lignum! Me shepherd 'em long time. Know you come sometime!"

Kidman was delighted. He had looked forward to a big mob of fats on Bulloo Downs and here was this black stockman knowing of a mob eighty miles from the homestead. Probably he had not told the manager all he knew, keeping something up his sleeve for when the "big fellow boss" came along. He could not have chosen a better time.

Another eighty miles through bush brought the party to the Bulloo track and fifteen miles from the homestead the girls met Galloping Jack.

"Good day, boys," he said. "Where's the old man?"

"He is coming along behind."

"Good. Some of the blacks told me he was coming with a couple of young jackeroos. You're—"

He stopped short, puzzled. They smiled sweetly as Kidman drove up.

"Hullo Jack, I see you've already met my girls."

"Your what?"

"My two daughters, Gert and Edna." Galloping Jack slowly lifted his hat.

"I want some cattle, Jack, as many as you can muster."

Watts raised his eyebrows.

"You want a big mob then!"

"I do badly!"

"Oh, in that case I might be able to let you have a few."

"How many?"

"Oh, between 3000 and 4000—at a pinch!"

"Good!" exclaimed Kidman. "I'm glad of the pinch," he laughed. "I'm pinched myself. Can't you make it 4000, Jack?"

"I'll see what I can do."

Kidman was delighted. Here he had 4000 marketable cattle.

They should average from twelve to fourteen pounds per head, say £52,000. That plus £41,000 makes £93,000. The £116,000 was almost within sight.

They rode then up along the Bulloo River to Thargomindah station where the girls, after causing the usual sensation, watched the cutting out, the lassoing, and branding of cattle. Here, the manager promised Kidman a probable 1000 head of fats to be ready for sale in Brisbane in three months' time.

"I can only allow eight pounds per head in Brisbane at three months," mused Kidman, "still—that is another £8000. Added to £93,000 makes £101,000. I'll do it on my head."

Still travelling north-east, Kidman inspected beautiful Norley station, then through Ardoch on the Bulloo by Noondoo station across to Tilboroo station. Near Tilboroo homestead the girls passed a drovers' camp, and stopped for a yarn. Later at Tilboroo the drover rode up to Kidman and his nephew Tony.

"I say, boss, those two chaps or girls who are travelling with you! They rode up to our camp and there's a heated argument about them. Are they jackeroo boys, or jackeroo girls? Look, there they are now!" and he pointed to the two girls who had come into the homestead garden with Tony Kidman's wife.

"They are my daughters," explained Kidman.

"What! You don't say so now!" He went back to his camp in rather a daze.

"Those blokes down there are girls," he explained to the men. "They are Sid Kidman's daughters."

At Cunnamulla the girls' 1000-mile ride ended.

33

The Mustering of Warenda

In Brisbane Kidman urgently wired Jack Edge to inspect Warenda, report by wire to Brisbane, then personally in Adelaide. He busily set about arranging the sale of the mobs he had bought, then wired his agent that he would shortly be in Sydney to discuss finalization of Warenda and Tinapagee.

To the hour almost, the wire came from Edge: "Warenda all right. Good country. Estimate herd anywhere between 30,000 and 40,000."

Kidman clenched the telegram in delight. Thirty thousand head! He could finance the deal easily. But the selling of 30,000 head, in addition to the yearly increase of his own herds and the mobs that he must continue buying, would take two years. Still, it was a wonderful deal. He seized his hat, and by wire finalized his purchase of Warenda and Tinapagee stations. He had committed himself now.

He hurried then to Adelaide, for his horse mobs would soon be arriving at Kapunda, and the drovers with their mobs of cattle would soon be arriving at their respective railway depots. He must sharpen his wits to successfully negotiate every one of those sales.

In Adelaide, a thought suddenly struck him. "Why not sell the station now, without the stock!"

He acted immediately and to Brabazon and Williams sold Warenda for £20,000. Delivery to be taken in twelve months.

Highly elated, he took that cheque to the bank. Here was another £20,000 ready money.

"What about Warenda?" asked Kidman of Edge in Adelaide.

"Good. Excellent country, 4000 square miles of it. Hasn't been properly mustered or branded for years. The bullock paddock alone is 400 square miles. Fairly well watered by waterholes, and seventeen flowing bores. Impossible to estimate correctly the stock in the short time you gave me; but I should say between 30,000 and 40,000 cattle, and about 1000 horses."

"What kind of horses?"

"Good. Saleable draughts, clumpers, team horses."

"Any fats?"

"The usual percentage."

"I want them shifted immediately—everything."

"What!"

"I have sold Warenda—bare, on a twelve months delivery."

Edge whistled. "Twelve months. Christopher Columbus! Four thousand square miles of country, anything up to 40,000 cattle— I'll swear thousands have never known a branding-iron. All nice bush to muster in; the cattle can poke away in any direction they please and I doubt if there are sufficient yards on the place."

"Well then—broncho them!"

"The wild and woolly west! I'll want the smartest horsemen, the slickest cattlemen in Queensland, an army of drovers. By the way, was it twelve months or twelve years you mentioned?"

"How long will it take you to brand them?"

"Oh, that's nothing! We have only to muster them first! After which, not having many yards, we will have to lasso and brand them."

"I'll be jolly pleased if you brand 10,000."

"Of course you will. And what fun we'll have doing it!"

Kidman laughed.

"Start on your fun right away, Jack. Go straight to Warenda; take delivery; form your mustering-plants and get to it right away. I'll arrange for the drovers from this end."

Thus started the world's record for stock movement off one station, 38,176 head of cattle mustered, branded, and moved away within 20 months. And 1000 head of horses as well!

Among some shocks, several mild surprises confronted Edge on checking up Warenda. In the store was a ton of long-handled shovels, a ton of Fruit Salts, a ton of Epsom-salts. What any of these three articles could be wanted for on an outback station in such quantities, he could not imagine.

"What on earth did they want all this Epsom-salt for?" he asked of the book-keeper.

"I don't know. Since Kidman bought the place there's been movement enough without it."

"H'm. Well, get busy and see if you can sell that Fruit Salts to travellers for baking-powder. It makes johnny-cakes rise well, and cook white as snow."

"That's a new one on me," said the book-keeper. "Do you know any recipe for the long-handled shovels and Epsom-salt?"

"Not yet," replied Edge. "See what you can do with the Fruit Salts first."

The sale of the Fruit Salts—in cases as baking-powder—was a great success, until a case of Epsom-salt got mixed up by mistake.

As the drovers with their plants arrived, each took delivery of his mob and started on the roads to either Townsville, Brisbane, Sydney, Melbourne, or Adelaide, for sale, or to Mundowdna, Monkira, Annandale, Bulloo Downs, Norley, Glengyle, Durrie, Sandringham stations to be fattened.

The first 5000 head Kidman sold to the Townsville meatworks at five guineas per head. Soon he saw that not only had he paid for Warenda and Tinapagee stations, but he was going to make thousands of pounds profit.

Back at Kapunda, he thought over the position.

"I have handled Warenda very badly," he said to a friend. "I should not have sold it at all. I should have kept the cattle on it, and sold them as they fattened."

"Still, you did not know how you were to raise the money!"

"No, it looked impossible."

"And you will make a big profit?"

"Not so bad; probably between £40,000 and £50,000. I'm satisfied."

"And Tinapagee?"

"Oh, I get that for nothing now, with £7000 cash thrown in."

"So there is corn in Egypt yet."

"Yes, and not only for me."

"For whom else?"

"I sold Warenda bare for £20,000."

"Yes?"

"Well, it has been stocked with 80,000 sheep and resold for £150,000."

"Oh!"

Kidman smiled. "I'm not the only one content with quick profits. I am satisfied with the deal."

"But you say nothing about the fight to pull the deal through; the thought and organization in getting all the station mobs on the roads; the organization of the marketing; then the mustering, branding, and droving of 40,000 cattle in eighteen months and selling each mob in the right market at the right time, all dove-tailed so as not to interfere with the movements and sales of your own station herds, as well as of the other mobs you continually buy."

"The pleasure was greater than the money," Kidman admitted with a smile. The mustering and shifting of the stock on Warenda *was* a great feat. Within the time thirty-one mobs of cattle were put on the roads from that one station.

In 1910 Kidman had twenty-five stations and shares in several others. Cattle were bringing a good price. Yearly now a large mob of fats left each station bound for a New South Wales, Victorian, Queensland or South Australian market. Besides which, drovers came down from the Northern Territory, from northern Queensland, with mobs of "Kidman" cattle or sheep bought from other stations. Each year, big and successful horse-sales took place at Kapunda. Despite the failure of a few stations, this "snow-balling" of profits quickly paid off station after station and supplied thousands of pounds to improve property and, above all, to bore for water.

On returning home to Kapunda feeling just a little tired, he stepped out of the train and into the "chariot". The old ponies puffing and grunting did their level best to gallop through the streets of Kapunda. At the home, an almost featherless cockatoo shrieked, "Hullo father!" Needle, who always seemed to know when he was coming home, came running to meet him. Old Nelson rested now, down under the willows by the creek.

34

The Little Things

Kidman was travelling on inspection. Already the restless movement of this tall, strongly built man was familiar in every carriage in the train. His large, keen brown eyes seemed to see everything; the bold, well-shaped nose, the high cheek-bones lent an air of strength to the face as the long limbs did to the figure. The quick smile, the short easy sentences in which not a word was wasted, invited every confidence.

In the long trip of this little train slowly creeping up towards the centre of the continent, he had yarned with every man, with the crew too, and to the few women aboard—his usual custom, for they were mostly station men aboard, drovers, stockmen, dingo-shooters, settlers, or prospectors, all men of the bush, and each man probably knew something that Sid Kidman wanted to know. He had an uncanny knack of engaging in friendly conversation while leading up to something he wanted to know. A man told him everything and hardly knew he was telling it. How naturally he cloaked his powers of observation by that easygoing bush manner! No chance of learning by his facial expression or even conversation what his real thoughts were. And when, lazily and naturally, he moved away to yarn with someone else, he left a pleasant feeling behind him.

It was pitch dark on the second night when they reached Farina. Jack Brooke met him.

"Where are the horses, Brooke?"

"In the railway yard."

They walked across, feeling their way in the dark. While Kidman was putting the collar on a horse he said:

"I know this horse by its shape; it is a chestnut?"

"Yes."

"Well, don't feed it any more, it is not much good. Let it go bush."

"When did you see it last?"

"A year ago at Kapunda."

They drove away, Brooke in surprise at a man who could identify a horse on a night as black as pitch, a horse he had not seen for twelve months. They drove on in the long silences fairly common among bushmen. At last Kidman said:

"I have made a lot at selling horses, £33,000 in one year. So whatever you do feed your working horses well; it pays to feed them if you've got the work to do; feed them right and they will do your work. But don't waste time or feed on a horse that will not do the job."

Next morning, Brooke, as usual, was up with the birds. His boss was not. Brooke, giving the men their orders for the day was thinking of two great cattlemen, Kidman and Tyson. He had worked for Tyson for years. Tyson was always up before the birds. Kidman, except when special work was to be done, never. This morning he did not turn out of bed until late for breakfast, which meant that Mrs Brooke's housework would be disorganized. When he did get up he spoke on every topic except cattle. Brooke let him meander on; he was beginning to get used to this man who could camouflage his thoughts so easily, then at an unexpected moment learn all he wanted to know in a few short sentences.

After breakfast they strolled outside. Near the old pioneer homestead, low built, of stone and pug coated with lime, clustered a dozen stone outbuildings, yard, cart, and wagon sheds. Encircling all were low sand-ridges covered with dead-finish, bluebush and saltbush. Half a dozen men were saddling horses in the yard; a boundary-rider was emerging on his camel from a distant haze; hens were busily foraging among the sand-dunes, Kidman picked up a stick and called a lubra.

"Hi Lily! Bring a tin!" He pointed to a bolt on the ground.

"Here, pick that up and put it in your tin, that is money!" He walked around the dray sheds pointing to discarded nails, bolts, buckles, screws.

"Here, Lily, pick all this up. This is money!" The lubra followed him, staring at the ground as if she had lost her eye-sight.

Brooke seized his chance and left them at it. Half an hour later the black gin came sneaking around to him.

"What name that one feller, boss!" she demanded. "That one no money. Mine thinkit him crazy feller!"

"Brooke!" came a distant shout. But Brooke went on with his work. The boss must have his little way until he was ready to talk real business. Brooke knew him for a great man who probably would not be so great were he not particular over small things. He could not stand the sight of a leaky bucket. He was so capable he could see waste at a glance, he thought the other fellow a fool if he could not see waste for himself. He would pick up a discarded length of pencil, sharpen it, and put it away for future use. He could not bear to see a jam-tin thrown away that still had jam in it, yet he never questioned the ration bill on any station. More than that, he always insisted on good food.

A station-hand came along, hiding a smile.

"The boss wants you, Mr Brooke," he said.

Brooke strolled across. The boss was flat on his back under a wagonette, a screw wrench in his hand.

"Here you are, Brooke," he drawled, "here you have a bit of an idea how I made my money. These nuts are loose. You might be driving along one day and lose them. That's bad. You might have an accident too." Brooke looked on, interested but unimpressed. He had known Tyson be careful about similar little things but he knew that it was in the combination between the little things and big things that these two men had done the big things they had.

Mail-day came around, and towards sundown the lad rode to Mundowdna Siding for the mail. It was a pitch-black night. Near twelve o'clock Kidman said:

"The lad is very late, I hope he hasn't got lost." Then they heard his footsteps at the door. He came in, staring straight at Brooke:

"I've brought the mail. But I've had hard luck; the mare broke her neck."

"What!" said Kidman.

"I was cantering and fell over a wire fence in the dark. But," drawing something from his shirt, "I've got two magpies— they're not hurt!"

"That's fine," said Kidman heartily. "We've got plenty of horses but we've got very few magpies."

With black boys following with packhorses, Kidman and Brooke rode off on inspection. The first night out they camped at a cattle-camp; the drover had just arrived with a mob of Glengyles for Mundowdna. Next morning at daylight the watch came riding to the campfire. They could tell by his face something was wrong.

"Wing bullocks away!" he said laconically.

"What?" exclaimed Kidman.

"Bullocks gone," replied the stockman.

"Where?"

"Across the sand-hills—lost."

"Why?"

"Tracks blown out."

"Never!"

Kidman mounted and in a minute was cantering away. He found the tracks, and the missing cattle before midday.

They reached Tarkaninna waterhole very late the following night, put on the quarts and unrolled their swags. After a hearty meal they lay out on their blankets, staring up at the stars; the black boys around their fire joked in low tones; the horse-bells tinkled out in the shadows. Suddenly Kidman jumped up, feeling his pockets.

"I've lost a shilling."

"Look in your blankets," drawled Brooke.

On his hands and knees Kidman searched the blanket.

"Ah, here it is. That's fine."

His mind at ease he stoked the fire, sat by Brooke, and at last talked business, going into the minutest details in the travelling of great herds that would yearly be coming down the Birdsville track, of Brooke taking over from drover after drover, the clockwork organization of fattening and subsequent trucking from Mundowdna. Details in which a slip might well mean the loss of thousands of pounds.

Old John Brooke listened intently, smoking as he gazed at the fire. He might not take much account of odds and ends, a few horses or an old buggy or two, a few nails and buckles, but big business in his line he understood thoroughly. He has trucked successfully from Mundowdna to date over 250,000 cattle and many thousands of horses and sheep.

35

Kapunda

The Kapunda horse-sales were well established now, making a busy fortnight yearly for the little town. The sales, very noisy, were conducted amidst riotous fun making.

At one sale "Old Archie" Bevis, who had grown into an institution, wired from a country town his sorrow at not being able to attend. Kidman wired back: "You must come or I'll have to postpone the sale. All Kapunda awaiting you. Will meet you at station." The circus had come to town as it yearly did for the sales. So "the boys" hired the band and dragged out one of Cobb and Co.'s old coaches from the back shed. They greased it, harnessed in six horses, put the band aboard, then with Kidman at the ribbons swept out of the yard to the railway station, cheered down the street. A crowd was there to meet Old Archie, all in holiday mood. The engine whistled "Cock-a-doodle-doo", as amid thunderous cheers Archie was carried to the coach. The band struck up, and with men clinging to the coach, or escorting it on horseback and with dogs barking, they went full pelt round and round the town.

The saleyards, in the very centre of the little town, were packed with horses. Men sat on the rails like rows of black crows; people were at the windows and on verandas and roofs overlooking the yards. Charlie Coles climbed up into the auctioneer's box amid shouts and greetings from the thickly packed throng. Buyers were there seeking all sorts and conditions of horses. From the ring Kidman leapt on to a horse's back and with marvellous agility, from back to scurrying back, leapt down in the yard centre ringed in by plunging bodies.

"The sale opens, boys!" he shouted. "We won't haggle over a pound or two so you must bid quickly if you want a horse. These horses have no tickets on their tails; you've got to put your own price on them. Let her go, Charlie!"

The sale started, and was kept going at high pressure for ten days.

Bidding was always spirited, the horses selling at the rate of one a minute in a very lively atmosphere, men overbalancing or being overbalanced from the fence to fall in among the flying horses and leap back to the rails amid shouts of laughter. Some enterprising fellow at the back of the fence with a bundle of fish-hooks and a long line would hook numerous coat-tails together. A gentleman sitting reminiscently on the rails with his newspaper on his knee suddenly fell backward as the paper burst into flames. An Indian buyer unobtrusively dropped a lighted cracker bomb in a neighbour's pocket; in the resultant explosion half a dozen men fell backward and forward off the fence. The Indian buyers had a debased fancy for evil smelling and noisy Chinee bombs which would explode on the crown of a man's hat, underneath him or in his pocket, at the most inconvenient moments. But the sale always went on; Kidman in the centre keeping the horses moving, Coles and his assistants roaring themselves hoarse.

At a busy stage a telegraph messenger climbed the auctioneer's box waving a telegram towards Kidman.

"What's it say, Charlie?" he shouted.

"Three inches of rain on Annandale."

"Hooray! Knock 'em down, Charlie. Knock 'em down! Rain on any station means plenty of feed to grow more horses. Knock 'em down, Charlie."

Each horse as sold was drafted into a branding-yard, where they were passed through at the rate of between 250 and 300 per day. As horses were drafted out others were drafted in; so a mob was kept circling around the big yards.

After each day's sale there was always fun when the buyers came for their horses. Good horsemen, of course, would immediately draft their purchases and have them into the lane quickly trotting down the street. A farmer, who had bought a single horse, started home using a clothes-line for an improvised halter, one end of which he had tied around his waist. But the horse bolted immediately it reached the street, the man leaping and plunging along fifty feet behind. Luckily the line broke and the crowd roared in reaction from the threatened tragedy.

After each day's sale Kidman would wave an arm that embraced all: "Come and have a bite, boys!" And the wife would rapidly count the little troop coming noisily across the street. "Ten, twenty, thirty," she was never "caught". At every sale every man he brought home for a "bite" found a comfortable seat and meal ready for him.

But Mrs Kidman and the girls had to work all hours during those sales. The men little guessed the planning and organization done by the womenfolk.

The sales realized from £32,000 to £33,000 a year.

They have been a yearly feature since 1904. In recent years motor transport has made a big difference.

In 1911 Sid Kidman visited Delhi Durbar. It was magnificent. But, amongst the gorgeous splendours there, he was delighted to recognize numerous horses that he had previously sold to Indian buyers at Kapunda. Though visiting numerous cities at a time when a great part of India was *en fête* he enjoyed himself thoroughly and did business too by securing a contract to supply horses to the Indian Government.

In all of his trips overseas he was out not only to see the world but to see if he could not do business with the world. He travelled right up the Nile, visited Europe, enjoyed the beauties of England and Scotland, visited the great meat markets and ranches of America, and the pastoral country in Africa. And though he enjoyed himself throughout every hour of travel he also sought keenly any avenue of expansion whereby he might sell produce from Australia to the world.

In 1912 Kidman, with brother Tom, bought Morney Plains station, 908 square miles, in western Queensland, for £25,000. A good speculation. Then Galloping Jack Watts went "halves" with him in Tobermory. There were 4000 cattle on it. They did very well. In a few years Watts bought Kidman's share, resigned the managership of Norley, and went to live at Tobermory. Kidman then bought Durrie for £30,000. Just north of Birdsville, it covers 3000 square miles of country, and has a seventy-mile frontage to the Diamantina. He knew it as great fattening country when the floods came.

These stations strengthened the south-western Queensland portion of the main chain.

36

The Yellow Flood

Having bought or taken up a few more small stations in the north of South Australia Kidman decided to venture farther north into Queensland and became interested in Fiery Downs, a well-grassed, well-watered area in the Gulf country. So, too, was Augustus Downs, a big station into which Kidman and another great cattleman, William Angliss, bought a controlling interest. On behalf of a syndicate he bought this station for £80,000. Lord Rochdale and several other Englishmen were shareholders. The station, carrying 18,000 cattle, is on the Leichhardt River, the steep banks of which shelter beautiful and permanent waterholes. In these holes are crocodiles, and many unwary beasts fell victims to them. This syndicate also bought Lorraine and Talawanta stations adjoining. Now, Kidman's Queensland chain of interests stretched from the Gulf down through south-western Queensland to the New South Wales border. There it joined the New South Wales and the branch South Australian chains. More links yet were to be forged north, east, south, centre, and west.

Kidman now found an Adelaide office essential to his evergrowing organization.

Then came the four years of horror. The Cattle King was beyond the age limit so did his bit in other ways. He immediately offered Fulham Park to the military authorities as a remount depot, gave cattle, horses, sheep, money; fitted ambulance cars, gave several battle planes; helped Red Cross appeals in numerous towns; circularized his managers to help in every way efforts made by local patriotic bodies. When the cry for wooden ships went up he was asked to build them, and suffered a loss of considerably over £100,000.

And he had his own particular fight. Old Man Drought came raging through western Queensland to test his chain of stations.

He set the wires busy calling up every resource available against this determined attack. It was the main chain, the south-western Queensland chain with its subsidiary New South Wales and north-eastern South Australian branches that were threatened; the secondary Central-South Australian chain, running parallel several hundred miles to the west, partially escaped this particular drought-belt.

Each station in the main chain, besides having to fight its own local battle, also had to fight in co-operation with the chain for the common good. Each station must immediately muster fats and get them on the roads, destinations would be wired them, drovers would be wired where they had to pick up their mobs. This action immediately left more water and more grass upon each station for the "stores" and breeding-herds that remained. These mobs of fats would come week after week into all the markets of Australia, their routes regulated by time and distance so that no market would be flooded. Another great advantage in the chain became immediately apparent. As the drought came slowly down from the north and the herds travelled slowly south, they were held on feed at each station before moving another stage on their allotted time and course to market. At the Queensland border some were sent along the southern branch through New South Wales to railhead at Broken Hill, others along the south-western branch through the north-eastern corner of South Australia, to Farina. At these trucking centres foresight told again. The depot stations there were waiting with water and grass to receive each mob preparatory to its train ride. So let Old Man Drought wield the whip as he liked, these travelling mobs would be saved anyway.

Immediately the drovers had taken the fats upon the road, the store cattle and breeders on the various stations were mustered in mobs within easy reach of the waterholes, the bore drains, and grasses. As the lesser waterholes began to dry up, the cattle were moved before too late to permanent waterholes. As the grasses around the ever-flowing bore drains were eaten out, those cattle, too, were moved farther south along the chain.

Living became very dear, freight charges terrific. Only the strongest teams could travel, because, besides carting stores, the teamsters had to cart chaff and corn for their horses. As the waters gradually dried up, the teams were almost driven from the roads. Only the camel-teams could travel. In a few places the new-fangled motor trucks were tried, but with little success. The motor lorry then was far less efficient than it is to-day.

As the drought tightened its grip the moving of the herds that remained was not always unattended by catastrophe. The danger lay in the rapidity with which a waterhole dries up once it has fallen below a certain level. The remnant vanishes under evaporation with frightful rapidity. Such a waterhole, if found dry by a perishing mob at the end of a sixty-mile feedless, hot stage, possibly means disaster, for the mob must then keep travelling. And thirst-crazed cattle are difficult to handle.

A mob of 1200 set out from Cooncherie, travelling a corner of then sheer desert—the sand track between Coongy and Birdsville. The drover with his men started the mob in late afternoon, travelling in stages throughout the night. Next day it was blazing hot. Crows followed the thirsty cattle. The following day at sundown they arrived at the waterhole. It was dry!

After three hours' spell the men managed to drive the cattle from the caked mud and start off again. Their horses were tired, hungry and thirsty; the cattle in distress. The sun rose like a furnace. By ten o'clock several horses were staggering, weak cattle began to drop out. The mob pressed on, heads low to the burning ground, eyes bloodshot and dust rimmed. (Along this track several men had perished some time before at the Deadman's Sandhills. They were going across country to the Birdsville races, and it was not drought-time either. One man cut his horse's throat and drank the blood but he perished beside the track.)

The drovers held the mob until midday. Then some refused to travel, others dropped; others simply staggered out into the desert. When a beast goes like that nothing can turn it. The horses were done; no man knew of any water ahead.

The drovers turned back for the station they had left. They just reached there—with only two horses. The mob perished.

As the drought crept down upon and over link after link, the decreasing herds were shifted to the last of the bore-sites and waterholes. Then came the last phase in the terrible struggle. Over a huge area in scattered little mobs the remnants of the herds waited marooned: each within a circle of fifteen miles. Fifteen miles to walk for feed; fifteen miles to walk back for water.

Filling up their bellies almost to bursting, then the slow walk away out into the blazing sunlight. Strings of lean-ribbed cattle branching out from every last waterhole, one behind the other, patient eyed, doggedly walking. They would stay out two days. Then, their bellies loaded with dried grass, leaves, sticks, anything, one behind another, the tired strings would come, over burning earth in hazy mirage, slowly in for water. The calves all dead now, long since pulled down by the dingoes. But the killing of the calves would give the crazed mothers a chance of life.

Day by day, growing weaker and weaker, they walked fourteen ... thirteen ... twelve ... eleven ... ten ... nine miles. And then—every vestige of grass, every fallen leaf, every root, every stick had long since been eaten out within a radius of nine miles of the boresites, of the last of the permanent waterholes. Time fast coming when they could stagger out no more.

A ceaseless, losing fight between the scattered bands of stationmen and the withering clutch of drought. Their jealously guarded and hand-fed stock-horses now helpless against the waterless distances were themselves marooned around some mudhole or boresite. Camels were used by every camp until the final remnants of the herds became too poor to move. Bags of bones, they waited listlessly for the end. This was Old Man Drought, pitiless as the dingoes, set as firmly as the brazen sky.

And then, far away in the Gulf country the sea winds blew in clouds across the coast. Slowly they began to travel inland, to bank up over the land. Rain fell.

Far to the north-east a lacy fleece of clouds spread over the sky. Light rains began to fall. Then heavier.

Far north-west in the Territory clouds gathered; thunder muttered; rain began to fall.

Several nights later down south, all along the parched Three Rivers, men sprang from homestead and hut; out in the arid lands they leapt from blanket and camp and stared up at the sky. A brilliant sky with not the sign of a cloud, stars like sparkling eyes undimmed by tears. Hark! A shrill whistling, a trumpeting, a blast as of a coming wind, a trumpeting from a clouded host swiftly flying. With rush of wings, whistling, calling, trumpeting, the host of birds sped by. Shouts of excited men, prick ears of horses. Screaming hysteria in scattered aboriginal camps; skinny mothers clutching skinny babes as they shrieked to the skies. From bush and tree and lignum, wherever a hardy bird had survived, came a chirp in answer to that trumpeting in the sky.

A flood was coming; a flood! a flood!

Nightly came the flight of the water-birds, long lines of them, wedge-shaped Vs of them, clouds of them.

Far to the north, over a great arc, rain was steadily falling. Dripping down from the tablelands, rippling down from the ranges, soaking into the flats. Millions of gutters were trickling into gullies; gullies were running into creeks; the creeks were swelling! Then, from north-east, from north, from north-west, thousands of creeks "came down". Into the river-heads. Sand and parched river-beds soaked up the stream. The river-heads then "came down", faster, stronger. Long, spreading, creeping snakes of water began appearing in the river-beds. They were swallowed by sand. Then a spreading volume of water appeared, while ever ahead of it trailed out again long, spreading, creeping snakes of water.

The rivers began to run. From east, north, and north-west three yellow-brown walls of water came creeping down, softly, silently, surely: the Cooper, the Diamantina, the Georgina. Gently the yellow floods came, slowly growing faster, noiselessly gathering weight. Then each came rolling down, rolling yellow volumes down the Three Rivers; growing stronger, coming swifter, a faint murmuring in the air.

They rolled down through south-western Queensland; they rolled across the borders and rolled on into South Australia, on towards the salt-lakes system. Alas, not to fill it. Too choked up were the old river-beds for that. Not since 1906 had grim Lake Eyre been really filled.

Still the rain fell, away to the north, cold sheets of driving rain night and day. The earth, its great thirst quenched, could hold no more and all the waters sped into the three yellow rivers. Over their shallow banks to east and west went creeping many snakes of water that quickly spread out into claypans. Hundreds of channels filled, then spilled more water on to plains and flats. Every depression became a swamp, every claypan a lake. At last the Three Rivers had covered the earth with a sea of water twenty miles out from each river's banks. Such an inland sea was what Sturt and others had dreamt of seeing in the old exploring days.

The drought had broken. But it had shaken the Cattle King.

Of cattle alone, 85,000 head had perished. His chains of stations were not quite complete. Immediately he started to build up again and then spread farther just as the Three Rivers had spread over the land. As the flood-water receded, the country over scores of thousands of miles smiled to the skies under beautiful feed. For years to come now, the earth here would bloom. But well he knew that time would bring another Old Man Drought. It was up to him to beat it.

"The good God gave me brains, Bell. And if I don't use them, then it serves me right if a brainless drought wipes me out. I feel sorry for the poor chaps who have not had the opportunities I have."

"Here is my chance for a little praise," answered Bell, "and I want it. If you had not married me you would be stuck out on some lonely station and would never have built up your chains."

"You are the best drought resister any man could have, Bell. With a few more like you Australia could laugh at the biggest Old Man Drought that ever was."

Kidman bought Bootra sheep station in partnership with nephew Tony for £20,000, and Monolon to add to his New South Wales chain. And at last he bought Forders. He had tried harder and longer to secure this tiny fifteen square miles—had waited longer for it than he had for any great station. He would not have got it then only that the brothers who owned it decided to give up bush life and live in the city. Forders selection was as strategical to the Broken Hill and Adelaide market as Mundowdna was to Marree and Farina railway. He secured Clyde and Yandama. The fact that, as a boy, he had ridden over this country, added pleasure to his ownership now. Of 3128 square miles, it is situated just below the New South Wales "corner", portion of it in New South Wales, portion in South Australia. He bought it from Bill Naughton and Jack Linnane. It was stocked with 10,000 head of cattle and 300 horses. From wild country he had seen this grow to a station supporting 40,000 sheep. But the sheep and rabbits had partly eaten it out. He kept cattle on it, and would soon put bores on it to solve the water question. When he bought Callabonna adjoining, he paused a moment with old memories of riding across this country with Jack McDermott.

From the Quinyambie boundary to the Queensland border their country extended 120 miles, while from the eastern boundary to Lake Callabonna was 124 miles. On the rare occasions when the Strzelecki floods down from the Cooper it slowly dribbles into this big old prehistoric lake, now parched and dry. Here is where the petrified skeletons of *Diprotodon* are,

264

giant monsters that roamed the land before the sand came. The once great lake is a real lake no more. But insect man bores down. The Tilcha bore at 2345 feet gave 1,000,000 gallons every twenty-four hours. It made a "dead" creek come "alive" again, and created a deep waterhole across which Pat Kennedy swam 500 head of bullocks. And down that once dry creek the water now flows for twenty-five miles. Wild ducks swim and nest upon it, birds chirp from trees that draw their life from the stream, tame and wild animals come to drink where before there was sandy desolation.

As a great change from the arid lands he, with a syndicate, secured Rutland Plains (650 square miles), Iffley Park and Vena Park (1087 square miles). Rutland Plains was in wild country on the western coast of Cape York Peninsula, 1150 miles from Brisbane. The blacks were fairly numerous. But very soon these unfortunate people were to be decimated by Spanish influenza, a legacy from a great war about which they knew and cared nothing. No wonder the stone-age man cannot understand the fate which has doomed him to extinction. Iffley and Vena Park, 800 miles south-west, were in the Gulf country. Stocked with 20,000 head of cattle, these stations cost £105,000. Rutland Downs, particularly, was in the tropics subject to the tropical wet season. No sandstorms there; no saltbush either unfortunately, though abundance of other natural grasses. Forest country, the plentiful timber was a change from the more sparsely timbered interior.

These stations were some hundreds of miles north of his main south-western Queensland chain. From them he would drove cattle south to the railway line pushing out west from Townsville, and truck them to Swift's meatworks. If these stations paid, his share of the profits would be subsidiary links helping the south-western chain.

Kidman next bought Undilla (566 square miles), carrying 4000 cattle and 600 horses, for £25,000. He was to spend a further £25,000 on this place, and finally abandon it, letting the manager keep what few cattle were left. He admitted his error with a laugh.

"A mistake is good for a man," he drawled to Sid Reid. "Pulls him up with a jerk. I remember years ago I made a loss on a line of sheep I bought from C. B. Fisher. He just said, 'That mistake is the best thing that could have happened to you, my boy; that is what I call a steadier. If you go on winning every time, you will get ahead of yourself. A failure now and then pulls you up and makes you think.'"

With his nephew, Hurtle Kidman, and the Taits, he bought Weinteriga (771 square miles) on the Darling, near Menindee. He had driven his bullock-wagon past it when it was in its pioneer stage; it was here that a squatter had galloped past him and sprayed his seven-and-sixpenny hat with dust. Now, with fine homestead and beautiful garden, it is one of the big sheep stations of the west.

His last purchase in 1916 was Glenroy station in the north-western Kimberleys.

And there trouble awaited Kidman. He was venturing far away, over the rugged King Leopolds, into the land of the wild man. Plenty of water there, rock-bound rivers, pandanus-palm creeks, grass, trees, lily-covered lagoons. But a wild, inaccessible country. Only half a dozen pioneering stations were in that area; to the north and north-west, none at all. It was a frontier job stocking that place, driving the cattle along the valleys and through the gorges of the Leopolds. And almost as bad a job driving the fats back to Derby and the cattle boat. They built up the herd eventually to 16,000, only to see it dwindle to 9000. And worst misfortune was to befall.

On a long trip of inspection the Cattle King called in at Durrie. He had great hopes of this station with its 3000 square miles of saltbush and lignum flats; its deep waterholes shaded under coolabahs along a sixty-mile frontage to the Diamantina. Rich fattening country after floods, he hoped in time with bores to make it drought-proof.

Durrie boasted a wonderful cook, Albert Tilmouth, famed not only as a cook but for his yarns, which Kidman delighted to retail. It was Albert who rode the notorious outlaw until it "bucked its brands off". It was Albert too who owned the "high jumping dog". All hands had told of their wonderful dogs one evening, when the dingo-poisoner sagely remarked:

"The take-off is the thing; no dog can jump high that does not take off from away back."

"There's something in that," admitted the head stockman. "My dog takes off from ten feet back and will jump a five-foot fence easy."

"How about yours, Albert?" inquired the rouseabout.

"Oh, he'll jump a sixteen-foot yard easy."

"What! That's a good jump!"

"Yes, not many dogs can do it," admitted Albert.

"How far back does he take off?"

"Oh, about from here to the yard."

The yard was fifty yards away.

One evening the isolated station had the unusual experience of a number of visitors, travellers curious to see this little-known track. At evening coffee-time quite a crowd rolled up to the kitchen. After coffee they sat around, swapping yarns. The manager told of the big flood which had first appeared as a spreading grey sheet coming slowly across the plain. It brought countless reptiles. The blacksmith made tin leggings for the men as a safeguard in walking about after dark. One night when the manager was playing the concertina in his bedroom a snake appeared on the rafter above. Another carne slithering in at the open door. He took the lamp and stepped out on the veranda to see two snakes coiled around the veranda posts. He called the men, and all hands indulged in an hour's snake hunt within the house and under it.

Then one of the travellers, who had recently been through America and India, took his turn. He told them tales of the terrible rattler, and the Indian cobra. He finished a good effort with a few thrilling ones about the poisonous snakes of the Malay Peninsula.

"Have you ever known any poisonous snakes, Albert?" inquired a stockman.

Albert spat reflectively, without shifting his pipe. "Yeh!" he drawled reminiscently, "I've known one or two. I was chopping a tree down by the creek one day and missed and chopped into the sand. Up popped a snake's head and bit the axe-handle— and the wood swelled so much it burst the eye of the axe."

37

The Windmill

Before 1917 old James Tyson had been the acknowledged Cattle King of Australia. In that year another had taken his crown, and the new king's Adelaide office had become the heart of a great organization. In this office he had to attend board meetings, for he was now associated with companies, syndicates, and private interests.

One afternoon Kidman attended a meeting where important matters were to be discussed, involving huge responsibilities and great sums of money. He had been thinking all day of Cyclops his one-eyed horse of long ago. From the crowded passage outside by a doctor's waiting-room came the wail of a sick baby. Kidman pushed back his chair.

"Just a moment," he drawled.

He went outside and looked down the passage. A poorly dressed woman stood there, rocking a baby in her arms. "Come with me, lady, and sit down," he said, and took her gently by the arm. He led her into his secretary's office, and helped her to an easy chair. "Stay here as long as you like. When the doctor is disengaged one of my girls will tell you. Don't be afraid that the baby will bother us." Then he carried on with the meeting.

Kidman had grown with the nation.

"It is wonderful, Bell," he drawled. "When I ran away from home, a little boy of thirteen, Adelaide was only a town. There were only just over 1,500,000 people in all Australia. Now we have 5,000,000, and Australia is a nation. We have an army of almost 500,000 men fighting in the Old World; and a navy that has been in action with the mightiest. Because of that we sit here safely in the Adelaide hills. And to-night our guns are thundering on many battle fronts. Poor lads. We have moved some, Bell, since I rode away on the old one-eyed horse."

"You have helped in the movement," she said.

"Yes, I've done a bit. But I have hardly started yet!"

He gazed out into the night, his eyes very bright. She sat there, watching him dreaming. A strong, handsome man of sixty, his clean-cut face but little lined, the thick, wavy brown hair only just dashed with silver. The brown eyes looking out into the night, a set, faint smile at the corners of the mouth. She knew this man's heart was far out in the back country. Impossible to keep him at home—he would never retire, not until old age or sickness forced him. She dreaded such a day; what sort of a patient would he make. She coaxed him to take another trip, this time to see the cattle country of America. He did so, and enjoyed it. But his greatest joy was in returning to Australia. And now the wife wanted a home in Adelaide. So lovely "Eringa" was purchased in the garden city. And he gave his big Kapunda home to the South Australian Government for use as a high school.

A breathless midsummer day. The woman working at the well felt nearly done in. Her hands, hardened by toil, felt sore and stiff around the iron windlass handle. Slowly the bucket came up. She had been turning this handle for an hour, and still had another hour to turn before the trough would be even half full. What a tremendous amount of water cattle drink! And the poor brutes would be perishing on a day like this. The heavy oil drum, full of water, came slowly to the lip of the well. Holding the windlass handle with one hand, she landed the bucket, sighing as the logs took the weight. She manhandled it to the edge of the well, then tipped the water into the trough. It seemed like a drop to the ocean. Wiping the sweat from her brow she lowered the bucket again, with a glance towards the slab-built home. She was always afraid of fire! But the children were playing under the bauhinia-tree; the tiny homestead stood shadowless under the sun. She bent to the windlass again.

The dog growled, staring down the road. She looked. Two horses drawing a buggy were coming in a whirl of dust. The dog walked out with a threatening growl as the buggy drew level. Over the selection fence the driver saw the woman toiling at the windlass. Although he was in a hurry to catch a train and had sixty miles yet to go, he pulled his horses in towards the fence. Jumping out, he tied them there. A cattle-dog leapt from the buggy, dived through the fence and stood there, showing teeth to its oncoming foe. But as the man vaulted the fence the foe stood undecided; it did not even growl; it actually allowed the tall man to pat it, to pull its ears. With cheery words he walked across to the well.

"Good day, missus. I was wondering if I could water my horses?"

"You are welcome," she replied.

He climbed the dump and took the windlass handle quite naturally. "Then I'll fill the trough," he smiled, "and earn my horses a drink. Hot day."

"Yes," she replied.

"You are lucky having a well like this. Well timbered too — a tradesman?"

"My husband."

"Knows his job."

"Yes," she faltered.

"Is he out on the run?"

"No — he is dead."

"I'm sorry."

"It is quite all right. He died a few months ago."

"You will have a job carrying on here alone."

"Yes. I can do it, though, if it would only rain and fill the waterholes out on the run. There is plenty of feed in the back paddocks, but no permanent water. We know—we knew we could get water by sinking wells. My husband sank this one just before he died. If I can only keep our few head of stock alive until rain fills the waterholes I will have a chance of pulling through."

"It may be a long time before it rains," he replied gravely. "How long does it take you to fill this trough?"

"Four hours."

"Does that satisfy the cattle?"

"No. I pull water for two hours before sunrise to give them a morning drink."

"No help?"

"No. The neighbours are very kind," she explained half defiantly. "They have helped me a lot. But they live a good many miles away and I cannot expect them to be always riding over here."

"Of course not. Well, I'll feel like a drink of tea when I've finished here. What if you put the kettle on. Go across to my buggy, there's plenty of tucker there, there's tinned fruit and biscuits and tinned sausages, and all sorts of good things. We'll give the kiddies a picnic."

It was two hours later before the man drove away. And he left quite a lot of food.

"I don't want it," he urged. "I'm catching the train in Broken Hill to-morrow night, and all this tucker will be of no use to me."

He drove away, waving his hat to the children who followed him to the fence. The woman stood there, staring at the vanishing dust. It was just a week later that the dog again gave a warning bark. The children came running to the kitchen. Men were coming in at the gate! The woman went to the door. A heavily loaded lorry was already pulling up down by the well. Two men jumped out and deftly began unknotting the tie ropes. Fear clutched the woman's heart, the selection was not quite paid for——

272

Bravely she walked down to the lorry. Both men raised their hats.

"What are you doing here?" she demanded.

"We've brought the windmill," answered the driver.

"Brought the what?"

"The windmill," smiled the man.

"Nonsense. I ordered no windmill."

"Perhaps not, missus. But we've got a windmill here for your selection, and a lot of troughing. We've got another load to bring from Broken Hill—a little crude-oil pumping engine, some piping oil, and accessories. When we bring the second load we'll bring the men who will erect the mill and show you how to work the engine."

"There is some mistake," she insisted. "I never ordered any of these things!"

"It's all right, missus; it's Kidman's orders."

"Who?"

"Kidman. You know Sid Kidman, or you've heard of him surely ... Sid Kidman, the cattle-dealer."

"I've heard my husband speak of him."

"Well, he is putting this windmill up for you; that is all we know. We are working for Mr Kidman's agent in Broken Hill."

"Broken Hill?"

"Yes."

"What is this man Kidman like?" she asked slowly.

"Well, he is a tall chap, very active, thick wavy hair going grey, I should say he was a good-looking chap years ago. Got a drawly voice and a smile."

"I believe I have met him," she said slowly. "A man like that passed through here a week ago—in a buggy—he had a dog, a very old dog."

"That's him," they both exclaimed. "Now you know it's all right."

"But," she protested, "I have no claim on Mr Kidman. I have no money to pay him—I just don't understand."

"You don't have to, missus," said the driver ... "Look here, missus," he said reassuringly, "you don't have to pay anything.

This is not the first job of this sort we've done for Kidman. He doesn't want any money. Very likely he was just passing by, and he saw your cattle perishing for a drink, and if there's one thing Kidman hates to see it is cattle perishing for a drink! Come on, Bill, let's get this load off. And missus—when we've finished we'll be ready for a drink of tea. It's a dusty ride out from the Hill."

38

The Men Who Work the Stations

By the end of 1920 the Cattle King had bought, taken up, or secured an interest in Lake Elder, Allandale, Stuarts Creek, Merty Merty, and Hamilton stations for his South Australian chain, with Crown Point and Bond Springs just north in the Territory.

Lake Elder is in the heart of sand-hill country on the South Australian border north of Cockburn. He paid £25,000 for it and later sank thousands more in boring for water. After the scanty rains this area would be a mass of flowers and herbage; in a dry summer, dust-storms and desolation. But, as a pasture land in a good season, it was strategically placed for topping up cattle for the Adelaide and Broken Hill markets.

Bond Springs in the Macdonnell Ranges was 1800 square miles of good country, but lacking in permanent water for big herds. Crown Point, just over the Territory border, with Allandale farther south in South Australia comprised 6863 square miles, and was to prove a proposition requiring many years to develop. These three stations cost £115,000—a disappointing investment for the syndicate.

For the main chain, on the New South Wales side he bought Nundora, Yancannia (1487 square miles), Corona (1359 square miles), Urisino, Thurlow Downs, Momba, Purnanga, Cobham, Packsaddle, Boxhole, Wyarra, Mount Arrowsmith, and Wonnaminta (2660 square miles). All in the north-western corner.

Yancannia, Corona, Cobham, Packsaddle, Boxhole, Wyarra, Wonnaminta, and Mount Arrowsmith were sheep stations destined to increase his wool production.

Among these New South Wales stations were some that he had long wanted. Corona was desired ever since he had been shepherd-boy for Harry Raines. And that boy gradually turned it into one of the show stations of the Western Division, under the managership of W. I. Foulis. Momba also was a place of old memories; he had driven his mail-coach through it, hurrying to catch the mail for Hungerford. He knew it in the pioneer days when it was a cattle station, and later when it carried 450,000 sheep. But over-stocking and rabbits caused havoc. Yancannia, a great station now, has been greater. Once it carried 196,000 sheep. The homestead, sheltered on all sides by coolabah-trees, rests beside a beautiful waterhole where Burke and Wills once camped. That tree-shaded waterhole is three miles long and has never been known to go dry. He paid £85,000 for Yancannia, with 35,000 sheep. Then spent thousands in cleaning out huge tanks that had sanded up, and in scooping new ones. Rabbits and sand-storms had caused deterioration here, but it became a highly payable station.

Wonnaminta was another place of memories. As cattle-boy for old German Charlie he had ridden over it. When he was a young drover it was in its hey-day. The Kennedy pioneers had taken it and built it up to a station, running 80,000 sheep. He remembered Frank Kennedy driving eight dashing greys around the station, and the brothers driving a blood team four-in-hand to Wilcannia, 110 miles, in ten hours.

But drought, overstocking, and rabbit plagues had played havoc with the carrying capacity of all this country. He gave £93,000 for Morden, Mount Arrowsmith, and Wonnaminta, and spent thousands in improvements, apparently unavailingly. Then he gave the country a five-years' "spell", and it "came again".

But Nundora, for which he gave £20,000, he used as a depot for fat cattle from Queensland. Its once fine homestead and beautiful garden, the love and pride of a woman, was closed up when it was again amalgamated with Wonnaminta and Morden.

The year 1921 was an especially happy year, for it saw knighthood conferred upon him. Of this honour for war services he was justly proud.

On one of his last trips to Yandama he rode to a little tree near the homestead, took off his hat, and stood by the grave of Jack McDermott. With a trace of a stoop to his shoulders he walked away. At a little hut not far away sat an old, old man quietly smoking. One of his old pensioners, Tilcha Frank.

"Old Frank lasts well, Monty," he said to Monty Winton, the manager.

"Yes, but he is a bit of an old tyrant. The wife looks after him more carefully than she does me."

Sir Sidney chuckled as they walked across to this one of the very last links in his chain of far-back memories.

"Well, Frank, how goes it?"

"Not too bad, not too bad."

"How is it you haven't made money as I have, Frank?"

"Well, sir, some of us has got to keep the roofs over the pubs."

Kidman laughed. "I wouldn't be surprised if you still wangle a wee drop now and then?" he queried.

The relic took the pipe from his mouth with a startled: "Ssh! Ssh! Sir!" He peered across at the homestead. "Mrs Winton has got eyes like a hawk," he mumbled, "and what she don't hear no one else does neither. If you so much as whisper, sir, you'll get me and the boss into a cruel row!"

At Wonnaminta Sir Sidney's face grew lined and troubled as he noted the bareness of hill and dune and plain. Where had all the mulga gone, the whitewood, and acacias, and turpentine bush, the black oak and nelia, and bullocky bush, the thick shrub life that had carpeted this country when he rode through here as a boy? He noted the exposed roots of much of the timber left, the topsoil blown away, roots bare to sun and wind. The little clump of dust and sand around every tuft of bluebush—not the sweetly edible bluebush that once was. Dead mulga! "Dead" creeks too! In the old days the creeks did not run so fast nor flood so easily. Now, so much topsoil had been washed and blown away that the creeks had silted up. Only the hard earth surface was left. The rains, now, just ran off this hard crust into the silted creek. In old days, much of that rain would have been absorbed by the topsoil. And the saltbush and grasses and shrubs and trees which then bound the topsoil together would have flourished and carpeted the earth with rich feed for stock.

He found Con White away out on the run supervising the scooping of a 25,000-cubic-yard tank. A hot day, with away west a yellow haze overspreading the sky, telling of a coming dust-storm. The teams down in that great tank were straining at the chains as they pulled the heavy scoops.

"How is the country out west, Con?" asked Kidman as he nodded towards the reddening haze.

"All dry," answered Con. "The shower cleaned the saltbush, then the sand-storm came and dirtied it so that nothing can eat it."

"These sand-storms are the devil."

"Worse. They kill the country and they fill the fleece with sand. The sheep have not only got to carry their own wool, but from six to ten pounds of sand in it."

"My word, that poor fellow is handicapped, Con," Kidman nodded down towards a man willingly toiling with a badly crippled leg. "Has he had a bad accident at some time?"

"He is a returned soldier."

"Ah." He looked west again.

"Well, Con, Wonnaminta doesn't carry the sheep it once used to, but you are making a do of it all the same."

"Yes, sir, I'm glad to say."

"How much are you paying the men to sink this tank, Con?"

"Tenpence a yard."

"Make it a shilling, Con. It's terribly hard ground, Con. Make it a shilling." He turned towards his horse.

Con felt a little hurt. He was going to explain that tenpence per yard was a fair price for this tank. Then his glance fell on the crippled soldier. He smiled understandingly and turned and followed the boss.

With all other stations, sheep or cattle, that Kidman bought or secured an interest in, it was the same. Some paid magnificently from the start; others responded fairly well; others barely held their own; a few proved "soaks", which swallowed tens of thousands of pounds. But the striking of a flowing bore meant joy. The bore-drain carrying the water from the bore-head would meander for many miles, so saving the stock long distances of walking to water, and preventing them trampling and destroying large quantities of feed. Whenever a dry old creek-bed was near a bore he turned the water into it and that creek became a running stream, carrying water to thirsty stock for twenty, thirty, or more miles. In dry times, that water from the bowels of the earth has saved Australia millions of pounds.

Some stations he "spelled" for years, and they "came back" with renewed growths of vigorous grasses. Others never "came back".

Despite all his vast experience, all the wealth rolling in from successfully bred herds, and the profits from tens of thousands of cattle and sheep that he bought yearly, Kidman was still grimly engaged in a fight to a finish with the bush of the lesser rainfall areas. He made of life a fascinating game of chess. The board was Australia; the pieces were station managers, land, drovers, stockmen, bore contractors, tank-sinkers, water conservers, money, energy, thought, organization, markets, transport, distances, stock-routes, water, grass, cattle, sheep, horses, and camels. His opponent was drought, now slowly allying itself with erosion. It was a wonderful fight, lasting sixty-five years. Eventually the man won all along the line, though still fighting at the end.

Around him he had gathered a wonderful group of station managers, drovers, and stockmen. These men were of the type that gives of its very best. After a few early failures, he unerringly picked those that carry on through thick and thin. Some of these men were in his employ a lifetime; others for twenty, thirty, forty years, and are still carrying on. Each of his drovers has had a life's experience in the shifting of mobs over big distances in varying country under every difficulty of nature.

His little army of stockmen are among the finest in the world. Needs must, for they ride the frontiers.

And as loyal as they were to him, were their wives to the men. Many of the stations were out in lonely places; some had to be developed from nature at her loneliest and wildest. Then, in the sand country, life in summer for a woman was often particularly harsh. Kidman has more than once said to me:

"My men are loyalty itself and I love them for it. But then, they are men, doing men's work. I admire more than anything I can say the loyalty of the women to their husbands."

The Cattle King's main chain, through south-western Queensland into north-western New South Wales, was now very strong.

He turned his attention again to the far north-western corner of the continent, the Kimberleys. He bought Yeeda station, forming a company in which English capital was interested. Yeeda (1230 square miles) is on the Fitzroy twenty-five miles inland from the tiny port of Derby. Yeeda would be 1550 miles, as the crow flies, north-west from Adelaide. Thus he now had interests in the farthest north-east in Queensland's Cape York Peninsula and 3000 miles west of here in Western Australia's north-western "corner".

And these Kimberley stations were in altogether different country to the Territory–Central–South Australian chain, and as different as chalk from cheese, to the south-western Queensland–New South Wales chain. Problems, climate, beasts, grasses, insects, animals, men, diseases, and transport, all quite unlike. Transport for instance. Whereas in his chains of stations his men were used to moving the mobs over big distances on dry land, here the main road to market was the sea.

Kidman quickly learned yet more things about his beloved Australia when he ventured into the Kimberleys.

He bought a half-interest in Fossil Downs station for £75,000, and an interest in Mount House. Yeeda, in the Western Kimberleys, had been long since established, along the great Fitzroy River on which the well established cattle and five sheep stations are. The new company did well in their first year, for cattle were scarce in Perth, approximately 1500 miles south. And for other cattle they found a market in Java, a market supplied by northern cattlemen.

But the easy geographical and settled conditions at Yeeda did not prevail at Mount House and Fossil Downs. These frontier stations were well in among the ranges, and the rough track by which the fat cattle had to be brought to the coast often knocked the condition off them.

He next secured Isdell, a large area of country over the Leopolds, on the Isdell River, and towards the rugged coast. It was in the country of the wild men of the Isdell and Charnley gorges and of painted warriors from the rugged Leopolds. From their rocky retreats these emerged to harass the cattle. It was not the numbers they speared that counted so much (although the number killed was considerable) as the effect of their attacks on the rest of the cattle. Over many miles of country the cattle became terrified. At the faintest whiff of a black man, they would be off in a mad stampede. This constant stampeding down the narrow valleys effectually prevented the cattle becoming fat. To fatten, cattle must be contented. From the day they entered the Leopolds the Isdell cattle were never left in peace.

Kidman gave strict orders that nothing more violent than the stockwhip was to be used against the raiders.

"Give the jolly tinkers the whip," he ordered, "if you can catch them! But don't harm them otherwise!"

Catch them! How the wild men laughed. From their rocky crags they watched the lonely stockmen riding the valleys. They laughed as they chewed their good beef, then from the cliffs shrieked in naked pantomime, giving point to it with the most insulting gestures.

39

Teeth, Erosion, and Sand

But while the Cattle King planned and worked, while his army of cattlemen, sheepmen, drovers, office men, camp followers, with brain and hand and unswerving loyalty worked to his bidding, stock and vermin on lesser rainfall lands were eating him out. Eating all men out. Millions of hoofs trampling over the land, billions of claws rooting into the land, billions of teeth ceaselessly night and day eating deep into the roots of things.

The country might just have held its own had it not been for the rabbit plagues. They devoured not only the grass but the edible bushes. They destroyed the roots, the bulbs, the very source of life. In dry times they attacked the bush and shrub life in ravenous hordes, eating deep down to the last shreds. Then they started on the mulga-trees and leopard wood, eating the bark, ring-barking the tree life over huge areas, stripping the bark from the currant bushes. As time went on, clumps of dead timber reared dead limbs to a brazen sky. Nature provides for the continuity of tree life by sending up young trees. But these babies were rung and the bark eaten by ceaselessly gnawing teeth. Seeds of tree, shrub, and grasses were devoured literally in thousands of tons.

True, the driest times killed the rabbit hordes. So did floods and bush-fires. But always, here and there, over tens of thousands of square miles of country there was left some solitary rabbit, survivor of the fittest. When green grass sprang up again these survivors roamed the land to meet and mate. It has been estimated that given favourable conditions, one pair of rabbits will increase to 1800 rabbits in two years. Thus, in another three or four years, "The rabbits are about again!" men would remark on meeting. Then several years later would come another rabbit plague.

Man, before he became uneasy, had helped with careless fire and axe in this destruction of tree life. But to nothing like the extent with which his brothers ravaged the rich tree life far to the south and east. Out in the lesser rainfall areas tree life is scanty; quite a lot of it is edible. No ring-barking has been done here; no ruthless destruction. But in areas where sheep were tried, and before the sheep "ate the country out" the land was scoured for fenceposts, hundreds of thousands of posts in sparsely timbered areas. In those places where the sheep ate the country out, the men's labour was in vain, and their hopes died like the trees. It was necessary to have posts for fencing. Much timber, just as naturally, was used in the building of homesteads and outbuildings and station yards.

The real but not vandal destruction by man was in overstocking, and in the careless use of the firestick and in the cutting down of mulga and other edible trees in the hope of saving starving stock. For men overstocked in good seasons, then, when dry times came, found they had to put on men to cut bush to keep stock alive. Large areas of mulga were thus destroyed. On one great station alone, thirty men were employed for two years in cutting mulga. Naturally. It was man's last hope at times, a short-sighted hope, for it is a fact that on a large holding with plenty of tree life the sheep in a dry time live for weeks on the leaves that the wind blows down from the trees. Nature sought to remedy this massacre of tree life by sending up many clumps of young mulga. And then — the rabbits ring-barked the tender trees.

Bush-fires, though nothing approaching the fierceness of the great fires along the coastal forests, still did much to help kill the timbers. And this killing of the timbers meant the killing of the birds that have ever been a good friend to man, birds that destroy countless millions of insect pests.

Over an area at least 600 miles in length, at least 300 in width, the plant life had been greatly thinned out. The roots of grasses, herbage, vines, bushes, shrubs, trees, all that had bound the topsoil together had been eaten and destroyed year by year for seventy years. And this in the arid country, where shade and a thin matting of plant life combine to conserve a trace of moisture in the soil, that moisture repaying its host by keeping it alive in dry times! But with the roots gone, the already loosened soil was thus exposed to sun and wind and rapidly dried up. The strong winds that blow fairly constantly began to blow away more and more of the soil in dust. Men began to remark:

"The dust-storms are coming more frequently. They are lasting longer too."

In portions of the lesser rainfall areas, the barren clay is only a few inches below the soil. Every here and there, like faint bald patches on a man's head, new claypans began to appear. On each of these, no grass would ever grow.

In the sand-ridge country proper, little feathers of dust blew out from high up. On a windy day for hundreds of miles these little feathers were blowing out like smoke. And the strong winds carried the smoke away until the sky grew yellow, then muddy, then sullen brown. And this sand was a "drifting" sand. The wind would drop it miles away. But the next strong wind would pick it up and carry it farther—unfortunately, towards the south and south-east, ever towards the good lands five, six, seven hundred miles away.

For years now over many thousands of square miles all over the drier areas when rain did fall an unnoticeable little thing happened. Grains of soil and sand were washed down the hills and ridges by every tiny rivulet. The loosened, friable soil, with nothing now to hold it, was being increasingly washed into the ravines. And then, as time went on and other rains came, millions of deepening gutters and ravines carried their accumulations of mud into the creeks. In turn, these began rushing their accumulations into the few rivers.

It began to be noticed that waterholes were silting up. It really was worse than this. For with each infrequent flood the old riverbeds themselves were silting up. Unlike rivers possessing a constant volume of water to keep debris moving until it reached the sea, these rivers flooded irregularly for only a matter of days or weeks. As the waters receded, so debris sank, and was left in the channels. So with gathering accumulations, the channels themselves more and more noticeably began to silt up. It was noticed now that numerous waterholes with a life, hitherto, of twelve months, would now only last a couple of months after a flood. Worse than this, men began to hear with alarm that a permanent waterhole had "gone dry".

Thus gradually, for seventy years, but now, alas, with a rush, conditions have grown far worse. Not only waterholes in the last few years have dried up, but whole creeks have silted up. Erosion, sand, and wind are now definitely and freely combined. Millions of tons of the scanty topsoil have been blown away while the damage by water erosion is beyond estimation. And now, added to this, the sand has come.

From some creeks can now be seen only the top branches of dead trees. In places, stations and homesteads have been abandoned, suffocated by the sand fiend. If it was not for the bore-waters neither men nor cattle could now travel across quite large areas simply because the natural waters are buried through erosion or by sand. The stock-carrying capacity over great areas has diminished by sixty, forty, and twenty per cent. Worse, where country has to be abandoned.

And the sand fiend now comes howling down towards portion of our good lands.

Queerly enough, the movement of all these uncountable grains of sand and soil was taking place in possibly the oldest corner of the world, so geologists tell us; the first to rise above the sea. Certainly it is the oldest portion of Australia, where still exists the oldest animal life in the world. Here great rivers ran in ages past, and lakes made beautiful the land. Only in places here and there are the dried-up courses of these once great rivers visible to-day. Here grew mighty forests. We see their ghostly relics now in the petrified fragments lying upon the country. Herds of monster animals roamed the grassy plains and creeper entangled valleys. We dig their skeletons from the dry salt lakes to-day. Here crawled serpents of unbelievable length, while over all flew fantastic birds with a terrifying breadth of webbed wing.

Fitting that here should be the cradle of the weird beliefs of the oldest stone-age man still existing on the earth. He has lived, while all around him has passed away. He lives still, but is passing away. From here come his legends of the giant snakes, of the huge beasts and birds, of the half-animals and half-fish, of the flying animals and the animal birds. Of men too who were partly men, partly animal; and of queer women, strange mothers who mothered strange things.

In this old land the inland sea of fresh water has long since dried up, the mountain chains are mere fragments of hills fast crumbling away. Then the white man came and with his flocks and herds and rabbits destroyed the scanty binding that held the last of the soil together.

It looks as if man has upset the balance of nature.

The Cattle King, for some time now, had gradually been growing deaf. This, coupled with a habit of dropping fast asleep in the middle of a business discussion, caused misbelieving ones to remark: "Old S.K. is not so deaf as he makes out to be. Nor so sleepy either."

"I'll wake him!" declared Paddy Conroy one day.

The Cattle King lay asleep on an easy chair on the balcony of a Broken Hill hotel. As a matter of fact, he was thinking of the bare hills around for many miles. When he came here as a lad these hills, and plains and flats were covered with dense mulga. He wondered where all the birds had gone; he knew the reason of the increasing dust-storms. Everywhere around him was the battle of man against nature; he wondered which was going to win in the long run. But around him now was a battle of man against man. Stock interests were involved in a dispute with the master butchers. A deputation arrived to discuss matters with Kidman. They found him fast asleep. Efforts to wake him, short of pulling him from the chair, were unavailing.

"He only wants to gain time!" declared Paddy. "I'll wake him!" He tiptoed to the chair, then shouted "Fat bullocks!"

Instantly Kidman sat up.

"There you are," said Conroy triumphantly, "the only way to wake this old steer is to shout 'Fat bullocks!' "

40

The Stampede of Bill Hannigan's Mob

Tall and slim is Bill Hannigan, one of Kidman's men. The big mob of 2300 fats were coming down from Bulloo Downs. Bright moonlight, with tree shadows like ink; every grass blade in silhouette; the bullocks' horns shining. An uncanny quietness.

Well out from the mob rode the watch, singing. Mounted on a coal black mare, her rump and neck like polished velvet as she walked between shrub and tree and on open claypan. Her grandsire a Melbourne Cup winner, she was the love of the watch; he almost worshipped her.

Cooky's fire of gidgee logs burned merrily; the kerosene tin buckets were just coming to the boil; a heap of ash-covered coals showed where a big damper was cooking. Cooky's dog lay coiled near the damper. Among the scattered tucker boxes lay the blanket wrapped forms of men; each clothed and with his saddle for pillow. The night horses close by were ready saddled and bridled. Wagonette and cart stood there, harness upon poles and wheels. A short distance away a blackfellow, his wife and piccaninny lay coiled in a gunyah of boughs.

In a moment they were off! the night filled with the thunder of 2300 bullocks stampeding. Instantly each man had leapt for a tree, followed by flying fragments of cart and wagonette mixed with splintered boxes, spinning saddles, and glowing coals. The torrent tore on while a mulga cracked like a pistol shot. Then they saw her, a black glimpse flying around the lead, her black tail flying.

She vanished, then reappeared a coal black streak grazing the very horns of the lead as she swerved them from the aboriginal gunyah. Trembling with their arms around one another and the dogs huddled amongst them, man and woman and child shivered as the thunder roared by while the gravel, sprayed like driven hail, knocked the gunyah flat. The stockmen leapt for the night horses that quivered to be after that vanishing roar. From the bushes they plunged out on to a claypan where a demon mare flew before a thunder-cloud glinting with the gleam of horns and maddened eyes. It crashed into a clump of mulga. The trees split the mob in two unequal lots which charged in different directions. Then the stockmen were among the trees each man racing in a living nightmare with bodies thrashed by branch and twig.

Presently came a churn in the thunder as the mare turned one mob, which raced back out on to the claypan. Then the riders held their breath as the second mob burst from the trees. With a frightful bellowing each mob swerved head on to join the other. Impossible now to turn either aside. Crash! ... bullocks shot into the air like horn-tossed dogs as rank piled on rank. The flanks broke around one another in primeval hysteria.

While round and round them but far out flew the black mare, satanic in her knowledge. And with her now were the galloping horsemen ringing the maddened beasts in ... ringing them in.

The Cattle King had seen the deterioration of the arid lands coming. But he had an unshakable faith in the country and was certain it would "come again". As he acquired his stations, so he planned not only against drought, but against the lesser carrying capacity of the country. Over huge areas he fed proportionately small herds of cattle. They had "the world" to roam in, for there were practically no fences; while west of almost all his Queensland and South Australian properties was unoccupied country. Beasts could roam there at will, subject only to distance from a waterhole. West of his Territory and South Australian chain, conditions were closely similar. So that his country was really unlimited. Even so, he utilized large areas only as shepherding grounds, putting stock there only when rains had produced an abundance of feed, moving the stock immediately the feed began to "go off". He called to his aid all that science could devise: big water-conserving schemes; bores put down on station after station. Some huge flows were struck; other bores were failures, costing thousands of pounds. Some stations he closed up altogether, "spelling" them for years. Others he grouped together and formed one station where previously had been three or four, even five. With such vast resources he could now afford to do this.

So, as the Cattle King grew older the fight was carried on under changing conditions. He who was to control 125,000 square miles of earth was to fight against moving grains of sand.

He helped others fight too; helped selectors stock their country. He gave a helping hand even when some of his own stations were resumed for closer settlement; helped the selectors stock their country with sheep and cattle; and made more friends than he knew.

Far away out in the Kimberleys, where there were no dust-storms, no denudation; where there was plenty of water and grass, the Bush attacked the Cattle King.

Yeeda station succeeded very well for a time. Then bad times came, followed by the great flood which swept hundreds of cattle out to sea. In the twenty-mile bullock paddock 1000 cattle were apparently safe, but the brown waters rolled over those twenty miles and the cattle went to feed the sharks or die, stranded in the branches of the trees. Of those swept out into

King Sound many, battling gamely to the last, were swept back to near shore by the terrific tides, only to meet the rush of the river and be carried out to sea again.

One brave old bull managed to beat the river, the sea, the tides, the currents, the sharks, and the crocodiles. He put up a Homeric battle for many hours. Bruised and cut, battered and floundering, he managed to gain the wave-washed mangroves fronting the little Derby port. Rolled about the greasy mangrove roots he fought with fast-ebbing strength the last few hundred muddy yards to the shore. Gaining it, he stood for long with lowered head, his dimming eyes blistered by sun and wind and salt. Then slowly and nervously he walked through the little main street of Derby, straight back to the bush, admired by the townsfolk who watched him stumbling by.

After the flood came the cattle-ticks, causing mortality and tick-fever.

The cattle-tick came to northern Australia with Brahma cattle from Batavia in 1872. Slowly it acclimatized. With colonization it spread throughout the Territory herds, into Queensland, and from there into New South Wales. Travelling west from the Territory it was now in the Kimberleys. Another imported pest that cost Australia untold millions, is still costing millions. With the Yeeda herds just getting on their feet again pleuro-pneumonia broke out in the Kimberleys, which placed an embargo on the cattle-shipping industry to Java. Then the bottom fell out of the Perth market and the isolated Kimberleys found themselves up against hard times.

North on the Isdell, the wild men, too, found themselves up against a big disappointment. They had killed the goose that laid the golden eggs. Isdell was abandoned and the remnants of the herd driven farther east to Glenroy. This station was in wild country, but the labyrinthine gorges of the rugged coastline were missing. Still, the aboriginal feasted on the Glenroy cattle. But inaccessibility was the worst enemy. Fat cattle were poor when they reached port. Then there was the cost of the long sea trip to Perth. Kidman gave £25,000 for Glenroy; it cost him more than another £25,000 before he was forced to abandon it. When it was abandoned, a good droving trip was put up, across rough country through the Eastern Kimberleys, down through the Northern Territory to Crown Point station, adjoining the northern border of South Australia: T. E. D'Arcy in charge of 2100 cattle; Lee in charge of the bullocks; 1382 miles; time, from first week in June to last in December. An interesting trip.

Sir Sidney Kidman met Sid Reid at the Adelaide office and was very pleased. Reid had just returned from a long tour of inspection and told him that a young fellow whom Sir Sidney had helped as a boy had taken up a selection of his own with every chance of making good.

S.K. was as pleased as if he had made a big deal.

"I was sure young Tom had it in him," he said excitedly. "He come to me a lad of sixteen with not even a swag, not even a toothbrush. I told him that opportunity awaits every boy if he will only apply himself to his job."

"He has certainly done that," said Reid. "And now he has seized the opportunity."

"Good luck to him. I hope he grows and grows. That is the best thing that can happen to a lad—let him go out and acquire self reliance. I'm as pleased as anything about young Tom."

"I knew you would be," said Reid. "That is why I told you first. And now to my report; it is not too bright. We've lost a good many cattle in the Centre, and in the north-west the sheep country looks to be in for a dry time."

"That's all right," said Kidman. "The cattle and sheep will build up again, it's bound to rain sometime. How many head of stock did you say young Tom has put on his place?"

Reid replied, admiring this man who was so pleased with the success of a lad that he insisted on hearing all particulars before he would listen to his own vast interests.

He did his inspections now by motor car; though Sid Reid and Ted Pratt and son Walter were doing nearly all of it now since it had grown into a constant job of swift travelling all the year round.

Coming down from the Gulf through the south-west, Kidman and his travelling inspector pulled up at Bedourie. In Gaffney's he saw a whip coiled up above the bar.

"Old Jack Hall's whip!" he said.

"Yes," answered Gaffney. "Poor old Jack, seventy-six."

"He's gone then," said Kidman slowly.

"Yes. He was cutting out cattle with the Sandringham mustering outfit at Pulchera waterhole on the Mulligan. He was riding a young colt when a weaner calf broke away. Jack turned after it and broke into a swinging canter. The colt came off the sand on to a hard claypan and went straight over. Jack was killed clean as a whistle. He wanted to be killed that way—on a cattle-camp."

At Durrie station Sir Sidney listened to the conversation awhile. When he first rode up along the Three Rivers it meant hundreds and hundreds of miles of riding before a man could even reach a railhead, let alone a city. Now a man here leaving for holiday simply rode to the nearest township or stepped into the motor mail and was whisked away to a much nearer railhead.

Leaving Durrie, they passed through the Warri Gate at the border into New South Wales. A glance at a struggling selection told them that on it there was no strong guiding hand or experienced or willing worker who would here wrest a living from the bush. Sir Sidney nodded as they passed by:

"Pratt, I am going to help them."

Now, the inspector knew his boss had been approached for help, he knew also that the family of young men were not only lazy but liable to abandon the selection at any moment. It was his duty to warn his chief.

"The country is poor, sir."

"I know."

"The boys are lazy, will not do a hand's turn to help themselves. The only worker among them is the crippled lad."

"I know. I am doing it for the sake of the crippled lad."

Driving back through Milparinka from Yandama he met for the last time another old memory of bygone days—Bullocky

Bill. Bullocky's once fiery beard was snow white, his once strong back was bent; but his eyes were bright, his hand-grip firm. He nearly cried with delight. The two old friends strolled down to Evelyn Creek—it was Bullocky's last walk. They had so much to talk about. This was the very road along which Kidman had driven his tabletop wagon in the days of the Mount Browne rush, and along which Bullocky had punched his bullocks from Wilcannia. Alas, Milparinka now looked like a township that had suffered bombardment, only four or five houses were intact. But the old pub was still there, still run by an indomitable spirit of the pioneer days, Mrs Bonnett. To the little crowd that evening Bullocky Bill held forth. A little while back Evelyn Creek had "come down" and the motor mail had been bogged. They hitched a team of horses to it and pulled it out. It left a track two feet deep.

"Oh yes," said Bullocky scornfully, "it don't take much to hold 'em up these days. I remember years ago I was carting to Tibooburra time of the big flood. Coally Flats was ten feet under water, but I had to get through with the rations, the people was starvin'. So I climbed up on top of the loadin' an' set the bullicks to it. An' they took me right through."

"How could they?" asked a new chum. "The bullocks' heads must have been four feet under water!"

"So they was," growled Bullocky.

"Well then, how did you drive them?"

"Easy. Wherever I seen a bubble I hit with the whip."

From Milparinka they sped to the Darling *en route* to Weinteriga, Corona, then Broken Hill.

Busy times at Weinteriga; shearing was due. Old Harry Perry was addicted to sudden attacks of colic and at night he kept a bottle of chlorodyne beside him. Harry's "medicine chest" was awesome to the other men in the hut. One cold night he awoke in pain, and fumbling for the chlorodyne, raised a bottle to his lips and swallowed the contents. A hair-raising howl awoke the hut. Men sat up in bunk as again that howl hit the roof. Matches were lit. Harry had drunk the iodine.

They chased him around the hut as he held his stomach and howled. They poured salt-water down his neck; they held him down and poured soapy water down, while he howled and gasped and blew beautifully coloured bubbles. They mixed up mustard and water and almost killed him, but could not make him sick. When Jack Goddard, the manager, came hurrying into the shed, little Billy Graham was dancing before a window-pane in his little short shirt howling: "Oh Harry, if I could only catch a fly! If I could only catch a fly!"

41

Through the Cycles
of the Years

As time went on the Cattle King added a few other stations to
his chains until now, for some hundreds of miles, with a very
occasional break in between, his men could bring down herds
through Queensland and New South Wales and be on his own
property all the time—or on country in which he held large
interests. Time and the country's development had again helped
him, in the series of Government bores put along the Birdsville
track. Those flowing bores saved countless stock and kept the
great track open. Otherwise, through denudation and dust-
storms which had destroyed the local waterholes it would have
been closed to man.

"The bores have been a wonderful help in dry times," he
said to John Brooke at Mundowdna one day. "The seasons
seemed better in the years gone by, but even so I often marvel
how we brought the cattle down without the bores. We certainly
could not do it to-day."

"Much of the country would have been done without them,"
growled old John, "but all the better for the 'Ghans!"

Sir Sidney smiled.

"You have never liked the Afghans, Brooke. But in the old days they did a great service to this country in helping with their camels to open it. Even to-day, I have a few stations that I could not keep going if it was not for the camel-teams. But the motor lorries have just about got the 'Ghans beaten. Be kind to the Afghans, Brooke. Don't interfere with their camels when they stay on Mundowdna. They are strange men, friendless in a strange land, and the poor chaps have been of service to the country."

He strolled into the Adelaide office one afternoon in genial mood. That day he had been directing repairs to the fence at his home when a high official in the railways came along. He stepped from his car and they chatted a moment.

"Improvements, Sir Sidney?" nodded the official towards the fence.

"Yes. I'm always improving, whether it's a cattle station or making two roses bloom where only one bloomed before."

"We are planning drastic alterations in our railway system too," said the official. "Speed, comfort, greater efficiency in every respect. Can you suggest anything, Sir Sidney?"

"Yes," he replied. "In the cattle-trucks the small handle inside for opening the door sticks into the backs of the cattle."

"I will have the matter seen to immediately," replied the official.

Sir Sidney was very pleased; he was all smiles walking up the stairs to the office. Bird had his hands full of telegrams, pleased at the chief's pleasure.

"Well sir, for last year you certainly paid your fare on the railways."

"I've never jumped the 'rattler' in my life."

"Last year your South Australian railway bill was £58,581."

"Yes I know, I have paid away a lot of money to them. That £58,581 must have helped grease the wheels a bit, and bought a little coal too."

He sat silent awhile. Then: "That official spoke about improvements and keeping pace with the times," he said slowly. "When I ran away from home there was not 200 miles of railway in the whole colony. What is there now, Bird?"

"All but 2500, not counting the 622 miles of north-to-south line transferred to the Commonwealth in 1911."

"H'm. Well, the railways have certainly kept pace with the times. What did you say that bill was, Bird?"

"£58,581."

"H'm. That is more than the sum voted by the Government for the first railway on South Australian soil. I remember a little Scotch teacher who told me all about it."

"I'll show you something else of interest," said Bird. "You had five shillings in your pocket when you ran away from home?"

"Yes."

"Just a moment." He stepped into his office and returned with a sheet of paper. "Last year you paid in wages, apart from numerous other expenses, £61,316."

"Did I now! I am real pleased at that bill."

Bird laid the paper before him.

SIDNEY KIDMAN STATIONS

Amount Expended in Wages and Rations in One Year (Year 1925)

Wages paid	61,316	1	3
Rations to employees	23,427	8	4
Total	84,743	9	7
Railage paid to South Australian			
Railways Department	58,581	5	10
Total	£143,324	15	5

He studied it for quite a while then leaned back in his chair. "£143,324 15s. 5d.," he murmured. "That should help the wheels of industry a little bit."

"That is only three items," said Bird. "There are numbers of others in connexion with the organization."

But Kidman was dreaming; a cold dawn, a shivering boy on tiptoe leading a one-eyed horse out through a little cottage gate.

And now he was a grandfather. A keen and active one, he found it hard to realize that he was what the world called an old man. His brain, tempered by experience, was calm and alert.

Physically he could still handle a horse. He did not find in old age the terrors generally credited it. He had gone for another trip around the world, and enjoyed himself. When he returned he was not able to plunge into active life again, but still was as keen as ever.

He realized that the bush was changing fast. His old bush was disappearing except in isolated corners here and there scattered throughout the continent. Development, speed, elimination of distance, and time had done it. Was it for good or ill? Stations now employed less men. Gone were the blacksmiths, the wheelwrights, the teamsters, the saddlers. River traffic had almost gone. Motor transport particularly had done it, had affected even towns. For motor traffic passed by in a whirl of dust. What had represented a stage to the teams now hardly meant an hour's run to the motor.

Numbers of stations even had their own telephone system. Fancy the boundary-rider of thirty years ago being told that a day would come when his lonely hut would be in constant touch with the homestead, twenty, thirty, fifty, sixty miles away! Electricity, the motor, wireless, all had helped do away with manpower. Strangely enough, various station areas in the arid regions could not be carried on but for motor transport. With the lesser carrying capacity of certain lands, the cheaper and time-eliminating factor of motor transport and motor work helped balance the budget. As development work proceeded over numerous areas, fewer tank-sinkers, well-sinkers, and water-borers were employed, although the work of these men was still very necessary. Gone, too, were the old road shanties, and the old shearing-days. The shearing teams arrived by contract from the cities, and two hours after a shed was cut out they were away by motor car, dashing past the tiny townships which once they had helped so much to support. Gone were nearly all the station and bush "picnic meetings", the old concertina and fiddle dances, the "hard cases", the "characters", and the circus.

Gone too, except in far out corners, were the picturesque characters of the bush. The "Wild Colonial Boys", the

"Whistling Canaries", the "Red Stags", the "Dukes", the "Greenhide Billys", the "Gentleman Dicks", the "Jacks without a Shirt", and numerous similar Knights of the Road who had brought countless laughs to the tracks of the old time bush.

"Do you know, Bell," he said one day, "the old Jumbuk is a very hospitable animal. I give him his board and lodging and in return he grows me wool. He only needs a decent season or two and he increases rapidly. You know, Bell, I never thought I would be interested in sheep to the extent I am. We've shorn 190,000 sheep this year. They say it is just as well not to have all your eggs in the one basket, and with cattle prices being so low of late the old sheep has been a great help to us."

"You have done well with the sheep," she answered, "what about the horses?"

"We still have a few left, not so many as in the big horse-sale days, though; the motor cars and trucks have taken their place to a large extent, but they will never be able to do without the old horse entirely. I will always have a high respect for him."

"Now that Sid and Walter are running the stations you still keep on dealing."

"I must go on dealing, Bell, it keeps my mind occupied, it's the game I have been most successful at, the game I love. Besides, it is a wonderful game and I am playing a continent against drought. I think I have it beaten, Bell."

Even as he spoke his organization was making the first moves against the 1927–30 drought. There is an enthralling story in that three years' fight, the movements of a mighty organization now tested at every point by this long-drawn-out blow of nature, an organization which fought from the city throughout the farthest bush from coast to coast of a continent. And the man won.

He lost 120,000 head of cattle, 100,000 sheep, 6000 horses, hundreds of camels. Spent tens of thousands of pounds in boring for water on those areas where feed still held out, and huge sums in motoring chaff and hay long distances to keep cornered herds alive. In money, his losses and the losses of others interested reached £1,500,000.

He won out, with ample stock remaining throughout his chains to quickly build up again. But he was getting old. He saw some old friends "go out" in this drought and it saddened him. He now owned, controlled, or had an interest in more than 100 stations, representing an area of 107,023 square miles, found himself owning more of the British Empire than any other man. His main interest in the city now was watching the stock-sales at the Adelaide Abattoirs from his seat in the selling-ring, among the little crowd of friends whose business interests concentrated around every sale. Here came the uneasy lowing of the penned beasts, the cracking of whips, the restive answer of hoofs. Each beast in turn would come smartly and anxiously up the main race leading into the drafting-pen, and so into the selling-ring. Occasionally he would quietly say to his auctioneer:

"Sell that beast for the Salvation Army and that one for the Benevolent Society. They are having heavy calls on them now and are doing good work."

On his last trip through the sand-ridge country he suddenly realized that he soon would be an old man. Rheumatics struck him. It was the bush hitting back, taking payment for the years of rough living, swimming of rivers, riding in the rain for days at a time behind mobs of cattle, sleeping in wet clothes under a wet blanket. When he could, he limped to the top of one of the Cowarie sand-ridges, and sat there under brilliant sunlight gazing over the Sahara that lay west. Around him the "Cark!" of the crows, their glistening bodies like ebony balls on the sand-ridge crests. To the north, but behind him, were his beloved Three Rivers, upon whose saltbush on the flooded country he and his fellow pastoralists had fattened their hundreds of thousands of cattle ... an old, old country ... He was fighting grimly against something that whispered this was to be his last trip ... His last trip!

Memories of over fifty years came gently crowding around. His eyes blurred like the mirage slowly forming away towards grim Lake Eyre. Down below, the little clumps of needlewood-trees grew dark as the dark soil on the shadowed flats. A great silence was over the land. What had happened to all the aborigines who had swarmed along the Three Rivers when first he came? The tribes had died out; only two or three old pensioners on each of his stations remained. Pneumonia and influenza germs had killed them just as sand-drift was choking the country's arteries, the Three Rivers. He had seen the pioneers come and go; the teams come and go; the motor lorries come and—they had to bring back camels in places where the tracks sanded over.

He certainly was growing old. He had never been a pessimist. With a fierce faith in the country he gazed around. Oh! for another fifty years to fight again; to fight until he saw all this country regain its thousands of miles of saltbush, its plains of herbage, its great clumps of mulga ...

When he reached Adelaide he withdrew entirely from active work, leaving the management to a son and the men he had trained to carry on the business which had taken him a lifetime to build up. But he loved to come into the office and pore over the telegrams that rolled in from all over the continent. He loved, too, to read the letters from the managers of the various stations and thus keep in touch with stock movements and all that was going on.

The rheumatics eventually crippled him. Less and less he was seen at the office, though nothing could stop him hobbling to his seat at the saleyards. He fought to the last. A few days before the end, he told me some fine stories of the "old days", days of the saltbush plains and the gidgee, of the roaring silver-camp at Apollyon Valley, of moonlight among the coolabahs on the Three Rivers, of cattle stampedes and feuds of the Afghan camel-drivers. His old eyes sparkled as he told of chases after cattle-duffers, of great bushmen, too, among the duffers who hurried huge mobs of stolen cattle across the arid lands. As he spoke he forgot pain, and I could hear the murmuring of the mobs coming down the Birdsville track; see him galloping his coach among the Cooper sand-hills while clinging to a dying passenger; hear the dingoes howling as they pulled down calves at night; see the Three Rivers break the drought as their rolling, yellow flood came creeping down.

It was the last yarn of the old man. Lying there on the couch with the rug over him, all crippled but still bright of eye, he smiled as he shook hands and said:

"Ah, well, it is all over. I've had a wonderful life. When the good Lord gives me notice I'll pack up my swag and go."